PANDORA'S BOXES
The Mind of Jihad
VOLUME II

Laurent Murawiec

Prepared for the Director of Net Assessment
Department of Defense

The views in this book are solely those of the author. No opinions, statements of fact or conclusions contained in this document can be properly attributed to the Hudson Institute, its staff, its members, its contracted agencies or the other institutions with which the author is affiliated.

Copyright © 2007 Laurent Murawiec
All rights reserved.

ISBN: 1-55813-156-6

For more information about obtaining additional copies of this or other Hudson Institute publications, please contact Hudson's website at **www.hudson.org/bookstore** or call toll free: 1-888-554-1325.

About the Hudson Institute:
Hudson Institute is a non-partisan policy research organization dedicated to innovative research and analysis that promotes global security, prosperity, and freedom. We challenge conventional thinking and help manage strategic transitions to the future through interdisciplinary and collaborative studies in defense, international relations, economics, culture, science, technology, and law. Through publications, conferences, and policy recommendations, we seek to guide global leaders in government and business.

For more information, visit www.hudson.org

Table of Contents
PANDORA'S BOXES: MIND OF JIHAD, VOLUME II

Acknowledgments	1
Introduction	2

■ PART I: THE NOMADIC WAY OF WAR

Nomads of Eurasia and of Arabia	7
The Prophet's Nomads	21
"Jihad is Not an Event, but an Institution"	34
A Primer on Jihad	34
Jihad for All Places and for All Times	41

■ PART II: THE TAINTED PEDIGREE OF MODERN JIHAD

From Islam to Pan-Islam	46
Birth of Pan-Islam	49
"Jihad Made in Germany"	57
Max von Oppenheim's Grand Design	64
The Khilafat Movement in India	72
Bolshevisks and Pan-Islamists	76
The Bolsheviks Buy the German Jihad	77
Lenin's Jihad	86
Red Jihad, Green Jihad	94
Sultan Galiev, the Hybrid	99
Ideological Infectors: Communist Parties in the Middle East	109

The Nazi Contribution	118
The Mutated Virus: "Islamic Revolution"	129
Stealthy Borrowing	129
Maududi, the Terrible Simplificateur	133
Gnostic Mullahs and Smaller Satan	142
Navvab Safavi, Iran's First Modern Propheta	143
How to Organize Masses: The Tudeh	145
Ali Shariati's Theology of Liberation	148
Jihad and Revolution: Ayatollah Mutahhari	155
The Imam-Mahdi of the Revolution	159
Coda: The PLO— Soviet Test-Tube and Incubator	163

■ PART III: MODERN JIHAD AS TERROR

Futuwwah, Not Netwar	177
A How-To of Modern Jihad: Algeria	182
"Strike Terror in the Heart of the Enemy"	191

■ CONCLUSION   195

■ ENDNOTES   197

ACKNOWLEDGMENTS

It is my distinct pleasure to acknowledge the debt I have incurred in researching this subject and putting it on paper. I have received the invaluable help of highly knowledgeable scholars. I have had the benefit of their science, their advice and criticism, and this book would have been much poorer without their contribution.

In the first place, Prof. Wolfgang G. Schwanitz introduced me to entire areas and topics of research; his wealth of knowledge always was a prime helper. David Wurmser followed step by step the development of the research and the writing and was always helpful and encouraging. Dr. Hans-Ulrich Seidt also oriented me in the right direction, and was a highly valuable partner in discussion. Prof. Mohamed ibn Guadi's deep well of science and friendship was always open.

For their suggestions, remarks and criticisms, I would like to thank Dr. S. Enders Wimbush, Eric Brown, Dr. Hillel Fradkin, my friends and colleagues at the Hudson Institute, Michel Gurfinkiel of the Institut Jean-Jacques Rousseau in Paris, Dr. David Kilcullen of the Australian Army, Praveen Swami of Frontline in New Delhi, Prof. Lynn Addington of American University, Washington, D.C., Prof. Yossi Kostiner and Prof. Azar Gat of Tel-Aviv University, Prof. Efraim Inbar of Bar-Ilan University, Prof. Efraim Karsh of King's College, London, Juliette Minces, David Pryce-Jones, Prof. Joshua Mitchell of Georgetown University, Muhammad Akyol, Paul Goble, Prof. Wolfgang Leidhold of the University of Cologne, Germany, Prof. Michael Stürmer, Dr. Joel Fishman, Prof. Jean-Paul Charnay, Dr. Shmuel Bar of the Interdisciplinary Center in Herzliya, Alex Alexiev, Ramin Parham, Prof. Hussain Haqqani, Prof. Bernard Lewis. May they all accept the expression of my heartfelt appreciation.

Special thanks go to Mr. Andrew Marshall of the Office of Net Assessment at the Department of Defense, who commissioned this work and unflaggingly supported it with his keen interest. I would not have been able to sustain several years of this research without him.

This book is, *selbstverständlich*, dedicated to my wife Dr. Claudia Kinkela, first reader, first critic, first in my heart.

—*Washington, D.C., February 15, 2007*

INTRODUCTION

There is a dry wind blowing through the East and the parched grasses await the spark (...) The fact is beyond dispute. I have reports from agents everywhere—peddlars in South Russia, Afghan horse-dealers, Turcoman merchants, pilgrims on the road to Mecca, sheikhs in North Africa, sailors on the Black Sea coasters, sheep-skinned Mongols, Hindu fakirs, Greek traders in the Gulf, as well as respectable Consuls who use cyphers. They tell the same story. The East is waiting for a revelation ...

JOHN BUCHAN, 1916

The Communist International turns today to the peoples of the East and says to them: "Brothers, we summon you to a holy war, in the first place against British imperialism!"

GRIGORY ZINOVIEV, 1920

The first part of this study examined the tribal and religious roots of jihad, and their projection into the modern world. The second part will examine the roots of jihad in the nomadic way of war—the rise of a fully fledged Muslim conception of jihad, the never-interrupted practice of Muslim war against the rest of the world, the German and the Soviet contributions to jihad in the modern era, and finally, the development, from the Quran to today, of a notion of jihad as terror. Jihad, the war to uphold the writ of Islam or aggrandize its dominion over the world, did not start with the presence of American troops in Saudi Arabia after 1990, with the establishment of Israel in 1948, with the birth of India and the partition of Kashmir in 1947 or, for that matter, with any modern event.

Jihad started when the prophet Muhammad was preparing his forcible conquest of Mecca from his exile in Medina. By 1683, Vienna, one of the imperial capitals of Europe, was besieged by the Ottomans' jihad. At about the same time, Moghul emperor Aurangzeb was carrying out a bloody jihad against the "polytheists" of southern India. The Safavid rulers of Persia, such as Shah Tahmasp of the sixteenth century, had been no less zealous in the exercise of jihad: a millennium after its inception, the Muslim jihad was as virulent as it had ever been. This millennium of "tremendous military successes spawned a triumphalist jihad literature. For a thousand years, Muslim historians recorded in detail the number of infidels slain or enslaved, the cities and villages that were pillaged, and the lands, the treasure and movable goods seized."[1] There has been no time when the world of Islam was not involved in jihad.

For much of the two centuries that followed Bonaparte's 1798 landing in Egypt, however, Islam found itself in a position of geopolitical weakness. This persistent condition gradually imbued the non-Muslim world with a false sense that Islam was in retreat, and that jihad when it occurred was purely defensive or reactive in nature. Islam was reeling under the burden of its own feebleness and the expansion of the more dynamic West, but jihad did not grind to a halt. Countless local jihads were proclaimed in India against the Sikhs and the British, in North Africa against the French, in Central Asia and the Caucasus against the Russians, in Africa against "pagans," in the Arabian Peninsula against the rest of the world. Jihad was not in abeyance: it was merely drawing the short end of the stick. There had been times when jihad was victorious, and times when jihad was ineffectual and repelled. But jihad survived the lean times.

Reforming Muslims, such as the Anglo-Indian Sir Sayyid Ahmad Khan (1817–1898), keen to adapt Islam to modernity, encouragingly claimed that jihad in the modern world could be restricted and used only in the most extreme of defensive cases, or be spiritualized entirely. The school originally centered at the Anglo-Indian College at Alighar powerfully tried to shed the intrinsically aggressive jihad. Adaptations made by apologists of Islam such as the Egyptian Mohammed Abduh (1849–1905) and his disciple the Syrian Muslim "reformer" Rashid Rida (1865–1935) were essentially rhetorical: they verbally restricted jihad to mean "defensive war in defense of Islam," while indefinitely stretching the meaning of "defense." This was *taqiyeh*, dissimulation.[2] Devious post-modern scholars, notably in the West, have since crafted convoluted rationalizations to make jihad an innocuous spiritual exercise under the label of "Greater Jihad."[3]

Jihad never died, nor did it even fade away. It continued as the Muslim *umma* faced Western expansion. To fail is neither to disappear nor to give up.

As soon as some Muslims were able to believe that the time had come to launch an offensive jihad again, they did so with great zeal. But in the process, jihad had been cross-pollinated by contact with the modern world. It is a subtle irony of history that the Wahhabis, the Muslim Brothers, the revolutionary Shiites—in short, the standard-bearers of jihad in the modern world—waged modern jihad in the name of a supposed return to pristine seventh-century Islam unsullied by contact with either the bida, the accused, heretical "innovations" that the centuries deposited upon "pure" Islam, or by the evil ways of the West; but, as this study will try to show, there is no way to understand modern contemporary jihad without taking into account the incorporation by the world of Islam and its jihadists of important inputs from the West.[4]

The first volume of this study has shown that the revolutionary "father" of Pan-Islamism, Jamal al-Din al-Afghani, was also the father of the politicization of the religious idea of the Mahdi: his political religion of Mahdism, became the fountainhead of modern jihad.[5] The second volume will show that contemporary jihad, firmly rooted in the theory and practice of jihad developed by the prophet Muhammad and his successors, as well as the consistent consensus of the Muslim doctors' jurisprudence, also drew from other, Western sources in the modern era.

In Bedouin society, and farther afield in the Arab world, the purity of lineage is central to the family, the clan, the tribe. The bloodline must be known, unsullied and well-attested. In Islam, the *hadith*, the sayings of the Prophet, must likewise be vouched for by a clear line of transmission. But contrary to the firm rules that govern tribal purity of lineage, and the precise rules that governed the compilation of the prophet's sayings, the pedigree of contemporary jihad has been muddied by hosts of impure benefactors. In spite of the most fervent, and delusional, wishes of Islamists, no "closed circle" of Muslim innocence of contamination by the modern world has been able to preserve the Islamic purity of jihad. Ironically, today's jihad is a mongrel.[6]

"Jihad made in Germany" and "Jihad made in the Soviet Union" are two principal donors to the DNA of modern and contemporary jihad.[7] All of these were gradually grafted upon the "mainline" of Islamic jihad as inherited from Muslim history, and as resurrected and transmogrified into political ideology, especially by Afghani. By the time Afghani's intellectual heirs were politically active, they had come into contact with various ideologies concocted in the West, and with various European state organizations that were keen on instrumentalizing jihad for their own purposes.

This induces a difficulty: contemporary jihad is situated both in the continuity of traditional doctrine and practice, and in significant discontinuity with pre-modern forms of jihad. The injection and assimilation of heterogenous, "alien" concepts and practices—the "Leninist" input into the canon of Sayyid Abu Ala Maududi, Sayyid Qutb and Ali Shariati: their explicit concept of jihad as world revolution, as well as their conception of the Islamists as a "vanguard party"—cannot be reduced to Islam's traditional doctrines, even as it recombines the new with the old. As in all cases of "invention of tradition," the novelty is concealed or repressed even from the consciousness of the innovator, while rigid adherence to the letter of the old compensates for the change that has in effect occurred. The neo-jihadi conception draws enough of its fundamental elements from traditional Islam to remain within the boundaries of the Islamic *ijma*, the consensus of the doctors of the community: there is no "firewall" between traditional Islam and jihadi Islam.[8] The literalism of Islam, the infinite plasticity of words drawn out of context from the Quran, *hadith* and *sharia*, allows the recombinant jihad to be both faithful to tradition and to incorporate modern elements: anyone can invoke some verse, some saying or some ruling that will fit the occasion.

Another difficulty lies with the fact that outside the ranks of the self-confessed radicals, many Islamic clerics and spokesmen, worried by a degree of exposure to the Western media, have practiced doublespeak, double-language, double-entendre and Orwellian games whenever they speak or write in English or Western languages—a variation on the traditional practice of *taqiyeh*, dissimulation. Thus we will hear endless apologetic proclamations of the type: "Islam condemns terrorism, but suicide bombing is legal if practiced for resistance, in defense of one's land; ergo, killing Israelis [or others] is merely self-defense." Or: "This act of terror cannot have been committed by a true Muslim," whereas the act so described has actually been committed by a Muslim. Rhetorically denying the quality of "Muslim" to the guilty Muslim individual is a rather dense trick; it is nevertheless systematically used to distance the *umma* from acts committed by members of the *umma*, and in the name of the *umma*'s religion, and law and glory, as was done with regard to the 9/11 hijackers.[9]

This reinforces the confusion with which contemporary jihad has been seen in the West. Under the influence of Marxism and its various offspring, a systematic error of perspective has occurred in the Western mind: the Marxist-Leninist creed painted history as a whole as a class struggle between "oppressors" and "oppressed," an entirely ahistorical simplification, and a

Manichean and Gnostic falsehood. The West had fought World War II under the banner of freedom; it found it difficult to deny freedom to restive colonial peoples afterward. Intellectually and as part of propaganda warfare, the Soviet offensive against the West made great use of the argument of freedom, morally and intellectually placing the West on the defensive.

The West itself tended to adopt or at the very least adapt to, the bogus categories used by its Soviet opponent: "colonialism" and "imperialism," as if those were self-evident categories, whereas they were loaded concepts that rested upon Lenin's fallacious theory of imperialism. Just as the mendacious concept of "exploitation" ordered much of Western thinking about social and economic relations, the notion was generally accepted, especially after 1945, that Western imperialism and colonialism were a phenomenon of a somewhat unique, unprecedented nature in human history, with uniquely noxious effect, and, conversely, that the colonized peoples, nations and states were of a pristinely innocent purity, eternally untouched by the sins so uniquely ascribed to the West.[10]

As a result, through the fall of the Evil Empire in 1989–1991, "de-colonization" was one of the catchwords of the decades that followed the fall of the Axis. Freedom from colonial oppression and imperialist domination became the prism through which "Third World" affairs were often understood. To a surprising extent this warped view of the world informed the interpretation of events. A case in point was the war waged from November 1954 by the Algerian *Front de Libération Nationale* (FLN) against France: while it was presented to a credulous outside world as a "struggle of national liberation," which it was only in part, it was preached inside Algeria and the Arab world as a jihad, which it was in greater part. Likewise, the "liberation" of Arab countries from a—historically very short—occupation or control by Western powers, in conformity with the rhetoric adopted by leaders of those movements (Nasser in Egypt, an endless series of military dictators in Syria, etc.), was interpreted as the uprising of peoples for their "national liberation," rather than as a reassertion by Muslim Arabs of the Muslim self-conception which claims world supremacy for Islam and rejects coexistence with the Other unless he is a subdued *dhimmi* or a *kufr* liable to be attacked and subjugated.

PART I
THE NOMADIC WAY OF WAR

For, lo, I raise up [a people], that bitter and hasty nation, which shall march through the breadth of the land, to possess the dwelling places that are not theirs. They are terrible and dreadful (…). Their horses also are swifter than the leopards and are more fierce than the evening wolves: and their horsemen shall spread themselves, and their horsemen shall come from far; they shall fly as the eagle that hasteth to eat. They shall come all for violence: their faces shall sup up as the east wind, and they shall gather the captivity as the sand.

HABAKKUK, 1:6–9 [11]

Nomads, physically tough, logistically mobile, culturally accustomed to shedding blood, ethically untroubled by religious prohibition against taking the lives or limiting the freedom of those outside the tribe—learned that war paid.

JOHN KEEGAN [12]

Nomads of Eurasia and of Arabia

At the outset of his classic *L'Empire des Steppes*, the great historian René Grousset quotes the Biblical echo of the terrors felt by sedentary populations beleaguered by raiding nomadic warriors. The waves of pastoralists' invasions of settled peoples' lands, he avers, "have been one of the main drivers of the drama of history."[13] The earth-shattering role played over more than fifteen centuries by Eurasia's nomadic warriors found a match in the southern desert's nomadic warriors, the Arab Bedouins. The outcomes generated by these destroyers diverged substantially, though: the eruptions of the Eurasian nomads obliterated every kingdom and empire that stood in their way, but their energy dissipated soon enough that the conquerors melted away amongst the conquered peoples; the religion of the Arabs took hold of the vanquished, and with it, the political, juridical and ideological mode of organization that Islam entails.

Three belts of desert and steppeland gird the Old World. They breed a particular human type: the nomad. The great Eurasian steppe designated as the "Heartland" by Halford Mackinder is "a great continuous patch in the north and the center of the continent," a plain that stretches from Manchuria to Hungary, from Polar coasts to Baluchistan and Persia. Oases are scattered along the Heartland's southern rim; they became the stations on the Silk Road, but could not replace waterways (until the advent of the railway, overland transportation was always far more expensive than water-borne trade). This vast, landlocked expanse is the defining environment of the people who inhabit it.[14]

To the southwest, the Sahara is the world's largest, most unbroken natural boundary. Throughout history it has been a barrier: contrary to the northern steppe, its barren immensity has prevented it from becoming a breeding ground for a vast number of predators forever ready to swoop down on farming communities.[15]

Both the Sahara and the Eurasian expanse are landlocked. But "Arabistan," the region extending "from the Nile to the Euphrates, from the Taurus to Aden," is different. One half of Arabia is a desert, and the other half mainly dry steppes. Although it lies in the same latitudes as the Sahara, it is more productive and carries a more considerable population of wandering Bedouins. Moreover, it has larger oases, and therefore larger cities. Arabia is traversed by three great waterways in connection with the ocean—the Nile, the Red Sea, and the Euphrates—and the Persian Gulf, which distinguishes it from the Heartland. The steppes of Arabia that frame its deserts serve as a passage-land between the Northern and Southern Heartlands.[16] The Eurasian steppe is a vast avenue, the Arabian desert is a crossroad, the Sahara is a barrier.

The harsh natural conditions of the steppe and the desert enable them only to sustain a very limited population with low productivity. What populations do live in those environments only survive at the margin, "at the edge of subsistence."[17] The climate is extreme, with an 80°C variation between winter and summer: "[I]t is a climate for the hardy and it has historically been the home of the nomad." It is precisely the low-productivity habitat that creates nomadism: nomads cannot survive by remaining stationary. The nomads are forced to move in search of grassland and water, the critical resources they and their animals depend upon. "The true nomad is a migratory creature shifting his home twice a year between summer and winter pastures which are recognized by the tribe, and by neighboring tribes, even though they may be hundreds of miles apart or found at different altitudes. He travels as he does because he is a pastoralist.... However, the steppe will not feed the flock and herds all year around in a single spot."[18]

In this peculiar setting, the struggle for life leads to survival of the toughest. The nomad's way of life is his way of war: as peoples live, they fight. "War is … a natural consequence of successful nomadism."[19] In the desert and steppe, competition is unforgiving and intense among groups that must compete for rare resources. "The gain or loss of watering places and pastures made a difference for the nomad, between riches and poverty, even between life and death from famine."[20] Living on one's own for any significant period of time is impossible. The lonely days of young Temujin, the future Chingis Khan, as a fugitive described in *The Secret History of the Mongols* did not last long: days as renegades were just that—days. To survive the elements, poverty and the predatory behavior of fellow nomads, the group, in the shape of the clan and the tribe, of necessity forms the basic unit of nomadic life.[21]

The Mongols were the most successful of all nomadic warriors, an ideal type of the species. In this environment, "men learned to use their tools to the absolute limits of human skill and endurance. Here there was no margin for error." Men, horses, equipment were stripped to the bone, as it were. This "produced a warrior as cruel and free from ceremonialism as he was self-sufficient. And of these, none was harder and more ruthless than the nomadic Mongolian tribes living in and around the Gobi Desert, where in an endless combat among themselves and their neighbors, they perfected the sweeping tactics of ruse and lightning attack… [and formed] the most voracious fighting force ever assembled."[22]

The products of the nomads' animals, though supplying them with basic daily subsistence, are insufficient to keep them alive; extreme poverty can be mitigated only by contact with settled people: "The nomad, whether he wants it or not, must deal with settled people to some degree." In fact, the more "pure-type" nomad he is, the more his "survival depends upon either trade with or predation upon settled people."[23] The domestication of the horse made plundering practical. The use of archery made it irresistible. "Nomads could cover great distances to attack settled people, the distance protecting the nomads and at the same time allowing them to surprise their opponents.

Archery was a perfect skill to allow fighting without coming to close quarters... the nomads were the best horsemen because they rode every day to manage their herds."

The imbalance in wealth and the disequilibrium in warfighting abilities mean that "[t]he periodic onrush of the nomads toward the cultivated lands is a law of nature," writes Grousset, who adds:

> Whence come that this adventure succeeds nearly every time, that the same cycle occurs again and again over thirteen centuries—since there are 1,300 years between the entrance of the Huns into Loyang and the entrance of the Manchus into Beijing? The answer is that throughout that period, the nomad, while very backward by his material culture, enjoyed a huge edge and military advantage. He was the mounted archer. An incredibly mobile cavalry of unfailing archers, this is the technology that earned him a superiority over the settled peoples nearly equal to the superiority artillery, in modern times, gave Europe over the rest of the world.[24]

In the confrontation between nomads and settled peoples, both "species" behave according to utterly different operating principles. The nomad carries his capital with him, and wages war on the basis of much, if not most, of this capital. His capital investment—herds, horses; his labor skills—horsemanship, archery, speed, mobility, flexibility—apply evenly to war and peace. There is complete continuity between war and peace, as opposed to settled peoples' neat delineation of a state of peace and a state of war. As Miklós Jankovich puts it, "the nomads' life presented no great contrast as between war and peace."[25] As Spartans in Ancient Greece, settled people need specially to train for war, they need to muster themselves for war, they need to take time and energy out of their peacetime activities in order to be at war. Nomads' normal activities, herding and hunting, embody the selfsame ingredients as their warlike ones. As a rule, sedentary societies are not military societies—with a few exceptions like Sparta (a polity that entirely relied on slave labor for its livelihood). Inasmuch as this continuity obtains, nomadic societies are always military.

As a result, in Grousset's striking formulation, the zone of the nomads' habitat "had remained a repository [*un conservatoire*] of barbary. The survival of this humanity that had remained at the pastoral stage while the rest of Asia had long before that moved ahead into the most advanced agricultural level... led to something of a time-chasm [*un décalage chronologique*: an asymmetry in time,

LM] among neighboring peoples. Men from the second millennium B.C. thus co-existed with men from the twelfth century A.D."[26] Hence the peculiarly lop-sided relationship between predator and prey, one defined by one-sided violence. The nomad is "dumbfounded at the view of the miracle of sedentary civilization, the bountiful harvests, villages bursting with grain, the luxury of the cities. This miracle, or rather the secret behind the miracle, the patient toiling that was required to create those human beehives, the Hun has no means of understanding it. If he is dazzled, he is dazzled like the wolf—his totemic animal—that comes close to the farmhouses: behind the hedges, it glimpses prey. The age-old instinct of the Hun is likewise to burst in by surprise, to plunder, to flee with his loot."[27]

The brutality bred into the nomad by his environment means that the predator deals with the prey mercilessly, as if the latter were an animal to be gouged. "The nomad's contempt for the sedentary way of life was proverbial, and in this context the agriculturalist became virtually a separate species—to be preyed upon and exploited.... The record is full of ghastly tactical tricks played upon the nomads' opponents with horrific effect, and all are united by a uniform Mongol disregard for any shared humanity between themselves and those they attack."[28] The Mongols did not have a concept of other people as "humanity." There was "us" on the one hand, and all Others, lesser creatures, animals, prey— this is a constant in nomadic warfare wherever it ever took place.[29] War historian John Keegan's interpretation of the nomads' way of killing is that they apply to men the butcher's skills they practice upon their herds.[30] Chingis Khan's Mongols gloried in presenting themselves thus in the *Secret History*: "They pursue men like game. They slay them and take from them everything." They define themselves in this way:

> [Tayang] Who are those who pursue us like wolves hunting a herd?
> [Jumuga] They are the four hunting dogs of my brother Temujin [Chingis Khan] ; they feed on human flesh and are on an iron chain; their skull is of bronze, their teeth cut in rock, their tongues are like swords, their heart is of iron. Rather than whips, they have curved swords; the dew quenches their thirst and they gallop like the wind; in the battle they devour human flesh. Now they are rampant, they are foaming at the mouth, they are in joy."

Nomads all share some fundamental characteristics; bloodlust is one: "Amongst those descended from the Hiong-Nu, the Tou-kiue of the sixth century [A.D.], the number of stones that will honor the tumulus of a warrior was in proportion to the number of people he killed in his lifetime. The Indo-European as well as the Turco-Mongol nomads give off the same scent of blood."[31] To wit: "Any Scythian who killed his first enemy must drink his blood.... Any self-respecting Scythian makes it a point of honor, when he receives eminent visitors, to present his collection of heads."

Slavery logically ensues: "Subjugated populations were viewed as chattel to be exploited for their skills—or killed. The cruelty of Chingis Khan's armies is… legendary."[32] Tolstoy called the social organization of the pastoral peoples "a military state with the institution of slavery." The herdsmen's most valuable booty came to be the prisoner of war who could be enslaved. As the economic interests of many pastoral tribes widened they came to include an organized slave trade.

The disproportion is always impressive between nomadic aggressors and sedentary victims: "[G]iven equal populations, nomads will field a larger army than a sedentary people, and this, to some degree, will offset a settled people's advantage in numbers."[33] Thirteenth century Mongolia was home to no more than 800,000 inhabitants, but Mongol armies numbering no more than a few dozen thousand men took over a Chinese Empire of 115 million; among their principal other victims, Persia and the Khwarezmian Empire counted possibly 10 million souls, and the Abbasid Empire probably more. The numbers of the Turkic Ghaznavids who conquered much of India and absorbed it into the *dar al-Islam* were paltry compared to 80 millions Hindus. The entire "Turanian" area of modern Kazakhstan, Uzbekistan, Kyrgyzstan, Turkmenistan, and Tajikistan, home to much of the nomads, counted about 2.5 million. Arabia writ large counted no more than two million people by the time of Muhammad.[34] But 500,000 Arab warriors conquered populations of twenty or thirty million.[35] The concept of "military participation ratio" applies: the "MPR" is highest among nomadic peoples.[36]

Let us consider more systematically the shape of the nomadic way of war as it emerges from historical evidence. A first character is the exceptional mobility with which the mastery of his mounts endows the nomad pastoralist. "The force of a blow may be due as much to its speed as to its weight."[37] Another historian completes the explanation:

> The combination of the horse and the bow gave the steppe warrior a devastating combination of speed and maneuverability coupled with the most

effective missile weapon of the day. On the steppe, he would travel long distances quickly, maneuver on the battlefield, resist charges and re-form, and kill from a distance. He was not a practitioner of hand-to-hand or shock warfare because the steppe warrior had great mobility on the battlefield and such an ability to cover distances in a short time, the military style of these people was one of wide-ranging, quick contests and an unwillingness to come to grips with an enemy until victory was certain. This was in contrast to Western armies, who preferred to fight at close quarters and rely on the shock of their attack to decide the issue.[38]

The technique of war is inherent in the nomadic way of life.[39] As Herodotus recounted in his narrative of Persian King Darius' invasion of the Scythian nomads' steppe area, the Scythians' tactic was to retreat before the huge Persian army while it advanced and attack it if and when it retreated. Darius was frustrated at his inability to join battle—his forte; the nomads eluded and harassed—their strong suit: it was not the first time, and certainly not the last that an asymmetry of this kind occurred.[40] The Scythians even allowed the Persians a few minor successes to cheer them and lead them on, into the heart of the empty steppe. "This method was quite consistent with the steppe warriors' desire to wear the enemy without closing—to fight, if possible, with stratagem."[41]

The Parthians famously vanquished Roman triumvir Crassus in the first century B.C. in the Syrian desert. At Carrhae, as Plutarch relates:[42] the Roman Legions fell in battle formation waiting for the shock; instead of charging, the Parthians backed away as if they were breaking ranks, while in reality they were simply fleeing from view and enveloping the Legions. Crassus ordered his light infantry to run forward—volleys of missiles stopped them and forced them to retreat, smack into the heavy infantry, which caused some turmoil in the ranks. The volleys of arrows continued to kill and maim, until the Roman Legion cracked, and was slaughtered nearly to a man. "Carrhae is a near-perfect example of steppe tactics: shooting from a distance, shooting while retreating, the feigned retreat to draw and disorder an enemy, and encirclement to maximize the effect of archery by allowing as many horse archers as possible to have a target. Against those tactics in an open plain, the excellent close-fighting Roman infantry was completely unsuited to reply."[43]

The nomadic Goths who inflicted a terrible defeat upon the Romans at Adrianopolis (Edirne) in 378 A.D. used the same "whirlwind" tactics to devastating effect. On that battlefield, "the novelty consisted in [the Goths having adopted] the Hunnish tactic of repeated feint attacks which brought the ranks of their adversaries into such disorder that the battle ended in a devastating defeat for the Romans."[44] Attila's Huns wreaked extreme havoc in mid-fifth century Europe: "[their] sweeping and encircling maneuvers of bodies of men shooting from the saddle and rarely closing, at least until the fight was nearly done."[45] Roman historian Ammianus Marcellinus left a precious and similar description of the Huns' fighting tactics:

> They are very quick in their operations, of exceeding speed, and fond of surprising their enemies (…) they suddenly disperse, then reunite. After having inflicted vast loss upon the enemy, scatter themselves over the whole plain in irregular formations, always avoiding a fight or an entrenchment. And in one respect you may pronounce them the most formidable of all warriors, for when at distance they use missiles of various kinds tipped with sharpened bones instead of the usual points of javelin or arrow; but when they are at close quarter they fight with the sword without any regard for their own safety.[46]

Using another image, J.F.C. Fuller called this "whirlwind" tactic "cyclonic."[47] The great Byzantine warrior, military theorist and emperor Maurice (539–602 A.D.) "could see that all steppe nomads were cut from the same cloth and would exhibit the same military characteristics."[48] To wit:

> They prefer battles fought at long range, ambushes encircling their adversaries, simulated retreats and sudden returns, and wedge-shaped formations, that is, in scattered groups. When they make their enemies take to flight, they put everything else aside, and are not content, as the Persians, the Romans, and other peoples, with pursuing them a reasonable distance and plundering their goods, but they do not let up at all until they have achieved the complete destruction of their enemies, and they employ every means to this end.

To describe the "Tatars" of the thirteenth century, Marco Polo explains:

> When these Tatars come to engage in battle, they never mix with the enemy, but keep hovering about him, discharging their arrows first from one side and then from the other, occasionally pretending to flee, and during their flight shooting arrows backwards at their pursuers, killing men and horses as if they were combating face to face. In this sort of warfare the adversary imagines he

has gained a victory, when in fact he has lost the battle, for the Tatars, observing the mischief they have done him, wheel about, make them prisoners in spite of their utmost exertions. Their horses are so broken in to quick changes of movement, that upon the signal given they instantly turn in every direction; and by these rapid maneuvers many victories have been obtained.[49]

The description of the Mongol written by the Pope's envoy to Chingis Khan, the Italian Franciscan Plan Carpini (1246) eerily resembles earlier accounts of Scythians, Huns, Magyars, in short, of all nomadic warriors.[50] Grousset summarizes it:

Mongol tactic is the old, if perfected tactic of the Hiong-nu and the Tou-Kiue, the eternal tactic of nomads shaped by their regular razzias into the edges of cultivated lands, and also by the hunt's great beats [*battues*] in the steppe. "In full daylight, Chingis Khan is reported by tradition to have said, to lie in wait [*guetter*] with a wolf's vigilance, at night with the raven's eyes. In battle, swoop down on the prey like the hawk." The patient stalking [*affût*] in wait for the herds of deer, taught the nomads to dispose ahead of their march a line of silent and invisible scouts whose mission is to observe, and, while remaining unseen by the game or the enemy. Their use of a net of beaters [*rabatteurs*] in the hunt has taught them the practice of the flanking maneuver which allows them to overwhelm the enemy army on both sides, as a fleeing herd of savage beasts in the prairie is encircled. The mobility of the nomads' cavalry thus generates a surprise effect, an impression of ubiquity, which prior to any action disconcerts the opponent. Should he be numerically strong and hold fast, the Mongol squads do not insist, they scatter. They disappear like all the steppe marauders do, the better to come back as soon as the enemy's vigilance has relaxed (…) [The Mongol] practices the hunter's atavistic ruses who affrights the beast to bring it at his mercy.… The Mongols' [greatest campaigns] look like gigantic beasts that tire out the game, affright it, surround it, exhaust it and, at the end of the hunt, the methodical killing.[51]

A second characteristic of the nomadic way of war is to "affright" the prey, and use terror as a foremost method. "Terror had become a useful tool—purposeful terror could be just as useful as siegecraft, and caused fewer Mongol losses. The destruction that took place during Mongol campaigns was appalling."[52] Further, "terror was, in some cases, cultivated. Mongol generals used wholesale slaughter in tandem with selective sparing of small numbers of prisoners induced to flee to other parts in order to spread panic. The Mongols knew the value of calculated terror; as a campaign progressed, more and more cities and towns would surrender to them without a fight."[53] The effect of terror was striking: "Terror-induced passivity was the intent, and atrocity and rapid movement the major means of accomplishment," writes another historian."[54]

Thus the Huns slaughtered "two-thirds of the inhabitants of Gandhara," the admirable Indo-Hellenic kingdom that was heir to Alexander the Great's adventure.[55] The Southern Hiong-Nu captured the Chinese capital of Chang-An and slaughtered one half of the population.[56] Later, the Mongols took Peking, "slaughtered the inhabitants, looted the houses, and set the city on fire…." Grousset aptly calls them "the last levy of barbarism [*l'arrière-ban de la barbarie*] (…) a people that had barely crawled out of primitive savagery, which seeks to gain its enemies' submission but through a system of generalized terror; [it is] a people to which human life is of no value whatsoever."[57] The Mongols perfected a system they had by no means invented: they went to the extreme of methods natural to the nomads. It is estimated that the price paid for Chingis' conquest of Northern China was the loss of one third of the population, or 30 to 40 million lives. The entire population of Gurganj, the capital of Khwarezm, was slaughtered, and the city itself vanished, as the Mongols drowned it under the waters of the Amu-Darya River. In 1221, the male population of the great and ancient Persian city of Rey was exterminated. The population of Balkh was exterminated wholesale. The Mongol general Tolui "sat in the plain [outside the city] and observed the mass butchery of the population. Men, women, children, were separated and distributed in herds to the various battalions and they were beheaded. The same general stormed the great city of Nishapur and destroyed it altogether. "To make sure there would be no simulators, they cut off the heads of the corpses and erected pyramids of human heads, different ones for men, for women and for children." In Bamyan—where the Talibans recently destroyed the historic statues of the Buddha—"no loot was taken: everything was annihilated, no prisoner was made, every living creature was massacred." The next year, in and around Herat, a foundation of Alexander's, "the entire population was slaughtered—the butchery took a week." As Chingis moved West, Hamadan, Ardibil, Zandjan, Qazwin, all big cities, were treated likewise.[58]

The story is repeated *ad nauseam* in other places, wherever the Mongols went. As Grousset emphasizes: "Chingis Khan was one of the scourges of mankind. In his person he sums up twelve centuries of invasions of the old sedentary civilizations by the steppe nomads.... He elevated terror to a system of government and massacre as a methodical institution.... The mass butcheries of the Mongol conqueror were part of a way of war, they were the nomad's weapon against the settled peoples who did not prostrate themselves in time...."[59] Baghdad is besieged and stormed. On February 10, 1258, the caliph himself came out of the city to surrender to [Chingis' grandson] Hülagü. The latter told him to order the entire population to exit the city and surrender its weapons. The unarmed inhabitants came in droves to surrender to the Mongols who slaughtered them immediately. In the seventeen days of the sack, 90,000 reportedly lost their life.[60]

Tamerlane, though a Turkic son of Samarqand, was a proper heir to Chingis' legacy, and a pious Muslim. The insurgent Persian garrison of Sebzewar was caught: "Almost 2,000 prisoners were piled up alive on top of one another with mud and bricks and towers were built."[61] The rebellious Persian region of Sistan was treated identically: "Our soldiers," the hagiographical history of Timur entitled the *Zafernameh* recounts "made a mount of dead bodies and with the heads they built towers." In Zarenj, the capital of Sistan, Tamerlane "exterminated the people, men and women, young and old, from the centenarians to the babies." In 1387 he "ordered the extermination of the [entire] population. Each division of his army had to report to the board a set number of severed heads. The *Zafernameh*... reports 70,000 severed heads "piled up outside the walls of Isfahan."[62] Tamerlane also took Baghdad and exacted a body-count of 90,000. The conquest of "pagan" (Hindu) India produced the conqueror's worst massacres, symbolized by the killing of 100,000 prisoners before the great battle at Delhi, which underwent the same fate. Returning West to Syria and the Levant, Tamerlane inflicted the same fate on Aleppo, Hama, Homs, Baalbeck and Damascus.

The Mongols had merely brought to a systematic state of perfection a manner inherent to the nomads' way of war. The Huns or the Avars before them, the Turkic Oghuz and their kin the Seljuq, the Ghaznavids later and the Ottomans, practiced similar kinds of terror.[63]

Mobility and terror were the means and the result of the mode in which nomadic warfare was carried out: the raid. The supreme case of the deadliest of all, Tamerlane, shows that, strategically, nomadic warfare is essentially a raid. We are now in possession of all the essential characteristics of nomadic warfare: tactically, as we have seen, nomadic warfare very much relies on surprise (the ambush), ruse (the feigned retreat, the ghost horsemen) and intelligence (Chingis Khan's intelligence preparations were thorough and meticulous); it takes the form of a whirlwind ("cyclone"); it operates through the sudden concentration of scattered groups and one of its chief techniques is terror.[64]

Strikingly, identical characteristics, which together add up to an ideal type, will be found in types of nomadic warfare that are remote from steppe and desert: the great wave of Norsemen's raids into Europe which began at the very end of the eighth century display what we have identified here as the basic traits of nomadic warfare. The Vikings' long boats were as sea horses that endowed their crews of warriors with a mobility none of their opponents could match. "The tactics of the Vikings produced a most difficult pattern… the Viking raiding force was an elusive, swift, fleeting target." The "massacres, looting and burning [were] the normal pattern of Viking raids," military historians tell us.[65] Their endless raids were powerful enough to shatter and dislocate Charlemagne's empire. Just as the land-based nomadic warrior enjoyed a decisive technological edge with his combination of mount and archery, their ships' advanced design gave them unheard-of speed and seaworthiness, which in turn allowed their deep penetration raids to outflank all defenses. While there are some differences between, for instance, the Norsemen with their boats, and the Huns or Magyars with their horses, they were of the same species.[66]

Finally, this portrait of nomadic society must include the prominent role of the energetic and charismatic chieftain. Nomads are organized on the basis of the extended family, the clan and the tribe: the low productivity of pastoral life in steppe and desert conditions does not allow for larger groups. The constraints imposed by the low productivity of the environment are such as to preclude lonely, isolated existence such as that of the free farmer in Western Europe, and to prevent the formation of very large groups. Hence the existence of loose tribal confederations. The unit appropriate to the environmental and economic constraints is the family and at most the clan. Family and clan solidarity are a lifeline for all. Like that of all nomadic peoples, "tribal composition was fluid; chiefship was precarious and followings split and coalesced unpredictably." The instability had much to do with the opportunities for plunder the chief was able, or not, to offer: "Mongol (and Turkish) social organization was notoriously fluid and a given tribe depended upon the strength of its leader for stability and protection. Steppe nomads willingly joined other leaders whom they regarded as great warriors. Power on the steppe stemmed from the person of individual leaders rather than from established institutions, as with settled peoples. For a khan to rise to high station of ruling absolutely—over his own tribe and others—one must needs become an absolute despot… to achieve that he must start with a clean slate."[67]

This fluid organization needs to be nourished by outside loot. Pastoralist warriors are "a parasitic community of marauders."[68] Discussing Chingis Khan, a historian relates: "In order to keep his restive people in hand [he] had to offer them plunder—this was one of the main duties of a khan to his following."[69] It is equally the case for the Bedouin chieftain or Attila the Hun: "whether for attack or defense, the tribe must be well led and the leader must have absolute authority."[70]

Loot is a powerful lure. If the leader who leads his warriors to it is endowed with charisma, if he proves a great warrior, he will transcend the limits of mere traditional legitimacy of power and unite more and larger units of the loose tribal confederacy. A suggestive portrait of Attila and the sociology of his power is given by J.F.C. Fuller:

> Attila's rule over the confederacy he inherited was absolute, and though when he appeared among his people they received him with shouts of applause, their respect for him was based solely upon fear, for all stood in terror of him. 'He realized more clearly than any of his predecessors, writes [E.A.] Thompson, that if all the tribes could be united under an unquestioned and absolute leader, the Huns would form an unparalleled instrument for the exploitation of the peoples of Central Europe…. Instead of ruling on the unruly and divided tribal chiefs, he based his power on vassals… who were bound to him personally by an inviolable allegiance without the handicap of tribal obligations.'[71]

Power and stability of the fissile, fractious nomads were always threatened. Turks and Mongols "were similar and primitive… any confederation or polity depended for its existence upon the force of the leader's personality, so that his death often ended the state… a steppe state was inherently unstable… incipient divisions waiting only for the death of the leader to work their ways."[72]

Rarely, an exceptional leader rises and transcends the limits of nomadic life. This occurred in 1206:

> Now Chingis Khan held supreme power in the steppe, but as we know, steppe empires were intrinsically unstable; they exist as a consequence of the strength and acumen of the leader. Chingis Khan was, however, more successful than any of his nomadic predecessors. Why? He recognized the fluid nature of the

steppe tribes, their willingness to amalgamate voluntarily into larger units under the leadership of a man they respected, and he knew a corollary to this: defeated tribes could be effectively integrated into a steppe empire because they did not differ appreciably as a matter of culture. Thus he was able to build upon a base of those whom he defeated. However, he did not simply take all these different tribesmen into his army to create a mere congeries. Instead, he employed the technique of decimal organization to set it in order. This was familiar to the steppe, going back at least to the Hiong-Nu in the 3rd century B.C., and could be used as effectively to establish political control as to ensure military discipline.[73]

The nation-builder also legislated:

Chingis' favorite shaman, Kokochu, had long before predicted that it was the will of Heaven that Chingis Khan and his family rule the earth, and this too was played upon the superstitious nomads. With all means, Chingis Khan groped toward the creation of a sort of nation-state that might survive him, and he had some success in creating a polity of great military power for his use and that his descendants. An important part of this polity was a code of laws called the *yassaq*. Chingis Khan is credited with drafting it, though much of it merely codified existing nomadic superstition. It went further than this, however…. The *yassaq* stabilized the Mongol nation by removing some of the causes of its instability. The army, however, was the single most important institution of the Mongol state.[74]

As will become clear at a larger stage of this study, it is my contention that the emergence of Prophet Muhammad was an occurrence comparable to Attila, Chingis or Tamerlane; that his Bedouins were comparable to the Huns and Avars and Qiptaqs and other Turks, the Mongols and the Manchus; that the formation of the original Islamic state greatly resembles that of the more successful Eurasian nomadic states; that the creation of the Muslim *umma* and that of the Mongol nation are of the same nature—that is the gradual amalgamation of diverse tribal forces under one charismatic warlord who transcends traditional tribal loyalties and transfers them upon himself and the polity he creates; and that Muhammad's legislative activity resembles that of Chingis, the former's *yassaq*, resembles the legislative activity of the latter, as consigned especially in the Medina *suras* of the Quran. Thus, just as "Chingis Khan tried singlehandedly to form a new artificial nation called the Mongols which comprehended more than merely the Mongol tribe of old and to which these amalgamated nomadic people would thenceforward belong,"[75] Muhammad established the *umma* as an "artificial" nation based on religion, the nation of the Muslims, the super-tribe which entirely recast traditional tribal affiliations.

The Northern and the Southern pastoralists, the steppe nomads and the desert Bedouins resembled each other. Already in the fourteenth century, Ibn Khaldun remarked of the latter: "they are the most savage human beings that exist. Compared with sedentary people, they are on a level with wild, untamable animals and dumb beasts of prey. Such people are the Bedouins. In the West, the nomadic Berbers and the Zanatah are their counterparts, and in the East, the Kurds, the Turcomans and the Turks."[76] The similarity extended to their geopolitics, as the Belgian medievalist Henri Pirenne observed: "The Arab conquest unleashed both upon Europe and Asia [was] unprecedented; the speed of its successes can only be compared to the speed with which the Mongols empires were erected, Attila's, later Chingis Khan's or Tamerlane's. But the latter proved to be as ephemeral as the Islamic conquest proved durable."[77]

The Prophet's Nomads

The decisive difference between all Eurasian nomads, Mongols included, and Muhammad's Arabs was religion. The Mongols' religion and their primitive culture faded away, the Arabs' persisted and spread to much of the Old World. As we stated at the beginning of this study, the outcomes of the nomadic expansions, that of Eurasia and that of Arabia, diverged substantially.

Much of the difference between Eurasian and Arabian nomads stemmed from differences in their native environment's productivity, from their access to waterways that were not landlocked and from their proximity to and participation in international trade flows. Scythians, Huns, Goths, Avars, Alans, Bulgars, Magyars had no towns. At best they had what Grousset calls "ambulatory towns," convoys of chariots like the Huns. By contrast, the Arabs of Arabia had oasis towns. The Eurasian nomads had no merchant class of their own, whereas the oases merchants traveled far and wide and provided a connecting link between outer cultures and the deep-desert Bedouins. Whilst the Arabs derived a writing system from their neighbors, the steppe nomads had neither a literate culture nor a writing system. The Eurasian nomads raided and traded on the edges of the great civilization: the Roman armies had employed the Arabs of Syria for centuries, cousins to the Arabs of Arabia, as auxiliary and border troops, and so had the Persian Empire, to the point that both had long sustained Arab client-statelets. Cultural influences seeped into Arabia from the north and south, from *Arabia Felix*, the Yemen, which had been a Jewish kingdom until the early sixth century, from Christian Abyssinia, an ally of Byzantium; merchant ships plied the Indian Ocean from India to Oman and the Persian Gulf and back, transporting wares from the Far East to the Nile and the Mediterranean that often trans-shipped through the peninsula across the Red Sea. With trade came culture and religion. Primitive though the Arabs of Arabia were, they were led by an elite, such as Mecca's merchant tribe of Quraysh, the Prophet's own. The Quran is shot through with Jewish and Christian folktales, echoes from the Torah and the Gospel, with Gnostic inputs, often conveyed through Nestorian and Monophysite heresies. The texts assembled under the title of the *Quran*, whatever their intrinsic value, testify to a level of civilization far higher than, for example, that of the Mongols, as measured by the latter's *Secret History*.

Tengri, the Mongols' supreme deity (Heaven) was a vague divinity. The Mongols' religion was inchoate, as are all shamanic cults. Their animistic cult of nature and the elements had little consistency. They were possessed of "a universal superstitious disquiet" which "created a universal tolerance." In their "pantheon," there was room for every possible deity. As a result, all enjoyed their benevolence: "Nestorian priests they found amongst the Keraits and Öngüts, the Uighurs' and Kitans' Buddhist monks, the Daoist magicians from China, Tibetan lamas, Franciscan missionaries, Muslim mullahs, [all of whom] were likely to hold some supernatural powers."[78] Later, Chingis' grandson, the Yüen (Mongol) Emperor of China Kubilai Khan, became thoroughly Sinicized, and his grandson the Il-Khan of Persia was correspondingly Persianized. The amorphous, primitive Mongol culture dissolved into the far larger numbers of the cultures it had subjugated, just as their religion melted away. The Mongols ended up being thoroughly absorbed by their subjects, even to the extent of losing their own language.

Some of the nomads' shamans were not only endowed with magical powers, but also sometimes vested with royalty.[79] Chingis Khan was content to be the Great Khan, and was no shaman; he had no prophetic revelation to offer.

However, the Arab warlord Muhammad, who became the unifier of the Arabs, did have one. Prophet, fortuneteller, the oracular diviners, clairvoyant and seer, he was one of several such prophets who appeared at the time in Arabia who, like the shamans, practiced the art of prophecy.[80]

Where Chingis Khan was a warlord, and a legislator, but not a shaman, Muhammad the leader was warlord and prophet, a formidable combination of military, political, charismatic, poetic and, in the eyes of his followers, preternatural power. This was "as if Arminius had been a prophet as well and had united all the Germanic peoples under his leadership," the great German historian of war Hans Delbrück wrote.[81] Like the Arabs, the Germanic barbarians of the *Völkerwanderungen* had served as mercenaries guarding the peripheries of the civilized empires, Roman, Byzantine and Persian. But "the Germans had nothing and brought with them nothing but their warriorhood. They were still pure barbarians."[82] The difference: "[t]he Arabs had… for a long time a double element: the warlike barbarian nomadic element, the Bedouins of the desert; and a city-dwelling, merchant citizenry with a considerable degree of culture. Both elements were held together by their common ethnicity, their language, and a common religious culture, which no doubt was intentionally fostered by the traders in Mecca in order to moderate and control the hostility and the savagery of the Bedouins."[83]

The Arabs' wars of conquest were a great historical novelty. Not because nomadic raids were unable to assemble a vast empire in a very short period of time. Both to the east and the west of Eurasia, the Huns, the Avars, the Bulgars, to mention but a few of them, had done just that. For the very first time in recorded history, however, the nomadic way of war had been merged with an aggressive and conquering religious faith. The new mix was mighty. For the first time, the nomads' religion became the rationale and the justification for plunder and conquest, rather than mere *aura sacra fames*. "The Arabs transfused warfare with a new force altogether, the force of an idea." They fought for Allah, the Prophet and the *umma*.[84]

What Muhammad, merchant, *kahin* and warlord, did was to fuse everything "into a political-religious unity. Islam is… a political-military national organization based on the power of religion." What he did, to proselytize and recruit the raw, explosive energy of primitive tribesmen, would serve as a template for all future Islamic history.

In 1910, the future King Abdulazziz ibn Saud sent Wahhabi missionaries to proselytize the illiterate pagan Bedouins of the deep desert of Arabia. The envoys turned the "untamable" energies of the tribes into a mighty, fanatical force, the *Ikhwan*, who conquered him a kingdom in torrents of blood and destruction.[85] "When the [war] is one of religion, we exterminate everybody," as one of the king's parents put it.[86] Like so many would-be Mahdis, religious "reformers" and other founders of dynasties in Muslim history, the founder of "Saudi" Arabia, Ibn Saud, and his associate, the Wahhabi al Al-Sheikh, were replicating the process whereby the Prophet's armies and state had been forged thirteen centuries before that. It is the association of the *sheikh* and the *jawad*, of the theologian and the warrior, that is "the double reality of Muslim power."[87] Every wave of revivalism in Muslim history, the ascent of the Almohads, the rise of the Almoravids, the "Mad Mahdi of Somaliland" as well as the Sudanese Mahdi in the late nineteenth century, repeats this deep-seated pattern: the neophytes burn with fanatical zealotry, and they are put in the service of some messianic warlord.

To study this "raw material" that fed Muslim revival wars, and how it was turned into new armies and new polities, no better guide is available than fourteenth-century sociologist and historian Ibn Khaldun. The North African born thinker drew a comprehensive and compelling portrait of those whom he calls "the Arabs," meaning the nomads of the deep desert—the Bedouins. His depiction bears out the species-kinship that unites the nomads of the Eurasian North with those of the Arabian South.

The Bedouins portrayed by Ibn Khaldun are feral in their behavior. They "lead a life of misery and want" in a hostile environment, "the desert, this place of dearth and scarcity."[88] Their way of life has made them intrepid and courageous as a second nature, and "more apt to dominate the others." As a result, "because of the nature of their life away from [civilization], the Arabs are practitioners of plunder and destruction. They loot whatever they can grab… the [fertile] plains are the object of their greed." This is because they are "accustomed to living in isolation… the Arabs are a fierce nation. Their lonely life is part of their character and their nature. They enjoy it because it allows them to be free from the yoke of authority." Nomadic, "they usually spend their entire life on the move, traveling, which stands in opposition and in contradiction with a settled life, which generates civilization." They are destructive: "It is natural to them to loot what belongs to others. To earn their daily keep, they count on their spears alone. Their taste for extorting other people's chattels is limitless."

These "Arabs" are a lawless people: "Under their government, the subjects live in a state of anarchy." And the Bedouins themselves "all want to command.

Seldom will an Arab concede power to an other.... Hence are found among them a multitude of governors and emirs. Their subjects must obey multiple authorities."

Such was Muhammad's "raw material" and such were the workings of the prophethood that channeled the savage energy of the nomads into Islamic war.

As amongst nomadic groups the world over, the pre-Islamic way of war in the Arabian Peninsula was the razzia, or raid, a word derived from the Arabic word *ghazwa*, sometimes transcribed as *rezzou*. It is variously described as "the basic feature of tribal life,"[89] or "an ordinary part of the routine of tribal life."[90] It "aimed at aggression or revenge upon a rival tribe, and achieved by killing the enemy's fighting men (thereby crippling its power and ability to survive in the harsh environment of the desert), and by carrying off its camels or wealth and captives from it as slaves." In the desert environment, the structural function of the raid was to effect a "redistribution of wealth and women:" it took stock of the fluctuating balance of forces amongst tribal groups; it measured it and translated what changes had occurred in manpower and warring skills into loss or acquisition of wealth and human chattel. Even more importantly, the raid was meant "to secure the supremacy of the nomads over the peasants."[91]

The raids were "always limited operations for a specific purpose, and the so-called 'wars' of the pre-Islamic Arabia such as those of Basus (late fifth to early sixth century) and Dahis (late sixth century), were in fact strings of small-scale campaigns spread over a period of many years, and not full-scale operations with set battles."[92] Just as elsewhere, warfare in the Arabian Peninsula was a seasonal affair.

The Arabian horse- and camel-mounted warriors' principal tactics *karr wa farr* "flight and return," looked much like the steppe nomads' tactics: it consisted in successive mounted charges aimed at dislocating the opponent's line, sudden retreats which drew the enemy cavalry and infantry forward in search of easy pickings, and equally sudden *volte-face* on prepared ambush positions where the now-isolated horsemen and spearmen were caught. Raid and *karr wa farr* went together: "The ordinary method of fighting in vogue in Arabia at the beginning of the Prophet's career was that of the raid, in which a sudden charge was followed by prompt retreat and a sudden return to the onslaught. This method was retained by the Prophet's earliest converts when they went out against the [Meccan] Quraysh caravans."[93]

The treatise on warfare written by or attributed to Byzantine Emperor Maurice (582–602), the *Strategikon*, explains "how to fight the Scythians, that is, Avars,

Turks and other peoples whose way of life resembles that of the Huns." They "prefer combat at a distance, ambushes, encirclement maneuvers, feigned retreats and brisk voltes, as well as wedge formations, that is, dispersed groups" and "harrying."[94] The *Tactica* later written by the Byzantine warrior Emperor Leo (717–41), who successfully repelled the last major Arab attack upon Constantinople, pinpointed the "importance the Saracens attached to speed and mobility"[95] which in turn enabled their swarming tactics.

During the first phase of their conquest of the Middle East, the Arabs relied on traditional razzia tactics, with light cavalry and infantry.[96] Most long-distance campaigns were undertaken by small numbers of camel-mounted infantry, with some horse cavalry; the self-sufficient units lived by foraging and were able to do without supply lines. They "easily marched through barely secured territory to concentrate their forces where needed. The basic strategy was to weaken a foe with raids before a more serious invasion."[97] The small but highly mobile bands of warriors bypassed fortified cities that were only tackled in a second phase, after reinforcements flowed in. The absolute numbers, though, remained small: 27,000 Muslims soldiers fought the decisive battle of Yarmuk, which opened Palestine and Syria to the Muslim invasion; Caliph Abu Bakr sent an army of 7,000 to conquer Syria; 5,000 were sent to Iraq; only 7 to 10,000 reportedly fought the crucial battle of Qadisiya which broke the Persian army, while the conquest of Persia as a whole by Khalid took 18,000 men. Egypt was conquered by but 8,000.[98] The Muslim campaign against Byzantium in 630 A.D. mustered 30,000 men. As the wars of conquest of Islam started, "most of the operations in which the men were engaged were little more than raids on a large scale, and in the art of raiding, the tribesmen needed little instruction."[99]

The desert continued to give the Muslim armies a decisive edge: they were able to retreat to their arid fortresses that they used as "interior lines." The caliphs "were able to send out simultaneously on all sides armies that were far superior to their opponents;"[100] the desert provided an "inexhaustible supply of warriors," nomads desirous of joining in the quest for booty: "The bursting forth of the Arabs from their desert fortresses in the … 7th century under the inspired leadership of Prophet Muhammad was a mass movement of their adult fighting men, one which gathered momentum as reports filtered back of the rich plunder to be gained in Syria or Iraq or Persia."[101] Caliph Umar (634–644) disposed of a total force of about 50,000 warriors. He created regional armies, the *jund*, based on tribal origin, with seniority reflecting the date when the family or tribe had converted.[102]

In the initial phase of the conquest, "neither their methods nor weapons showed much change, yet a mighty transformation had taken place.... Muhammad had set off one of those explosions of human energy which transcend ordinary considerations of arms and tactics... such explosions have inevitably led to aggression. Defenders, however brave and patriotic they may be, are never charged with quite the same mystic fury."[103] Muhammad had reportedly effected "few changes in the age-old Arab fighting habits. In their first encounters with the Byzantine armies the invaders came on in irregular waves, sweeping around flanks or pouring into any gap of the line. Of discipline they had little, and still less of routine or organization. Their effectiveness lay almost entirely in numbers, mobility and a wild fervor carried far past any charted limit of morale."[104]

Here we touch upon what has often been the puzzle of the great Muslim Conquest: how could so few conquer so many in so short a time? The enigma is diminished by our earlier examination of other nomads' wars and empire building: the Muslims were neither the first nor the last of the nomadic warriors to erect huge empires at breakneck speed. The real riddle is that of the persistence of the religion and the *umma* based upon it. As to their beginnings, let us trust Ibn Khaldun:

> Because of their fierce character, the Arabs, are less disposed than any other nation to accept submission: they are coarse, proud, ambitious, and all want to lead.... But religion, thanks to a prophet or a saint, enables them to restrain themselves and lose their conceit and their spirit of rivalry. It then is easier for them to submit and unite themselves, as the common religion erases the coarseness and the pride, and restrains jealously and the spirit of competition. When a prophet or saint appears amongst them and calls upon them to obey divine laws, frees them of their flaws and teaches them virtues—which allows them to assemble all their forces for the triumph of truth—they unite and attain domination and power.[105]

In the debate about the causes of the Muslim conquest, many arguments have been presented, such as the vacuum left by the exhaustion of the warring Byzantine and Persian empires; the war-weary Byzantines and Persians cutting off subsidies to their Arab client statelets, the Ghassanid and the Lakhmid kingdoms, which not only created a power vacuum but removed a serious obstacle in the way of the Muslim armies.[106] The resentment of the subject populations of both empires, crushed by fiscal oppression and religious persecution, guaranteed that they would not rise in defense of the faltering rulers; the populations of Syria, of Jazira (northern Iraq) and of Egypt had been under foreign rule for so long that they could not remember anything else; Persian resistance was uncoordinated after the army collapsed.[107]

Yet, it was not any type of military superiority, or an edge in military technology and tactics, that gave victory to the Arab warriors. C.W.C. Oman, the British historian of Medieval warfare, proposes that it was "[t]he fanatical courage of the fatalist [which] enabled them to face better-armed and better-disciplined troops."[108] Motivation was essential: "The powers of greed and fanaticism united to draw together every unquiet spirit between Khorasan and Egypt. The wild horsemen of the East poured out in myriads." British historian Reuben Levy concurs: "When the foreign expeditions began under the first caliphs, the motives inspiring the tribes to flock to the standards were combined with anticipation of plunder from the fabled riches of the lands to be invaded."[109] But plunder does not suffice to explain the transformation of the despised "eaters of lizards and gerbils," as the civilized Arab tribes of Syria called them, into world-conquerors.[110] Delbrück adds: "The military strength of the Bedouin element, which had long been known and feared in the world, was multiplied by the religious teachings of fate (*kismet*) and of Paradise and military obedience was assured by the authority of Allah."[111] A *hadith* is quoted which has the Prophet state: "The best theology is to help God with the sword," as a result of which "the plundering Bedouins were glad to conform to a spiritual authority added to the inherited warrior strength of the sons of the desert the element of discipline...."[112]

As we also saw above, the conjoining of religious charisma with the explosive, raw energy of the nomads goes a long way towards solving the problem. Muhammad told his warriors that "[t]he sword is the key to heaven and of hell; a drop of blood shed in the cause of God, a night spent in arms, is of more avail than two months of fasting and prayer: whosoever falls in battle, his sins are forgiven: at the Day of Judgment his wounds shall be resplendent as vermillion and odoriferous as musk; and the loss of his limbs shall be supplied by the wings of angels and cherubim."[113] So were the warriors inspired.

The Arab breakout and the ensuing conquest was a strategic surprise of the first magnitude. There is no appearance that anyone had any notion of the witches' brew that had been simmering in Arabia and was now going to overflow. In Henri Pirenne's summation:

Prior to Muhammad's time the Byzantines had never considered the Arabian Peninsula as a flashpoint, nor assigned large military forces there. It was a watch-line [*une ligne de surveillance*] criss-crossed by caravans.... The Persian Empire likewise, Arabia's neighbor, had treated it similarly. In sum there was nothing to fear from the nomadic Bedouins of the Peninsula, whose civilization was in the backward tribal state, whose religious beliefs had barely advanced beyond mere fetish-worship, and who spent their time warring with each other or plundering … caravans (...). Too preoccupied with their age-old conflict, neither the Roman Empire nor the Persian Empire had the faintest clue of the propaganda that Muhammad, amidst a confusing tribal fight, was administering to his people, and the religion he was soon to project upon the world alongside its supremacy. The Empire was already being overwhelmed when John Damascene only saw in Islam some form of a schism similar to earlier heresies.[114]

In sum, "at the death of Muhammad in 632, there was no prophesying the peril that was to strike in such a thunderous way two years later. No measure had been taken to strengthen the borders... the Arab attack was a total surprise. In a way, the expansion of Islam was an accident [*un hasard*], whereby we mean the unexpected consequence of several causes that conjoin."[115] But if this conjunction was greatly accidental, it still begs the question of what it is that gave the new assailant his irresistible might, which turned accident into durable reality. Did their way of war endow them with some irresistible quality?

"What made the Arab victories all the more astonishing was the relatively poor quality of their armies." After all, Arabs had long served as mercenaries and auxiliary troops, but never as a force on their own account. Unification of the tribes by Muhammad gave them an extraordinary impetus, very similar to Chingis Khan's unique achievement in uniting all Mongols under his khanate. But contrary to the skillful Mongols, "The Arabs, despite centuries of desert feuding, had no real experience of intensive warfare; they were indeed 'primitive warriors' (...). Nor does their generalship seem to have been particularly cunning (...)." Having exhausted all contributing, partial explanations, Keegan's concluding argument is powerful: it was "Islam itself, which lays such heavy emphasis on the fight for the faith, that made them so formidable in the field." Tactics of flight (*karr wa farr*) and reliance on natural obstacle were primitive, but "primitive tactics become more effective if the warrior is inspired by a belief in the certainty of victory and is always willing to return to the struggle, however often he disengages when a particular fight goes against him."[116]

The Muslim warriors scored stunning victories, and more Arabs migrated out of the Peninsula to join in the great rush. It is estimated that in those years a total of half a million Arabs left the Peninsula. As they left, power ebbed out of the Peninsula and flew northwards. Contrary to many conquering armies, though, the victors did not become a landed aristocracy or a gentry that expropriate and replaces the vanquished gentry. The warriors became the ruling class, but did not disperse. "It was the great luck of the Arab expansion—which allowed them to continue in its stride and pile up more successes—not to have turned soldiers into farmers, at least during the first century [of Islam]."[117] They stuck together instead as soldiers in garrison cities, the *amsar*, a decision ascribed to Caliph Umar.[118] In the conquered lands, co-opted local elites were left to administer the subjugated people. This concentration in garrison towns kept the warriors together as a military elite, as a result of which the Muslims "were free to devote most of their military energy in the first few hundred years to expansion."[119]

For about two hundred years, it was this fervor that raised the men to arms *fil sabil Allah*, in the way and for the cause of Allah. The *amsar* were all located on the edge of the deserts. The new, garrison cities founded by the Muslim warriors—Kufa, Basra, Fustat, Qayrawan—all grew virtually overnight into major settlements. A quarter-century after its foundation, Kufa was able to muster 40,000 men able to serve, and Basra 60,000! Older cities were also given major garrison status, such as Damascus, Merw, Qum. Together they were "the Gibraltars and Singapores of the Arab Empire," as Bernard Lewis put it.[120] They "acted as concentration points for Bedouin reinforcement," protected the frontiers of the expanding *umma* and controlled the conquered regions.

It is noteworthy that the Arabs who settled down in the *amsar* did so along tribal lines: for decades to come, the tribe remained the basis for social and military organization. The Muslims were the army and the army was the Muslims. As a result, in the early decades of the *umma,* since the Caliph "had no army separate from Muslim society…"[121] his army was a loose confederation of autonomous tribal armies; thus was sown one of the seeds of future fragmentation.

Muhammad created the synthesis of the nomad and the believer, in the form of the Muslim warrior, variously described as the *ghazi*, the *murabit*, the *mujahid*, the *muttawwi*. The latter were volunteers "moved to fight by zeal for their faith. They came at their own expense," and came and went at their own will, unruly fighters who had little discipline. Many of them were Sufis or some other type of ascetics. They played their role until the end of the twelfth century, as they were replaced by the regular army.[122] From the 900s developed another type, as *ribat*(s) sprouted in great numbers along the Muslim *limes*, borders and coastlines, from the Atlantic Ocean to Transoxiana. The *ribat* was a fortified barrack-monastery, home for the *murabitun* who keep watch against the Infidels, based on the Quranic injunction "Prepare against them [the enemies of Allah] all that ye possess of strength and places for horses." The *ribat* was the institutionalized form of holy war. The *murabitun* were being actively prepared for martyrdom.[123] Transoxiana alone reportedly counted no less than 10,000 *ribat*, some as small as watchtowers, some much larger. Today's Moroccan capital of Rabat was established as one and bears the very name (*Ribat al-Fath*). The Berber dynasty of the Almoravids also drew its name from them. The murabitun, more often than not, were Sufis. "Wherever Sufi groups went, they took both aspects of jihad with them," the ascetic and the warlike.[124] The culture of the borderlands of Islam, such as Anatolia, long a principal battlefield between Byzantines and Turkish armies of the Caliphate, "was dominated by the concept of Holy War, while the nomads' traditions, especially in the military field, continued."[125]

The *ghazi*, the religious volunteer, was named after the *ghazwa*, the raid. Muhammad's campaigns, which occupied the last decade of his life, are known and retold as *al-Maghazi*, "The Campaigns" or "The Expeditions," in other words the story of the raids, "a revealing name [that displays] the warlike nature of Muhammad's career."[126]

What the Prophet's armies represented was a halfway progression from the old tribal raids to the great raids of the conquest. Centuries later, the *Iskandername*, the versified chronicle written by Ahmedi in the fourteenth century to celebrate the ascent and power of the Ottomans, memorializes them as *ghazi* in the hallowed tradition of the Prophet: "Who is a ghazi? A ghazi is the instrument of the religion of Allah, a servant of God who purifies the earth from the filth of polytheism (…): the ghazi is the sword of God, he is the protector and the refuge of the believers. If he becomes a martyr in the way of God, do not believe that he has died—he lives in beatitude with Allah, he has eternal life."[127]

The *mujahid* designates the fighter in the *jihad*.

> It must be admitted that there is some truth in the medieval and the later stereotype of the Muslim warrior-fanatic, the *ghazi* or *mujahid*. And memories of the religiously-inspired desperadoes, the Assassins in the 12th–13th century Syria and Persia have retained a favorable enough connotation in the modern

Islamic world for the Arabic term applied to such a desperado, *fidai*, to be revived in the Persian and Arabic worlds and applied to religiously or politically motivated terrorists, the *fedayeen*: those eager to sacrifice their lives.[128]

Religious fervor, then, powered the Muslim wars of conquest. "The role of the volunteer religious enthusiasts remained important all through the Muslim Middle Ages, and those *ghazis* often formed a significant element of the Islamic armies (...). The brunt of frontier defense in Anatolia, Northern Spain, Central Asia and the Indian borderlands devolved on these volunteers, who usually manned the frontier posts or *ribats*."[129] The saying attributed to the Prophet, that "there is no monastic life [*rahbaniyya*] in Islam. Each *umma* has its form of devotional journey: that of my community is jihad," emphatically demonstrates the complete imbrication of self-denial, duty to God and holy war.[130]

But extreme religious fervor seldom lasts long: revivals come in waves, in paroxysms that exhaust themselves in their manifestations. After the violent discharge of energy come times of latency.[131] The conquest elite had been "small, tribal, homogenous and warlike. But it did not retain those characteristics for long."[132] "After two hundred years... the original strength which had been brought along from the desert was consumed and used up.... The artificially blended elements of warriorhood and religion, which were already in conflict from the time of Muhammad's death on, were pulling away from each other.... After the beginning of the 9th century, mercenary units replaced the believers."[133] The Turkish tribe of the Seljuq converted to Sunni Islam, and now provided the warriors. "The Turks... Islam's frontier warriors, [were] the *ghazi* who taught the Quran with the sword."[134] In other words, as the religious fervor abated, the Muslim world developed three remedies: first, it took to employing slave mercenaries as the mainstay of its armies; second, it recruited new barbarian nomads drawn from the peripheries of the *umma*—two solutions that were not mutually exclusive; no more than the third, which was the professionalization of the army, now called the *jund* (the professional soldier was the *jundi*). Islam continuously required fresh supplies of slaves, not only for economic reasons—slavery was ever one of the mainstays of Islamic economies—but also for military ones.

When the second Muslim civil war (684–692) broke out, the original Muslim army, whose soldiers were Arabs from Arabia, was transformed into an army of Syrian-Arab Bedouins. It was "[a]n infusion of fresh desert Arabs....

Emigration from Arabia had petered out by the 680s and no new attempts to raise new armies in Arabia are recorded."[135] The next injection of primitive tribesmen was the recruitment of Khorasan troops by the early Abbassids, who soon added Transoxianic nomads. It was the Abbasid Caliph al-Mutasim (833–842) who first established the Muslim military slave system—barely two hundred years after Muhammad's *hijra* from Mecca to Medina. He set up a retinue of 3–4,000 Turks, designated as *mamluks* ("those who are owned," a synonym for slave). By 861, the Turkish praetorian guard had murdered the Caliph's second successor and turned the new Caliph into their puppet. The Samanid dynasty of Transoxiana had their military slaves, the *gulhams*, and later, in the fourteenth century, the Turkish emperor Murad I (1362–1389), who conquered the Balkans, created the corps of the janissaries—"new soldiers"—based on the *devshirme*, the forced enslavement and conversion of Christian children from the region: they were turned into military slaves and an elite corps which ranks amongst the most effective in history.[136]

The Islamic polities ever needed to tap the raw energies of fanatical converts, who were to be found amongst the nomadic populations of steppe and desert. Thus Berbers of North Africa conquered Spain from the Wisigoths, and twice reconquered the Iberian Peninsula in waves of nomadic-borne revivalism; freshly-minted Muslims of Turkic race, the Ghaznavids, conquered India; newly-converted Mongols and Tatars secured Central Asia and southern Russia for Islam; just as the Bedouins of Muhammad had originally burst forth from Arabia: in Muslim history, there is a close correlation between the intensity of jihad and that of religious revivals.

As a warlord as well as a legislator, a theologian and a jurisprudent, Muhammad's new synthesis systematized tribal mores and merged them into the new religion for the sake of which the new war was being waged. Between pre-Islamic war and Islamic jihad, there is as much continuity as there is discontinuity. Much of the "genetic" material of Islam is of tribal-nomadic origin. The Muslim conception, practice and doctrine of war was a new synthesis: "In large measure it was derived, like much of the practical side, from the experience gained against the Persians and Byzantines, but it was elaborated in ways peculiar to the Muhammadan way, the joint influence of the precepts of Islam and the reported sayings and doings of the Prophet."[137]

Central to the conception and practice of war by Islam was a basic fact: "The new religion... was a creed of conflict. It taught the necessity of submission to its revealed teachings and the right of its believers to take arms against those who opposed them."[138] War was enshrined in theory, that is, theology and law; it was equally enshrined in practice: "As the Medieval Islamic world evolved, much of its governmental apparatus, and especially its land tenure system, became geared to make war."[139] And war it waged.

"Jihad is Not an Event, but an Institution"

Most people, and certainly all members of Western civilization, are thus born into a world which differs radically from that of their ancestors, with the result that most of human history is a closed book to them (…). We all take the world in which we were born for granted and think of the human condition as ours. This is a mistake. The vast mass of human experience has been made with quite different conditions.

PATRICIA CRONE [140]

A Primer on Jihad

"We cannot repeat it enough: in Arabic, the way to say 'to win' [Arabic root n.s.r.] is 'assisted by God.' The victor, nasir, is not Man but God Almighty."

ALFRED MORABIA [141]

Strategic consequences will flow differently whether it is agreed that "Islam is a religion of peace" and that jihad is a "spiritual exertion," or, to the contrary, that jihad as war is firmly rooted in the very nature of Islam. Words are not value-neutral: time burdens them with complex legacies. A concept as ancient and as central to Islam as jihad does not escape the common fate. It is a layered, complex concept. "Warfare with spiritual significance," Prof. David Cook writes, "is the primary and root meaning of the term as it has been defined by classical Muslim jurists and legal scholars and as it was practiced by Muslims during the pre-modern period."

Jihad flows naturally from the innermost core of Islam as a belief-structure (*din*), an all-encompassing law (*fiqh*), and as a practice of the Muslim community as a whole, the *umma*. Not only is it integral to Islam, it stems irrefutably and authoritatively from the Quran, from the corpus of the *hadith* and from *sharia* as a necessary and relentless consequence. It is not a temporary, an accidental, an epiphenomenal aspect of Islam. There has never been an Islam without jihad: "the jihad is an institution, and not an event, that is to say it is a part of the normal functioning of the Muslim world."[142] Jihad did not start in some remote past and then stop, only to be restarted as a response to "colonial aggression," "imperialist encroachments," "Zionist intrusion" or "American crimes." Jihad never stopped. Islam is inherently expansionist: the writ and word of Allah must be extended to the entire world. "Once the war machine was set into motion, its march forward continued until it reached an impassable obstacle"[143]

Islam caused itself to be unwilling and incapable of keeping up with the efflorescence of European science and technology, of industry and the military that started in the 1100s, accelerated with the Renaissance, and went exponential as the Industrial Revolution gathered steam. As the balance of forces between Europe and the *umma* was upturned, centuries of Islamic siege of Europe came to an end and were even reversed, as Europeans encroached indeed into lands that had long been conquered and ruled by Muslims.[144] Muslim imperialism was *de facto* in retreat. But the spirit of imperialism remained even as it was vanquished: it has merely stopped being victorious. It remained ever ready to resume its imperial dream. As soon as some in the *umma* could nurture again the belief that jihad could be victorious again, that the balance of forces would again favor the *umma*, sizable groups and schools of thought went back to the offensive. Several events taken together may describe the resumption of that ambition: the (largely U.S.-inflicted) Anglo-French withdrawal from Suez in 1956; the French skedaddle out of Algeria in 1962; the first oil crisis in 1973. Today we face the flames of this rekindled ambition.

This hallowed and persistent practice of jihad expressed the core nature of Islam: in its own self-description, Islam is God's last word. Muhammad is the "seal of the prophets," since he is the last prophet God will ever send to mankind; his predication and prophethood therefore represent not only the complete, but also the final truth. Islam trumps any earlier or other revelation and is intrinsically superior to any of them. Islam's revelation further is the exclusive source of truth and no other source is admissible. The validity of the Quran, God's *verbatim* word, uncreated and preceding Creation, is absolute, unconditional and eternal. Allah's word and His law are immutable. The corpus of the *hadith* represents a source equal in dignity and value. *Sharia* draws from both.[145] Quotations from the Quran serve as the point of departure for discussions of war and peace, and of course of jurisprudence and policy-making.[146]

This sovereignty of the Muslims over the Earth is justified: "Believers are superior to Infidels" (Q., 91:6, 50). This is so because "Ye are the best people evolved for mankind, enjoining what is right, forbidding what is wrong, and believing in Allah." (Q., 3:110). The message of revelation holds for the entire human race: "We have sent you forth to all mankind" (Q., 34:28). The *umma* that believes in it and carries it out is superior to all other human groups, past and present: "You are the best community that ever rose among men" (Q., 99:111, 106–110). To superiority, the creed adds supremacy: "The Arab Prophet preached a doctrine of universal sovereignty of his religion:"[147] "Allah promised to those of you who believe and do pious work to make them the owners of the earth" (Q., 107:24, 54/55): this revelation does not only have a monopoly on truth, but by divine decree it must inherit the dominion of the world. "Allah showed me all corners or the Earth. I saw the East and the West. My community will possess of it what he showed me from it. The keys of the treasures of the Earth were brought to me and deposited in my hands."[148]

The result of those tenets: "something of a general trusteeship exerted by the *umma* upon the Adamic race."[149] The community of the Muslims is entitled by God's law and obligated by it to hold sway upon all other groups. The world is considered the sole domain of Muhammad" and his followers. It is Allah's explicit will that the world be divided between believers and unbelievers: "If your Lord had wanted, He would have made only one community of all mankind," and, "If Allah did not neutralize one part of mankind with an other, the Earth would be corrupt."[150]

The oft-cited Quranic verse "no compulsion in religion," advanced to buttress the largely fantastical claim of Islamic religious "tolerance" ("toleration" would be more precise), was abrogated[151] by the later "Verse of the Sword" (Q., 9:5): "Then, when the sacred months are over, kill the idolaters wherever you find them, take them [captive], besiege them, and lie in wait for them at every point of observation. If they repent afterwards, perform the prayer and pay the alms, then release them. Allah is truly great." Lest anyone misunderstand this, a well-known *hadith* has Muhammad assert: "Behold! God sent me with a sword, just before the Hour [of Judgment], and place my daily sustenance beneath the shadow of my spear, and humiliation and contempt for those who oppose me."[152]

During his *hijra* [migration] at Medina, Muhammad himself organized the *umma* as a polity ruled by Revelation: a theocracy, or, better, a logocracy: God's word is in power.[153] The religion that must extend its writ to the entire world took on the form of a state that later received the name of caliphate. That state is a divine instrument, "a necessary and coherent part of God's providential dispensation for mankind."[154] In turn, this dictates its "geostrategy," to use an anachronistic word. "The state [that] is regarded as the instrument for universalizing [Islam] must perforce be an ever-expanding state."[155] "Islam rules and nothing is higher," a *hadith* states.[156] To follow Majid Khadduri's formulation, it was "a divine monocratic state on an imperialist basis."[157] The Islamic state will be expanding in size and space until the end of Time, until the entire world has "made Islam," that is, has made submission to the revelation. "Allah in his own good time will make all religious communities disappear, except Islam," claims another *hadith*.[158] And another saying tells us: "Jihad is in force until the Day of Resurrection."[159] Muhammad said elsewhere: "and fight them [the unbelievers] until there is no more tumult and oppression, and there prevails justice and Faith in Allah altogether and everywhere" (Q., 8:39). A canonical *hadith* states: "Jihad will go on from the moment Allah sent me [to mankind] to the day when the last troops of my community will kill ad-Dajjal [the Muslim equivalent of the Antichrist], without a break in the continuity of the combat."[160]

In sum, "the purifying war is the instrument of the Alliance between Allah and the *umma* which has become destiny. By imposing upon earth the Order willed by God, jihad ends war by means of war.... Many Muslim doctors would second al-Qasani's statement that 'Killing the Infidels' has been decreed as a means of leading to Islam, by exhortation in the most abrupt way, once all hope of obtaining it by the easiest road, invitation by words, has been exhausted."[161] The great student of Islamic law Joseph Schacht writes: "The basis of the Islamic attitude towards unbelievers is the law of war; they must be either converted or subjugated or killed… the third alternative, in general, occurs only if the first two are refused."[162] To wit, the great Muslim historian Tabari records the recommendation given by Caliph Umar to the commander of the troops he sent to the conquest or Iraq in 636 A.D.: "Summon the people to God; those who respond to your call, accept it from them… but those who refuse must pay the poll tax out of humiliation and lowliness. If they refuse this, it is the sword without leniency."[163] And so they did.

As we saw earlier,[164] Islam divides the world into two parts that differ in essence: *dar al-Islam*, the world of Islam, where Islamic law rules, and the world designated as "abode of war," where Islamic law does not prevail, *dar al-Harb*.[165] The use of force by Muslims against unbelievers stems naturally from the doctrine: "The inhabitants of the *dar al-Harb* are *harbis*, who are not answerable to Islamic authority and whose persons are *mubah*, that is, at the mercy of the believers."[166] It is incumbent upon the *umma* to go to war to subdue the unbelievers—the "abode of war" is also called the "abode of infidelity" (*dar al-kufr*). "Expansionist jihad is a collective duty (*fard al-kifaya*) which is fulfilled if a sufficient number of people take part in it…the most important function of the doctrine of jihad is that it mobilizes and motivates Muslims to take part in wars against the unbelievers."[167]

Historically, "Islam found war in its cradle. It fought from its inception, and in order to prevail it imposed the new truth it carried by force of arms. This weighed in a singularly heavy way upon its entire destiny."[168] Indeed, from the beginning, Islam was a warring religious polity, a religion in arms, we may say. "In this formative period of classical Islam, Islamic militancy was reinforced by the superiority of Muslims over their enemies."

Muslims are religiously obliged to disseminate the faith throughout the world. As such, disseminating (*dawa*) is neutral: it is the missionary word. But Islam considers that the institutions of the *dar al-Harb* are hindrances to the spread and acceptance of Islam, and must therefore be removed. They "stand in the way" of the mission. As a result, "Muslims believe that expansion through war is not aggression but a fulfillment of the Quranic command to spread Islam as a way of peace. The resort to force to disseminate Islam is not war (*harb*), a word that is used only to describe the use of force by non-Muslims. Islamic wars are not *hurub* (the plural of *harb*) but rather *futuhat*, acts of 'opening' the world to Islam and expressing Islamic Jihad."[169] The *futuhat* is the consecrated word that designates the "conquests of lands," and the "era of the *futuhat*" covers the first century after *hijra*, 632 to 732 A.D., the period of the initial Islamic military expansion.

The conquests—the "openings"—have always been the object of popular worship. Oral heroic narrative poetry, already a feature of pre-Islamic Arabia, flourished early on in Islamic society. The *qussas*, popular storytellers and lay predicators, sang both the exploits of the olden desert "knights" of the *jahiliyyah*, the pre-Islamic state, and the conquering exploits of the Muslim warriors in edifying and fabulous stories which flattered the public's sense of Muslim identity and mobilized it. "In the Islamic world, the *futuhat* have never ceased to be a theme resonant with popular sensibilities. The Book [the Quran] and the Apostle had announced the supremacy of the [Muslim] Religion. Jihad had made it into a concrete reality. Hence, Allah wanted his party to spread the Religion of Truth. The True Faith, to all surrounding countries. It was fated to spread some day to the entire universe, with God's effective support."[170] Allah, indeed, intervenes permanently in the war, sends His Hosts of Angels, and secures a victory that inevitably will occur. The chronicles of jihad are replete with tales of Allah's direct presence and intervention in battles: "O You who believe! Remember Allah's beneficence toward you, when armies marched against you and We sent against them winds and legions of invisible archangels [to fight] for you!" So supported, the terrestrial victory of the Muslims is pre-ordained and inevitable. "So, whatever the Unbelievers do, [my] community will inevitably prevail. Isn't Allah the best of those who plot?"[171]

In Islamic law, in the Islamic mind, it is the unbelievers who "stand in the way" who bear responsibility for the state of war. "Those who resist Islam cause wars."[172] The circular nature of the argument is rooted in the exclusive nature of revelation: since it is God's very word, to resist it is to "attack God." Everything in Islam revolves around, and returns to, that privileged moment in time, Muhammad's prophethood, and the first four, "divinely-guided" (*rashidun*) caliphs, Abu Bakr, Umar, Uthman, and Ali. Absolute perfection then prevailed, and the highest possible course of conduct for Muslims is to emulate the Prophet and his companions, the *salaf*. "The past is a privileged moment of history at which the law eternally intended by God was revealed in universal and definitive formulations… [the Quranic] commands are valid as such for all times."[173] The imitation of the Prophet and the *salaf* is the highest possible standard of Muslim behavior: "Whosoever does not follow my behavior [*sunna*] is not one of mine," and "Whosoever revives my behavior revives me" are two of the Prophet's traditions.

Since Muhammad spent the last ten years of his life in jihad within Arabia, and his successors conquered a world for Islam, jihad indeed is the highest possible calling. As the Hanbali scholar and revered ancestor of all radical Islamists Ibn Taimiyyah (d.1328) quoted the Prophet: "The head of the affair is Islam, its central pillar is the *salat* [almsgiving] and the summit is the jihad" and "a day spent in *ribat* [remaining at the frontiers of Islam with the intention of defending Islamic territory against the enemies] in the way of Allah is better than a thousand days spent elsewhere."[174] War to spread the writ and rule of Islam is a categorical duty for Muslims.

Innumerable *hadith* praise and extol the jihadi war. "Authentic" *ahadith* were manufactured in large quantity to do so and lend it overwhelming legitimacy. They furthered "the bellicose character of [Muhammad's] last years' Predication."[175] Three of the six canonical collections of *hadith*, those of Muslim (d. 875), Abu Daud (d. 889) and at-Tirmidi (d. 892), were compiled by Hanbalite scholars, the most radical school of Islamic jurisprudence. Ibn Hanbal himself, and his followers, "are the most prone to quote *ahadith* that promote jihad, and harsh regarding the Unbelievers."[176] Abdallah b. al-Mubarak's collection, one of the earliest (d. 797), the *Kitab al-Jihad* (the Book of Jihad), is entirely devoted to jihad.[177] There are "literally hundreds of sources for militant jihad in classical Islam with books and pamphlets devoted to the subject, as well as sections of every hadith and law book, along with most commentaries in the Quran and historical material, as well as anecdotal snippets in the literary sources, and martial poetry…."[178]

To sum it up:

> Quran was a powerful exponent of an aggressive jihad doctrine. The hadith literature follows in its footsteps. Whereas the Quran supplies with generalities and encouragement to fight, the hadith material takes us into a full-blown description of warfare with a heavy spiritual content. It is clear from even [a] cursory overview that the subject of militant jihad was of critical concern to Muslims during the formative first three centuries of Islam, and there is no indication from any of this material that the jihad being described is anything other than military.[179]

In the first centuries of Islam, the world looked like the revelation had said it would: "Because of the miracle of the conquests, jihad emerged as one of the core elements of Islam."[180] This shaped and structured Islamic legal doctrine and collective consciousness. A fair summation of the doctrine is offered by Ahmad Ibrahim Muhammad al-Dimashqi al-Dumyati, commonly known as Ibn an-Nuhas (d. 1411), author, in Cook's view, "of the largest and most significant book on jihad ever written (until the present day), the *Mashari al-Ashwaq ila masari ad-Ushaaq*,"—a book that Osama bin Laden's mentor Abdullah Azzam called "the best book on Jihad:"[181]

Know that jihad [against] the infidels is *fard kifaya* (obligation upon the entire community, not upon every single member of it) in their lands by general agreement of the ulama… the least number of jihad raids that should be accomplished each year is one, and more is better without any doubt. A year without raids is not permissible, other than as a result of necessity, such as the weakness of the Muslims, the superiority of the enemy, fear of complete annihilation if [the Muslims] attack them first, or because of a lack of provision or fodder for their mounts.[182]

Jihad is fundamental to the latent, underlying world-outlook of the *umma*. Jihad is an aggressive, expansion-oriented creed. The early conquests that led Muhammad and his raiders to the domination of Arabia, and the "well-guided" caliphs and their successors to the great *futuhat*, to the Pyrénées and the Punjab, were jihad in its first greatness. Eyewitness accounts and contemporary chronicles agree: they were destructive, merciless, fanatical.[183] Jihad as the instrument of Allah's dominion over the world is "central to the latent or implicit outlook of the people of the *umma* of Muhammad" and is deeply etched in their collective consciousness.[184]

Jihad for All Places and for All Times

Muslim theologians and jurists' rulings and opinions manifest a general consensus on the question of jihad. Whether they belong to the four schools of Sunni Islam, Hanbali, Shaafi, Maliki or Hanafi, or issue from Shia junists, they agree on its fundamentals. Whether they wrote during the early centuries of Islam and were amongst the first clerics to opine on the matter, or were active during Classical and Medieval Islam or later, pre-modern or modern: jihad, the war to make Allah's writ supreme over the entire planet, is always a fundamental tenet. The best and the brightest of Islamic theology and law all agree on the essentials of jihad.[185] Abu Hanifa (d. 767); Malik b. Anas (d. 795); al-Shafi (d. 820); Ibn Hanbal (d. 855); the eminent hadith compiler al-Bukhari (d. 869); al-Tabari who wrote a monumental commentary on the Quran and a *Kitab al-Jihad* (d. 923); the North African Maliki doctor al-Qayrawani (d. 996); the renowned al-Mawardi (d. 1058); Ibn Rushd—the famous philosopher Averroes (d. 1198); the literalist Zahiri doctrinaire Ibn Hazm of Cordova (d. 1064); Ibn Khaldun the great scientific mind (d. 1406); Ibn Taimiyyah, the hero of radical Islamists (d. 1328); Ziauddin Barani (d.1357) who wrote against the Hindus; al-Ghazali (d. 1111) who reconciled mainstream Sunni orthodoxy and Sufism; the Shiite al-Amili (d. 1621); Indo-Persian Sufi theologian Shah Wali-Allah (d. 1762); the Persian al-Majlisi (d. 1699); the Iranian Shiite Ruhollah Khomeini (d. 1989); the Egyptian Muslim Brother Sayyid Qutb (d. 1966); the Egyptian Muslim Brother Yusuf al-Qaradawi.

Whether it is jihad *de jure*—the authoritative opinions of leading Muslim jurisprudents through the nearly fifteen centuries of the history of Islam—or *de facto* jihad—the history of Islam's wars against the rest of the world, from the Prophet's early campaigns through today, neither ever went in abeyance or ever was denied. Scholars of Islam traditionally knew it: "The classical [Islamic] works define [jihad] quite baldly as the religious duty of spreading Islam by force of arms. They lay down five propositions concerning it:" Jihadi war is a duty ordered by the Prophet; it must continue until the entire world is under the sway of Islam; the sovereign must lead it, not any self-appointed leader; the "call to Islam" must be issued before combat; and the Muslim who dies fighting jihad is a *shahid*, martyr assured of Paradise and special privileges there.[186] Jihad is so fundamental that it is permanent: "[W]e are pointing out a permanent historic force, which is ceaselessly renewed through the generations, independent of race, color, climate and all external circumstances, never beaten, ever being reborn. This force is the deeply held conviction, rooted in the soul of every Muslim.... Holy War is a categorical requirement, pure and simple."[187] Islamologist Henri Lammens wrote in 1916 that "[t]he war against the non-Muslims, so frequently recommended in the Medinese suras, almost became... the sixth pillar of Islam."[188]

As the French scholar of Islam Alfred Morabia concluded but one generation ago:

> The doctors of the Classical era promulgated the requirement of waging jihad against the Unbelievers, not on account of the threat they represented against the Muslim order, but because of their Unbelief itself. All the schools of law eventually adopted the thesis of offensive jihad. The definitive rule is that an offensive and permanent struggle against the Impious must be waged even if

the latter do not take the initiative of the struggle. Their impiousness itself is an attack on Islam and the rights of Allah. It is incontrovertible that the thesis of a defensive jihad barely found any echo with the medieval [Islamic] jurisprudents....[189]

The chronicle of jihad since its inception is literally endless. It shows that jihad indeed never stopped. The list is tedious, though telling. It registers the innumerable cities that were pillaged and burned down, the provinces invaded, the coasts raided and devastated, regions depopulated and populations uprooted, enslaved and massacred. Spain was conquered and occupied by the Arabs and the Berbers; Rome was attacked; Genoa sacked; Toulouse, Bordeaux, Avignon, Lyons sacked and destroyed; the Dalmatian coast and Thrace ruined; Armenia devastated. India was repeatedly shattered by Turkic invaders recently converted to Islam. Anatolia was turned into a quasi-desert by their ceaseless raids: land went from being used for farming to being used for grazing sheep. The Caucasus was mercilessly reduced. Arab pirates and unending raids made life untenable all around the Mediterranean, in the Provence, on all Mediterranean islands. The Romans' *mare nostrum* had been the connecting link for all peoples from time immemorial; after the Muslim conquests it became an unbridgeable divide. The *futuhat* were brutal and devastating.

Jihad did not stop with the initial centuries of expansion. It took three great waves of Muslim raids and invasions over a period of five centuries (from the eighth to the thirteenth century) for the jihadi warriors to conquer the entire Gangetic plain of India. Millions were killed by the Muslim invaders who relished in the slaughter of Hindu unbelievers and polytheists. "My principal object in coming to Hindustan... has been to accomplish two things. The first was to war with the infidels, the enemies of the Mohammadan religion; and by this religious warfare to acquire some claim to reward in the life to come. The other was... that the army of Islam might gain something by plundering the wealth and valuables of the infidels: plunder in war is as lawful as their mothers' milk to Musalmans who war for their faith," said Tamerlane, "Amir Timur," the conqueror whose mass slaughters surpassed those committed by Mahmud of Ghazni, the Turco-Afghan conqueror, and equaled Chingis Khan's.[190] On the western side of the Islamic *umma*, the Balkans became the hapless targets of Turco-Muslim raiding and mass enslavement, as the Bulgars, the Serbs, the Rumanians, and deeper into Europe even the Hungarians fell to the jihadi campaigns and were occupied for lengthy periods of time. Vienna was besieged in 1583 and again in 1683. The Polish king Jan Sobieski, who broke the second siege, had perfected novel methods of fighting back the Muslim raiders; he intercepted a Tatar army heading back toward the Black Sea with 44,000 prisoners destined to be sold as slaves.[191]

From the beginning of the eighteenth century, the *umma* found itself rolled back or raided by its erstwhile victims. Jihad did not stop. It was carried out at the behest of the legitimate ruler, the Ottoman Sultan-Emperor; it met all the qualifications the clerics had always required. The Persian monarch and the Moghul claimed no lesser legitimacy, and their own jihad was no less canonical. And then there were more jihad wars. In 1744 the pirate of the sand dunes Muhammad ibn Saud and the madcap predicator Muhammad ibn Abd al-Wahhab—the *sheikh* and the *jawad*, the plunderer and the bigot—struck a business deal which resulted in a brutal series of raids, the conquest of Najd by 1785 and the spread of a new version of the eternal Muslim "reform:" back to the past, to the roots, to the *salafis*. The armed Wahhabi faith declared the entire world, not only Christians and Shiites, but virtually all other Sunni Muslims, to be apostates, *takfir*, liable to be killed and plundered, and lost no time in practicing what they preached. Lacking any sense of proportions, Abd al-Wahhab proclaimed himself head of the *umma* and declared jihad against the Ottomans. Wreaking a path of destruction, his warriors raided Karbala, the towns of Hejaz, including Mecca. The first Saudi empire was annihilated by Egypt's Mehmet Ali in 1818, but the Saudi-Wahhabi jihad had a future which Abdulaziz ibn Saud materialized in the early decades of the twentieth century and his son King Faisal made into a global power after 1973.[192]

Usaman Dan Fodio led his own messianic and apocalyptic jihad in West Africa against "pagan" Africans from 1804 to 1810, where he erected a jihadi empire. India, subject to Muslim rule for seven centuries, but now under British control, was proclaimed *dar al-Harb* in 1803 by Shah Abd al-Aziz Dihlawi; Sayyid Ahmad Shahid (d. 1831), a Wahhabi convert returning from Mecca, put it into practice. The great Indian Mutiny of 1857–1858 against the British was largely a Muslim revolt and a jihad.[193] Fighting off Russian encroachments in Dagestan and Chechnya were local jihad wars, just as Sufi leader Abd al-Qadir, hereditary amir of Mascara in what later became Algeria, proclaimed and led a fifteen-year jihad against the French (1832–1847).

Jihad was the *umma*'s second nature over many centuries of practice; it had become ingrained in the *umma*'s cultural programming. Wars against external enemies were naturally perceived through the culture of jihad and waged accordingly.

In 1880, Muhammad Ahmad of southern Egypt declared himself to be the Mahdi, and took Khartoum at the expense of "China" Gordon's life. He and his successor, the unsurprisingly-named Khalifa Abdallahi, launched into wars of expansion, having declared a jihad on Egypt, Ethiopia and Eritrea. After the passing of that Mahdi and the inglorious death of his successor in 1895, another one sprung up in Somalia, the Wahhabi-influenced "Mad Mullah" who held the British in check until 1920.[194] Amir Abd el-Krim of Morocco led his jihad war in the Rif mountains against the French in the 1920s.

On the Shiite side, the Persian religious leaders declared jihad during the Russo-Persian Wars (1808–1813, 1826—1828). Each and every Ottoman war was a jihad. A polity like the *umma*, which rules itself on the basis of the in-distinction of the religious and the political, cannot but tinge its wars with the religion that pervades and rules society. Jihad, as we have insisted, never stopped. What happened in the contemporary world, which resulted in the jihad war waged against the West (including India), is a continuation of, and stands in full continuity with, the entire history of the *umma Muhammadiyya*, the community of Prophet Muhammad, against the rest of the world, the *dar al-Harb*, the *dar al-Kufr*.

In 1924, Mustafa Kemal Atatürk who had been awarded the name of "ghazi" for his victories against infidels, deposed the Sultan and put an end to the sultanate and finally abolished the caliphate. Turkey was to be a secular republic. The continuity of the caliphate—which, with hyperbolic exaggeration and a great deal of disregard for the facts of history, a believer could trace back directly to the Prophet—had been broken. This was an earthquake for Muslims, as it would have been in medieval times in Europe if the Papacy had become extinct, or elsewhere if the Japanese imperial family had been overthrown. Further, the despised Christian *adhimmi* was calling the shots in the Arab Middle East, the *faranji* (a generic term for Western Europeans, from "Franks") booted out by Salah ed-din the Great were now back in force, with their Maxim guns, their mufti suits, their made-up women and their missionaries. Worse still, the even more despised Jews had successfully defended their establishment in Israel, while a secular republic arose in India, the land of such Muslim glory, power and supremacy. "Contemporary jihad theory begins from the time that overt military resistance to Western incursions ceased and the need arose to radically redefine the meaning of jihad, either for apologetic reasons or because the definition was no longer relevant to new circumstance."[195] Jihad for our times was being prepared.

PART II

THE TAINTED PEDIGREE OF MODERN JIHAD

A people bewitched
With a history written with chalks of illusion
                                    ADONIS

From Islam to Pan-Islam

Like all human societies' cultures and ideologies, Islam can be analyzed through its "genetic" makeup—the materials that were pulled together to create it, the operating system that lies at its core; in one word, the "genetic code" which is specific to Islam. Likewise, to understand modern jihad, we need to analyze its "DNA." The first part of this study showed that there has never been an Islam without jihad: jihad is an integral part of Islam.[196] In the modern world, jihad has fared no different than the religion it serves. Just as the jihadis use modern Western technologies to wage their wars, they also use, if more selectively, a number of concepts and practices that originated in the West, all the while extolling the pristine purity of the form of Islam they practice. Its present composition resulted from the splicing of modern messages into the traditional genetic material. This analysis will start from the first impact of sustained Western expansion into the core areas of Islam, toward the end of the eighteenth century.

Islam sees itself as "metahistoric, divinely guided" and "essentially outside and above" history. An article of faith in Muslim orthodoxy determines Islam to be timeless and immutable, in the image of its holy book, the Quran, emphatically said by itself and by most of the Muslim tradition to be "uncreated."[197]

Since it sees itself as self-enclosed and self-similar, Islam cannot possibly borrow from the times in which its adherents live or from alien cultures or peoples. Islam, self-described as perfect from the very inception of its revelation, is suspended out of time; it rests ever impervious to change in a *stasis* of sameness. "Few culture areas have been subjected to so much and so violent change as that of Islam; none perhaps has so consistently refused to accept the ontological reality of change."[198]

Instead, reverting to an idealized Golden Age that consists of Muhammad's prophethood and his first four flawless successors, the "well-guided" caliphs, allows the actuality of time to be denied. History in this conception is not an open-ended development but an entropic process of degeneracy straying farther away from the original perfection. For mankind, the only desirable and indeed possible course of action is harking back to that past. For example in 1925, Al-Azhar in Cairo, the most authoritative institution of theology, law and learning in Sunni Islam, used a particularly revealing argument to condemn the views expressed by one of its numbers. "According to the unanimous consensus of the Muslims, Islam is the totality of the precepts transmitted by the Prophet in regard to doctrine, and legal relations among the people. These precepts form one whole and cannot be dissociated from one another."[199] Islam is of one piece, and therefore unchanging.

On the Shiite side, Ayatollah Khomeini avers: "Islam is not constrained by time or space, for it is eternal… what Muhammad permitted is permissible until the Day of Resurrection; what he forbade is forbidden until the Day of Resurrection. It is not permissible that his ordinances (*hudud*) be superseded, or that his teachings fall into disuse, or that the punishments [he set] be abandoned, or that the taxes he levied be discontinued, or that the defense of Muslims and their lands cease."[200]

It is then a great irony that Islam should have been massively drawing upon a modern world that was not of its making, and the workings of which were completely foreign to its very principles. All orthodoxy to the contrary, far from remaining watertight to a constant immersion in its environment, Islam has absorbed elements of a world alien to it. Ever since the relative fortunes of the *dar al-Islam* and the West were reversed more than 250 years ago, osmosis with the modern world has "contaminated" a supposedly hermetically sealed Islam.

What goes for Islam in general goes for jihad in particular.

The proclaimed and sought-after ideal of a politically united *dar al-Islam*—one caliphate ruling over all Muslim lands, as had been the case in the times of

Muhammad and his successors the *khulafa*, Abu Bakr, Umar, Uthman and Ali—eluded the Muslims as early as a few decades after the establishment of an Islamic polity. Although it lived on as an ideal of undiminished appeal, it was never reconstituted. As long as Muslims lived in a Muslim universe stretching from the Atlantic Ocean to the Bay of Bengal and farther, political fragmentation was an object of sorrow but not of scandal. Alien impingements changed this complacent mood.

Starting with the gradual demise of the Moghul Empire in the eighteenth century, the dynamics unleashed by the West helped dissolve or even destroy various Muslim polities; Western expansion spurred on the surviving ones, such as the Ottoman Empire, to change. The retreat of the world of Islam was speedy. After centuries of relative stalemate, the British brought to an end close to a millennium of Muslim rule in India; the French effortlessly took Egypt and later Algeria; the Russians advanced along a broad front into the ancestral lands of the Golden Horde and the Turkish lands all around the Black Sea and in Central Asia; the Dutch strengthened their control over the Insulindian archipelago. Gradually, awareness of the changes afoot spread among the faithful: "Muslims in India became aware of the decline of Islam as a world power," notably though the great pilgrimage to Mecca.[201] By the end of the nineteenth century, "the existence of an almost universal Muslim predicament, one of subjugation by the West," was general.[202] The mental map of the world Muslims were able to draw was less and less Muslim, while Muslims in larger and larger numbers stopped inhabiting a world comprised essentially of Muslim empires, as the Muslim tradition had depicted.[203]

In this bygone "natural" Islamic order, under the Ottoman Caliph, Indian Moghul or Qajar Shah, policies and decisions had been arrived at by means of court intrigue, harem cabals and the closed-door interplay of elite groupings. Powerful local notables, imperial lieutenants, prominent clerics and soldiers were players. Politics in the modern sense did not exist, it did not involve public deliberation nor the engagement of broad social forces. Now, more and more, as a result of the impact of the West, the instruments of rule were political manifestos and programs, books and newspapers, parties and associations, and parliamentary assemblies and street demonstrations that competed with increasing vigor with the old instruments of power. What had been dealt with in the secluded privacy of the Topkapı Palace was now increasingly played out in the public realm. Larger masses once kept outside the magic circle were clamoring at gates for some form of participation. Muslims were acceding to politics in the Western sense at the same time as Western politics reached them. As a public life was developing, Islam was less and less able to order it.[204]

The *umma islamiyya,* the community of Islam, was increasingly despoiled of a visible, credible political embodiment. One after the other the Muslim polities shrank and fragmented. The Moghul emperors and the Ottoman sultans tried for more than a hundred years to achieve an offensive alliance against a fellow Muslim ruler, the Shah of Persia.[205] This encapsulated well the state of chronic fragmentation and dynastic warring that had characterized Islam for most of its real-life existence. As time went by, no ruler was able any longer credibly to claim and offer leadership to the *umma* and its members. Once the last surviving Muslim imperial ruler, the Caliph, was gone, Muslims were released from the *sharia*-based political order that had once aggregated them: Muslims now had to re-compose their political order. They also were compelled to do so lest all Muslim polity disappear altogether. In spite of themselves, they were thrown into the "free market" of politics. The adaptive change of Muslim societies to the strange new world which now surrounded them first took the form of the rise of Pan-Islam, or Pan-Islamism, in the second part of the nineteenth century. "The idea of Islamic unity remained an alien concept to Muslim rulers until the 19th century, despite the pervasive feelings of religious commonality and brotherhood among the mass of the believers. Prior to the 19th century, in spite of a few, vague and isolated calls for unity, the Islamic states failed to develop a concept of unity."[206]

Birth of Pan-Islam

Pan-Islamism, then, as it evolved from the early nineteenth century onward, was the notion that the political and religious unity (or union) of Islam was the solution to the ills that besieged the world of Islam. The new ideology was based on a few principles: (1) the need for a strong central authority to lead Pan-Islam and impose its ideology; (2) the rallying to the cause of the entire Muslim world; (3) obedience to the Caliph; (4) total solidarity with the cause; (5) readiness for common action.[207] A fair outline of the doctrine by Jamal al-Din al-Afghani, considered one of the fathers of the doctrine, went:

> [Under the] rule of Islam over contiguous lands in a single sequence, their government was undefeatable. Their great kings ruled most of the globe…:

The Kings of China and Europe trembled before a word of their caliphs and princes. Four hundred million Muslims, their hearts stout and ready to die as martyrs in war. Any Muslim under foreign domination is injurious to the *Umma*. After having been the world's teacher, Muslims now lag in knowledge and industry. Muslims have not forgotten that Allah promised they would inherit the earth. But their first problem is their arch-rivalries and internal discord. Unite on the Quran and Islam guarantees success: unity![208]

Pan-Islamism was the form Islam had to assume in order to exist in an international order that it had not made or defined, over which it did not hold sway, and which it needed to fend off. It was the *umma* in politics. It was now the prism through which the world of Islam perceived its new, scandalous situation of worldly inferiority and imagined remedies to rebuild its erstwhile supremacy. As "[t]he expansion of the West into Muslim lands redefined for Muslim peoples the meaning of their universality,"[209] Pan-Islam was the *umma*'s first coherent response to its new situation as a minority in retreat, one that found itself materially and militarily overwhelmed. It was the recombinant form taken by the concept of the *umma* in a world dominated by non-Muslim powers.[210]

The situation of the *umma* thus produced both a global demand for new policies, in response to Western inroads, and a supply in the form of proposed leadership and ideology. Muslim reactions took on two principal and often conflicting forms: Pan-Islam as an official ideology developed by the Ottoman Empire and its rulers, and Pan-Islam as a mass movement of religious anti-imperialism. Where the two approaches converged and diverged, Pan-Islamist action was the result.

The Caliph was God's shadow on earth, the executant of His decrees, one whose legitimacy was transmitted by an unbroken chain of succession and whom all Muslims should obey and support.[211] This was embodied in his territorial dominion. But in 1774, at the end of a long, lost war the Ottoman Empire signed the Treaty of Kücük Kaynarca with the Russian Empire. One of the treaty's noteworthy features was the assertion by the Ottoman Sultan of his spiritual jurisdiction over Muslims living outside the empire. What a change this was! Instead of conquering by force of arms as the Ottomans had done for centuries, and thus asserting his dominion over land and people, the Sultan now claimed a lesser form of suzerainty, one modeled on the Christian West: just as European powers had wrested from the Sultans the *capitulations* that made them the "protectors" of the Christian communities inside the Ottoman Empire, the Sultan now claimed a religiously-grounded relationship to, and "spiritual" dominion over, the Muslims who lived outside his writ, outside the *dar al-Islam*.

The Ottoman rulers had spread the legend that Sultan Selim I had inherited the caliphate from the last Abbasid Caliph in 1517.[212] Sultan Abdülhamid I had been addressed by the title in 1774, but had not claimed the title himself. The controversial claim was not taken seriously until the reign in the 1860s and 1870s of Sultan Abdülaziz,[213] who was the first to claim the title.

As Muslim uprisings occurred in many places—Syrian rumblings of jihad in 1853; the Great Mutiny in India starting in 1857; Central Asian and Caucasus rebellions and Turkestan wars against Russian rule or incursions; Aceh wars against the Dutch— their leaders looked to the Ottomans for patronage, leadership, and support: there was a convergence of a supply and of a demand for some form of leading political authority in the world of Islam.

The assumption of the caliphal title provided much-needed leverage for the embattled Sultan Abdülhamid II (r. 1876–1909), the "Sultan-Caliph." As his empire unraveled on its Balkan, Russian and Mediterranean edges, he was "drawn to claim a spiritual authority no longer dependent upon the possession of the sinews of power. His was a policy intended to conceal weakness, to create an illusion of latent strength."[214] On the other hand, the claim to the caliphate was a powerful means of rallying to the Ottoman cause Muslim nations and leaders fighting against Western powers. The Sultan-Caliph thus killed many birds with one stone. He himself articulated the creed:

> If we want to rejuvenate, find our previous force and reach our old greatness we ought to remember the fountainhead of our strength. What is beneficial to us is not to imitate the so-called Western civilization but to return to the *sheriat* [sharia], the source of our strength. (…) Our relations with countries inhabited by Muslims must be expanded and we must strive for togetherness. As long as the unity of Islam continues, England, France, Russia and Holland are in my hands, because with a word the Caliph could unleash the jihad among their Muslim subjects and this would be a tragedy for the Christians…. [O]ne day Muslims will rise and shake off the infidels' yoke. [Millions of them] are beseeching God for delivery from foreign rule. They have pinned their hopes on the Caliph, the deputy of the Prophet Muhammad.[215]

Abdülhamid was conjoining Pan-Islam and jihad. A British Ambassador to the Sublime Porte reported him as saying in official conversation: "Unlike the czar, I have abstained till now from stirring up a crusade and profiting from religious fanaticism, but the day may come when I can no longer curb the rights and indignation of my people at seeing their co-religionists butchered [by various Christian rebels] and once their fanaticism is aroused, then the whole Western world, in particular the British Empire, will have reason to fear."[216] The Sultan broached on the theme again and again: "The entire Islamic world is, so to say, connected by an electric wire. The hand of the great Sultan of Turkey [himself] rests on its button. The least pressure on the button can disturb the whole Islamic world."[217] The conjunction of Islam, jihad and a modern Western technology was noteworthy.

In 1882, Colonel Urabi led a revolt against British influence in Egypt; in the Sudan Ahmad Muhammed who called himself the Mahdi started the rising that brought him to power in 1881–1882; Tunisia was restive in opposition to growing French control, and Sultan Abdülhamid was considering sending the Ottoman Navy. He was also reportedly considering the establishment of an international Muslim League to assist the Ottoman Empire militarily. The Ottoman press was clamoring that "the Sultan [is] willing to shed his last drop of blood and to spend the last piaster of his treasure to defend the sacred religion of Islam."[218]

If the last drop of his own blood and his last piaster were saved for another day, a constant flood of emissaries was streaming out of Istanbul to convey the new creed. Missions were sent to Japan which stopped over in Suez, Aden, Bombay, Ceylon, Singapore, Saigon and Hong Kong; to China, visiting Muslim countries on the way; emissaries were sent to Muslim communities in an old tradition of propaganda which went back to the Fatimid caliphs of Cairo: "Messengers in the guise of religious preachers and expounders of the Quran were sent to all quarters of the globe proclaiming the pious feelings of the Khalifa, and exhorting the true believers to persevere in their faith and to unite in a common bond in defense of Islam," a confidante of Abdülhamid wrote.[219] It was "a constant stream of emissaries to and fro Istanbul, bearing the Pan-Islamic message. Many were sheikhs, some of whom were associated with [brotherhoods], other ulama and men of religion. More rarely, they comprised notables, traders and businessmen…. At various points, one hears of their having visited southern Russia, Iran, Afghanistan, Central Asia, India, China, the Philippines… and naturally Morocco, Algeria, Tunisia, Egypt, Sudan and Arabia" as well as the areas adjoining Lake Chad, Tanganyika, Natal and Zanzibar."[220]

While the Caliph turned to Muslims, the converse was equally true: in their hour of need, Muslims turned to him as the sole remaining highly visible and legitimate political authority in the world of Islam. The leader of the Algerian resistance to the French had rallied the Caliph as his leader as early as 1840, and called for his help. So did the Sanussi Brotherhood fighting the Italians in Tripolitania. So did the Aceh Muslims fighting the Dutch, and Yakub Bey, the East Turkestan (Xinjiang) leader in the fight against the Russians. Islam began to acquire a new international dimension that the West described as "Pan-Islam."[221]

Abdülhamid made an especial effort "to harness the entire Sufi structure to his Pan-Islamism under the supervision of the sheikh of the tarikat [Sufi brotherhoods], the *shaykh al-Turuq*." He even personally joined one of them, while reaching out directly to other such important brotherhoods.[222] The Sufi brotherhoods were indeed the most direct and efficient way of reaching the broad masses of the Muslim populations, within and without the empire: popular Islam was out of reach of the stale establishment ulama. At the same time, Abdülhamid was ambivalent about popular Pan-Islamism, given the risk that it might escape his control. When Sheikh Shamil, the larger-than-life Chechen hero of Muslim resistance to the infidel Russians, arrived in Istanbul on his way to Mecca (the victorious tsar had permitted him to go on the *hajj* after he had surrendered in 1856), "the population gave him an extraordinarily enthusiastic welcome that lasted for days, until the Porte, afraid that the popular demonstrations were escalating into anti-government shows, hastened Shamil's departure."[223]

The Caliph was willing to instrumentalize the "Ottoman street," to paraphrase a contemporary expression, but not let it overwhelm him. For rulers, the paradox was powerful and dangerous: in order to safeguard their realms, they needed to mobilize the masses. In so doing, they ran the risk of letting the genie out of the bottle, and being unable to stop the populace from challenging the old order.[224] He kept Pandora's Box slightly ajar, a difficult enough exercise, enough for the rumbling to frighten partners and opponents, never so wide open that the winds he liberated would sweep him off his throne. In this, he was perhaps a wiser ruler than many later sorcerers' apprentices who recklessly unleashed vast popular movements and were overpowered by the results.

Modernity was at work: it was not enough to rally the ulama. In order to mobilize the masses, the Caliph needed to talk to them—and to do so, to use the literati, the intelligentsia. The Caliph used the printing press, and soon, newspapers were appearing under his benevolent protection and conveyed a Pan-Islamic message, such as *Basiret*, which "appealed to the world's Muslims, especially in Mecca, India and Central Asia." As for the contents: "*Basiret* claimed that Muslims were endowed with a special inner bond (profound, heartfelt love) which had a permanent religious essence and compelled all Muslims to move toward central union and alliance."[225] Caught between the old and the new, the Muslims' "response [was] largely politicized.... [Their] response had (at least initially), a character of religious anti-imperialism."[226] Religious brotherhood turned into political activism.

The predominant Sunni tradition, best expounded perhaps by the great thinker al-Ghazali (d. 1111 A.D., known as the "Reviver of the Faith" and whom "Orthodox Islam regards… as the final authority"), was unequivocal on this point:[227] better an injustice than a disorder, better forty years of tyranny than one day of disorder. The fear of disorder, *fitna*, was the bugbear of Islamic political thought. As a result, the very thought of organized political action outside the purview of legitimate authority was quite unthinkable. New conditions, however, demanded, an ideology capable of moving the masses. What was needed to mobilize the Muslim masses was an ideology that went beyond the narrow bounds of the political quietism in Islam.

Ideology and mobilization: these were key modern ingredients in the new broth now simmering about in the *umma*. These modern creatures, the ideologues and the political agitators, were equally required. The first was the charismatic adventurer Jamala al-Din al-Afghani, whose heady words of jihad we have already heard.[228] His recurrent theme was the mobilization of Muslims (and especially their leaders and intellectuals) simultaneously against European aggression and corrupt tyrannical rule at home.[229] Both appeals were revolutionary, and the combination made them even more so. The problem with the intelligentsia and the demagogues was that they soon were busy developing their own agenda, which did not necessarily include the Caliph. This is likely why Abdülhamid kept Afghani first at arm's length, and finally in a state of gilded captivity in Istanbul (1892–1897) until his death. The danger that the populist demagogue would overstep the boundaries set by his master was too great.

As early as 1877 or 1878, Afghani had drafted a letter meant for the Caliph's eyes, aimed at inciting the ruler to send him on an organizing tour of India to rally Indian Muslims to unity and the Caliph. The letter conjures up a messianic vision, comes close to announcing the coming of the Mahdi, includes clever scheming and realpolitik in the cause of Pan-Islam." Afghani outlines a plan to bring together the Ottoman Empire and the Muslims of India, those of Afghanistan, and presents even more ambitious plans for the achievements of Pan-Islam. He offers to send ulama to remote parts of India, others from Afghanistan, to Kokand and Bukhara, and yet others to Kashgar and Yarkand —all as secret emissaries to mobilize support for the cause. "Here one has the embryo of a master plan, bold in its conception and execution."[230]

While there is no indication that the Sultan or the Porte entrusted Afghani with the execution of the master-plan, the union (or unity) of Islam, in Arabic *Wahdat al-Islam* or *al-Wahda al-Islamiyya* (in Turkish *Ittihad-i Islam*), was becoming a factor in world affairs. To sum up the new ideology:

1. All Muslims are part of one country, the head and commander of which is the Caliph.
2. Muslim countries all over the world face the danger of subjugation by Europe. The enemies of Islam have gained the upper hand and have occupied Muslim lands not because of the inherent inferiority of Islam...but because is the members of the [*Umma*] remained disunited, ignorant.
3. The weakness of Muslim society has resulted also from the weakness of *iman* [faith], and the believers' failure to understand properly and obey their faith. Muslims, therefore, should properly interpret Islamic principles in the light of reason and science. Predestination should not be interpreted as fatalism, and Muslims must attach importance to worldly aspects of their existence, such as material progress, rather than solely to the dogma of the faith.
4. The rejuvenation of Islam is possible through a return to its basic principles, and that, in turn, depends first and foremost on achieving the unity of the [*Umma*] under the guidance of its leader, the caliph, or *amir al-Muminin*."[231]

The ever-recurring themes of Pan-Islam were summarized: "Damn the Christian hatred of Islam, smash European aggression.... Islamic union is a civilizing force thanks to its humane character.... Islam could shake the entire world with its force, renascent in the near future in a young, united Islamic nation."[232]

The Ottoman Empire itself was soon to take a radically new direction; the Sultan was to be sidelined and replaced by an officers' junta, itself based on a secret society. Modernization was relentless, including in its ugliest aspects. Events in Turkey foreshadowed the fate of many Muslim nations in the century to come.

The Young Turks had first been established in 1889 by cadets. The Committee Union and Progress (CUP), a secret society of opponents, was in an osmotic relationship with the Young Turks. They were not set on a firm ideology. Rather, they alternatively or simultaneously picked from a hodge-podge of different beliefs: a "pan-Turanian" ideology which vaguely aspired to ingather all the Turkic-speaking peoples, or the "Turkic" race, from Western China to Anatolia; "Ottomanism," which meant to continue the Abdülhamid's efforts to rejuvenate the empire; and "Pan-Islamism." Impatience at the Sultan's inability to ward off external threats and encroachments would not allow the Sultan much longer to lead the Ottoman renascence he had promised. Anticipating the sorry string of military takeovers that blighted so much of the history of extra-European nations in the twentieth century, a secret society plotted to replace him and to do better what he claimed he intended to do. Even the Sultan's Pan-Islamism had failed to deliver tangible results, and did not appear to have impeded the enfeeblement of the Empire.

In 1908, the Young Turks took power, deposed the Sultan and enthroned a puppet monarch. Their policy was unequivocally indicated in the same year, when the island of Crete announced its union with Greece: "The CUP threatened the European powers that, should they support this act, they would have to reckon with the wrath of the Muslims everywhere."[233] The Young Turks used the *hajj* to rouse Muslims energies to that effect. "At the 10th Congress of the CUP, it was decided to continue to employ Pan-Islamist policies; the 1911 Congress, held in Salonica, elaborated on this further." A "more aggressive stance" in activities and propaganda was adopted. By 1913 the CUP had installed a Pan-Islamic league in Istanbul—the *Cemiyet-I Hayriye-yi Islamiye*, or Benevolent Islamic Society. The society, which published *The World of Islam*, a fortnightly which appeared in Turkish, Arabic, Persian and Urdu, and a nationalist newspaper in Egypt, among other activities, centralized Ottoman Pan-Islamist action: Pan-Islam had become a central tenet of the Young Turks' policy.[234]

When Italy invaded Tripolitania and Cyrenaica in 1913 and found itself at war against the Ottoman Empire, the local tribes rose up under the Senussi Brotherhood, in the name of Pan-Islamism: "It was the first resistance movement inspired by Pan-Islamism against Western occupation." Moreover, "the war was widely considered as a jihad. Enver Pasha [the Ottoman commander in Tripolitania] issued a proclamation to the warriors, urging them to fight the enemies of Islam and assuring them of the support of the world's Muslims.

The entire Muslim press in the Ottoman Empire and many Muslim newspapers abroad… supported the Ottoman government and its military forces, on Pan-Islamic grounds, emphasizing the need for unity and union."[235] The CUP's international arm, the Benevolent Islamic Society, contributed a big share in the support apparatus. "The war contributed to the institutionalization of Pan-Islamism as a force to be employed."[236]

By 1913, the CUP, which had been the puppeteer for the new Caliph and Grand Vizier, tired of governing at one remove. Through a swift military putsch, it installed a military dictatorship led by a triumvirate of officers, Talaat, Jemal and Enver, the "Three Pashas." They made the fateful choice of aligning the Ottoman Empire with the Central Empires and entered World War I against the Allies. All the while, Pan-Islamism had been gaining the upper hand among the spectrum of ideologies available to the Young Turks.[237] The war was going to thoroughly transform Pan-Islamism. The long-threatened Ottoman jihad was indeed declared against the Allies powers, not without the helping hand of the revolutionary Pashas' ally, Wilhelminian Germany.

"Jihad Made in Germany"

Germany's links with the Ottoman Empire were not new, especially in the military sphere. They had started with Lieutenant Helmuth von Moltke ("The Elder")'s private visit to Istanbul in 1835. A few years later, the Sultan hired Moltke to advise on the training of the new army. More Prussian instructors followed;[238] the military connection only expanded with time. Later, in the course of two missions (1886–1895 and 1909–1913), General Colmar von der Goltz reorganized the Ottoman army. In 1913, General Liman von Sanders was appointed general instructor of the Ottoman Army and, when war broke out in 1914, commander of the Turkish Army Corps of Constantinople. He was later to head the Ottoman General Staff. In the Great War no fewer than 30,000 German officers and soldiers came to fight on the Middle Eastern theaters of war on the side of the Ottomans, from Palestine to the Caucasus.

The diplomatic aspect of the bilateral relationship had been less intense. Under Bismarck's stewardship, Germany's attitude toward the greater Middle East had been rather detached: the region was of "secondary" interest in the Iron Chancellor's foreign policy, as opposed to his "primary" interest, which lay in

Europe, east and west. The Middle East was not worth the bones of a single Pomeranian grenadier.[239] In 1898, having ousted the old statesman, the rash and striving new emperor Wilhelm II was mounting his great challenge to the British Empire. The motto of his *Weltpolitik Ein Platz an der Sonne* (*A Place in the Sun*) implied that established imperial powers had to make way for newcomers. The pan-Germanic challenge was multifarious. The German Navy was growing at a fast clip, while an aggressive German policy was developing in Latin America, Africa, the Far East, and the Middle East.

The Kaiser's policy was anti-British in the first place, and the Middle East was a primary stage for challenging the British. In 1898, Wilhelm undertook a long tour of the region that led him from a triumphant welcome in Istanbul to highly publicized sojourns in Jerusalem and Damascus. There, on December 8, he proclaimed himself the friend of "300 million Muslims." He let it be known that he had personally paid for a new marble monument at Saladin's tomb in Damascus, which he had visited with much fanfare. German propaganda in the region referred to him as "*Haji* Wilhelm Mohammed" and spread the rumor that he had secretly converted to Islam following an incognito pilgrimage to Mecca. "Passages of the Quran were found that showed the Kaiser had been ordained by God to free Muslims from infidel rule."[240] Sheikh Abdullah, who had welcomed him in Damascus, in return assured him that he had not only earned the gratitude of the "300 million Muslims," but also their love.[241]

The Kaiser was following a script drafted by his chief adviser in the matter, Germany's leading Islamologist Baron Max von Oppenheim, whose enthusiastic supporter he was. Wilhelm believed in the latter's thesis regarding the "world-wide importance of the Pan-Islamist movement" and in Germany's ability to harness it for her own interests. Islam was a revolutionary force, and would play an essential role in winning the war against the English, the Russians and the French.[242] This revolutionary intent fitted in the German Empire's broader war strategy, the *Revolutionierungspolitik*, policy of revolutionizing, which targeted the British and Russian empires in the first place.

The policy of "war by revolution" consisted of two main projects. The first part was to set off a revolution that would knock Russia out of the war. To that effect, Germany would strongly assist the Russian Socialist movement and Nationalist opponents within the Empire. The second part was to incite the Ottoman Empire to launch a jihad against Germany's enemies, and to assist Constantinople in that effort in order to undermine the colonial possessions of the Allies. Germany's plans also aimed at prompting Mexico to enter the war on the side of the Central Empires. State Secretary Arthur Zimmermann was in charge of all of the revolutionary campaigns, and he made sure that Oppenheim's proposals were read by the top levels of the German military leadership.[243]

In the margin of a July 30, 1914, telegram from his ambassador in Saint Petersburg, Wilhelm II noted in longhand: we must "publicly tear off the mask of England's Christian peacefulness.... Our consuls in Turkey and India, our agents and so forth, must inflame the entire Muslim world and move them to rise in fierce insurgency against this hated, lying nation of grocers devoid of any conscience; for if we are to bleed, England should at least lose India."[244] There was much emotional energy behind the policy.

On November 11, 1914, the Ottoman Empire declared war on Great Britain and France and their allies.[245] Nine days later, on November 14, signed by the *sheikh al-Islam* Khayri Efendi the highest religious authority of the empire, a five-part fatwa was promulgated in Istanbul to justify the hostilities.[246]

The fatwa was highly assertive:

When it is verified that the enemies have committed aggression against Islam and the Muslim lands have been seized and plundered and Muslim populations made captive, and the Padishah of Islam thereupon gives orders for the Jihad in the form of a general mobilization, then, in accordance with the beautiful verse 'Go forth, light and heavy! Struggle in God's way with your possessions and your selves' ([*Quran*] 9:41), is the Jihad a duty (*fard*) on all the Muslims and does it become an individual duty (*fard' ayn*) on Muslims in every land, young or old, on foot or mounted... to hasten to the *Jihad* with property and person?

"*Answer*: It does.

"It being verified, by their attacking today... the abode of the Caliphate of Islam and the Imperial Guarded Dominions, that Russia, Britain and France are hostile to the Caliphate of Islam and are striving God Almighty forfend—to extinguish and destroy the sublime light of Islam, it is a religious duty for all Muslims under the rule of those powers and of states which are aiding and abetting them, to proclaim the *Jihad* against such governments and actively to hasten to the Holy War?

"*Answer*: It is.

"Whereas the achievement of the desired end is dependent on all the Muslims' hastening to the *Jihad*, if—God Almighty forfend—they were to lag behind, would it be a grave act of rebellion fore them to do so and would they incur the wrath of God and the penalty for this gross rebellion?

"*Answer*: They would.

"Even if the Muslim populations of the aforementioned governments, which are making war on the Islamic government, are compelled and constrained under pain of death for themselves and even of the destruction of all their families, it being totally prohibited in the Law for them to fight the soldiers of Islam, if they do fight them do they merit the fire of hell?

"*Answer*: They do.

"As Muslims who are under the rule of the governments of England, France, Russia, Serbia and Montenegro and their coadjutors will cause injury to the Caliphate of Islam if, in the present war, they take up arms against Germany and Austria, who are aiding the Imperial Islamic government, this being great sin will they merit painful torment?

"*Answer*: They will."[247]

The fatwa accompanied the Proclamation of Jihad against the Allies drafted by the Council of High Learning, also signed by the sheikh and issued under the authority of the Sultan-Caliph The Proclamation of jihad itself expanded on the fatwa:

> The Moscovite government seeks to reduce mankind to slavery… the governments of England and France… account it the most agreeable pleasure to keep millions of Muslims under the halter of slavery in the general conflict which is now ablaze. They nourish base aspirations, such as wresting away freedom and ensuring their own interests beneath their unlawful and tyrannical domination.

It skirted of course the thorny question of allying with one type of infidel against another in the course of a jihad, especially in the case of the Austrians, the Ottomans' eternal foe in Central Europe and the Balkans. Many earlier Ottoman wars had not been jihad wars. This one was, and it was a world war:

> [T]he Muslims in general who are under the oppressive grasp of the aforesaid tyrannical governments in such places as the Crimea, Kazan, Turkestan, Bukhara, Khiva and India, and those dwelling in China, Afghanistan, Iran, Africa and other regions of the earth, are hastening to join in this great Jihad to the best of their ability, with life and property, alongside the Ottomans, in conformity with the relevant holy fatwas.... O community [*umma*] of Muhammad! You have been established as a meritorious community to be taken as an example for emulation among mankind, by following the beautiful way of life of the exalted Prophet... of Muslims, who are the obedient servants of God! Of those who go to Jihad for the sake of the happiness and salvation of the believers in God's unity, the lost of those who remain alive is felicity, while the rank of those who depart to the next world is martyrdom. In accordance with God's beautiful promise, those who sacrifice their lives to give life to the truth will have honor in this world and their latter end is paradise....
>
> "O Muslims who are athirst and longing for honor and felicity.... The Commander of the Faithful, the Caliph of the Muslims, summons you to the Jihad. O warriors of Islam! By the beautiful divine promise it is corroborated and announced that you will destroy and annihilate the enemies of the Faith and gladden the hearts of the Believers with eternal felicity by the aid and grace of the Almighty and the spiritual assistance of our revered Prophet."[248]

The precedent was thus set in the modern age: it was not some local chieftain or *alim* or mufti who called for religious war against one or the other Western nation. The Sultan-Caliph was throwing in the full weight of his legitimacy. A worldwide jihad had been enabled. While the fatwa and the Proclamation of Jihad were in the straight continuity of the traditional doctrine and practice of holy Muslim war, new elements were creeping in. Modern jihad was not going to be a carbon copy of traditional jihad.

The "new" jihad was the instrument of the Young Turks' war of choice. The fatwas and the Proclamation were translated and distributed by the *Teshkilat-i Mahsusa* (TM), the intelligence service created by Enver (each of the triumvirs had set up his own intelligence operation) out of Ottoman officers who had served under him in Tripolitania and enlarged and expanded during the war. A high-powered and efficient operation, it earned a flattering description from Colonel Walter Nicolai, one of the leading figures in German military intelligence: "[a] far-spread, efficient and secret Ottoman political intelligence service, whose field of operations included Central Asia."[249] The TM combined intelligence, counter-intelligence and irregular warfare capabilities, as well as political warfare—and jihad.[250]

The agency sent agents throughout the Muslim world to spread the jihad; in addition, Muslim societies led by exiled Pan-Islamist figures, such as the Society for the Progress of Islam, were established in Europe to perform the same function.[251]

The call for jihad was also spread by the *Nachrichtenstelle für den Orient* (*NfO*, News—or intelligence—Organization for the Orient), a new political warfare agency for the Muslim world created in Berlin by the Ottomans' ally, the German Imperial government and its military intelligence service. This "translation-cum-agitation office," employing a staff of Orientalists, rapidly developed up to forty subsidiaries from Istanbul on to the rest of the Muslim world.[252]

On the Ottoman side, the chief architect of the jihad policy was Enver Pasha. Born in 1881, the young officer had joined the Young Turks while garrisoned in Salonica. In 1908 Enver's mutiny against the Istanbul authorities made him famous overnight and propelled him into the highest ranks of the CUP. He went to Berlin as military attaché (1909–1911), learned German and became friends with prominent German military leaders, such as General Hans von Seeckt, the future chief of general staff of the Ottoman Army and supremo of the post–World War I German *Reichswehr*. Enver even grew a handlebar moustache in the style of Kaiser Wilhelm II. He was then sent to North Africa to fight the Italian Army—rather ineffectually—though he emerged a propaganda poster boy, "The Hero of Islam." He then returned to the Ottoman capital and applied his military glory to changing the politics of the empire. "On 23 January 1913… the Unionists launched their surprise assault on the Sublime Porte. Led by Enver Bey, a small party of officers forced their way into the cabinet room, shooting the Minister of War Nazim Pasha as they did so. At the point of their guns, the aged [President of the Council of State] Kamil Pasha wrote out his resignation, which Enver triumphantly took to the [Imperial] Palace and presented to the Sultan." Bloody purges ensued. "From then until 1918, Turkey was governed by a virtual military dictatorship, dominated by three men, Enver, Talaat and Cemal Pashas."[253]

Enver and his colleagues were the first of the endless cohort of the

"Bonapartes" of the twentieth century—more or less victorious military leaders who gore their way to the top of the state and confiscate power in the name of whatever ideology they have chanced on. After oscillations similar to that of his Young-Turk peers he ended up espousing Pan-Islamism. Whether or not his heart was throbbing for Pan-Islamism is a secondary issue: in the real world, he threw his lot in with that ideology, to exploit it perhaps but to ride forward on its advancing crest nevertheless.

Enver had not accidentally been nicknamed *Napoleonlik* by his fellow officers. In 1914, he married a minor princess, daughter of the late Sultan Abdülmejid, which further enhanced his power. In the bizarre, conspiratorial world of the CUP and its triumvirs, Enver played the decisive role in striking the wartime alliance with Imperial Germany: Talaat Pasha was in favor of England until 1913, Cemal was rather pro-French. Enver had become minister of war; he appointed himself chief of the general staff, and, on August 2, 1914, signed the momentous accords of alliance between the Ottoman and German empires, the alliance that promoted jihad as a method to "revolutionize" and debilitate their enemies.

Max von Oppenheim, the engineer of the Muslim prong of the strategy, has aptly been called the "German *Abu Jihad*" (father of the jihad).[254] A twenty-year veteran of archeological and ethnological studies in the region, and of the German diplomatic service, Oppenheim could boast as few Westerners could of detailed knowledge of the tribal makeup of much of the Muslim world and personal acquaintance with many of its leading personalities. On August 2, 1914, he was recalled into the Reich's diplomatic service. His ambitious, detailed plan for a generalized anti-British, anti-French and anti-Russian jihad aimed at "fomenting rebellion in the Islamic territories of our enemies."[255] A first version of the project, a cable to the Chancellor, submitted in July 1898, had reviewed the potential of the Pan-Islamist movement as a strategic auxiliary for the Reich. It was the inspiration behind the resounding speeches of the Hohenzollern tourist of the Middle East. Oppenheim already then was banking on a pro-German, anti-British jihad.

Both Germany's political and military authorities demanded jihad action on the Middle Eastern front as soon as the war broke out. On August 2, 1914, and again three days later, von Moltke, Jr., nephew of the great field-marshal, now chief of the German General Staff, told the German Foreign Office in no uncertain terms: "[It is] of the highest importance… [to set off] insurrection in India and Egypt, and the Caucasus as well. Thanks to the [war alliance] treaty with Turkey, [we] will be able to implement those ideas and rouse the fanaticism of Islam."²⁵⁶ The famous Swedish spy-explorer and geopolitician Sven Hedin concurred and reported that the amir of Afghanistan was "raring to conquer India," and only needed German support to do so. A mission to Afghanistan was set into motion; plans to take the Suez Canal were hatched; contacts were renewed with Abbas Hilmi, the ex-Khedive deposed in 1914 by the British; connections were opened to the Senussi leadership in North Africa through Enver Pasha; ideas were developed to gain the alliance of both the *sharif* of Mecca and his rival Abdalaziz ibn Saud.

Von Moltke had urged Minister of War Enver Pasha to proclaim the jihad. As we have seen, the pliant Sultan and *sheikh al-Islam*, prodded by a triumvir characterized by "energy, remorselessness, cold-blooded determination, pitiless intention," complied.

Max von Oppenheim's Grand Design

Max von Oppenheim now presented his expanded and updated grand design, a blueprint for joint German-Ottoman action. His 136-page memorandum *Die Revolutionierung des islamischen Gebiete unserer Feinde* (The Revolutionizing of Our Enemies' Islamic Possessions) spells out the ways and means of a grand jihad. He neatly outlined the strategic rationale of the grand design, to wit: "England's colonial empire is her most vulnerable spot." Hence, Oppenheim wrote:

> [O]nly when the Turks break into Egypt and when red-hot insurgencies set India ablaze can England be tamed. If it be so, British public opinion will force the government in London… either to send a large part of the Fleet, perhaps half of it, to India, to save their many people there and their billions of invested capital, and Britain's world position, or, should [they] not be able to do so, [they would be forced to] sign a peace agreement in our favor. (…) The entire way in which our foe is waging war gives us the right and the necessity of our self-preservation the duty to take up such powerful weapons and make use of them in the struggle that has been forced upon us.²⁵⁷

The first phase, Oppenheim explained, should be to carry out "systematic and clearly-directed propaganda" which should "use the aura of the Sultan-

Caliph and be spread in his name," namely as a "call to Holy War." The effort was to be centralized in Istanbul, "but always under German leadership... but in such a way that the Turks may believe we are only a friendly adviser...." But Enver Pasha was in agreement with it all, he added. Stations would have to be created in Ma'an, Jeddah, Van, Damascus, Basra, Baghdad, Kerbala, Tabriz, Busher and ten more cities under the elastic rubric of *Nachrichten,* which means both intelligence and news; German agents would have to be sent to Mecca, Medina, Jeddah.[258]

Propaganda and preliminary organizing, recruitment, etc., should start in Egypt, so that, when the Turkish troops approached, a general insurrection would occur. "The whole of Egypt is anti-British," save the Christians. "We must especially bring to the fore the religious element, the Al-Azhar, the religious brotherhoods. We must launch little putsches, violent actions, etc., whether they succeed or not.... The more cruel the reprisals to be expected, and the more they strike the innocent, the more they will heat up the rage and the fanaticism of the people...[and will] move the urban masses and the fellahin to fight to the death to expel the British. (...) We cannot count on a popular insurrection at present, in spite of the hatred directed at the foreign occupier." However, the ferment can be helped along; when Enver's troops and a German army enter Egypt, the Khedive will tilt decisively, and then so will the populace. At that point, "the 'Holy War' on the Nile will break out. British civil servants will be killed in town and country. The British garrison in Khartoum will meet the same fate as Gordon.... As soon as the Turks have won the first battle, England's fate in Egypt will have been sealed. The Suez Canal will be locked, and violent risings will take place in India," which in turn will have a major impact on the overall strategic situation."[259]

Similar action was to be taken in the Caucasus where "it would be easy to raise 20 to 30,000 experienced and fanatical warriors against Russia."[260] Persia is not neglected, especially due to "its traditional significance for the Orient" since she "still possesses the greatest spiritual influence upon India, Afghanistan and Russia's Muslim possessions." Persia the gateway is "unanimously anti-British and anti-Russian."[261] Oppenheim's otherwise cool, calculating and well-informed view sometimes veers into delirious wishful thinking, such as when in defiance of all common sense he assures his reader—the Kaiser—that "Persia would make no difficulty in acknowledging the hegemony of the Turks."[262]

In spite of such arrant fantasy, Oppenheim's grand design was not wholly unrealistic—provided German arms had gained the upper hand in Europe.

The plan called for bringing together a Turkish-Persian-Afghan alliance "which would enable an Afghan march on Northwest India… [that] would cause a mighty revolution in the whole of India, which could mean the end of British rule in the Indian [sub-]continent." Therefore, "the task at hand would be to gain the support of the Porte for this plan. It would not be difficult to set off a rising of the fanatical Persians."

Afghanistan was central to the strategy: "I have long considered that in case of a war opposing Germany to England, the participation of the Amir of Afghanistan and his invasion of India to be of the highest importance. A great general Indian insurrection will only occur as Afghan troops march into the Indus Valley, naturally after India itself has made itself ready for revolution."[263] Hence, as will be examined shortly, came the ragged epic of the German mission to Afghanistan, the steppe-and-mountain counterpart to T.E. Lawrence's sand-dunes yarn. The great differences between them were that the Germans never had an effective public-relations agent and that they lost the war.[264]

The "fanatically Muslim Afghan people," Oppenheim continued, were enthused by the Sultan-Caliph's call. "Some Indians will join, members of a committee of fanatical nationalists who have come to Germany to prepare an Indian revolution." Their networks reached far and deep into India, where most educated classes, Oppenheim stated, were anti-British. The *Svadeshi* movement was promoting boycotts and sabotage, while the *Svaraj* movement "aims at bringing about independence by using all possible means, including political assassination.… There is a whole series of revolutionary associations and secret societies…." India's Muslims were increasingly dissatisfied, "and they are the most warlike and fervent part of the population."[265] Just as the Great Mutiny of 1857 broke out as a result of England's preoccupation with the Crimean War, the Great War in Europe would open spaces for India, Oppenheim reasoned. And more concretely, he added: "In complete quiet, I have established a committee of Indians who live here and in Switzerland, 18 members strong, highly imbued with our ideas, educated people of high organizing abilities and intelligence, and animated by a burning patriotism." Some of them, he reported, are ready to participate in our revolutionary propaganda.… Some are chemists, a profession they embraced because of their revolutionary intent. They have sworn themselves to die and committed themselves to kill traitors," and were being infiltrated back into India. "My friends have sworn to spare the lives of [English] women, old people and children, as much as possible. Our foe's own methods justify the measures we take in self-defense, including the attack in India.... I believe it possible to set India afire, to force England to make peace with us.... We must use all possible connections into India, as well as Mecca, the Muslim religious brotherhoods, Hadramut, etc."[266]

The German "Abu Jihad" concludes:

> In the struggle to the death against England that has been forced upon us, Islam will become one of our mightiest weapons. Egypt and India are the Achilles' heel of the mighty maritime British colossus. This is why England has for long done all she can to prevent us from connecting with the Pan-Islamic and nationalist movements of the Orient. But the ground was being prepared for the rising of Islam in connection with us.... Everywhere [in the Muslim world] prayers are made in mosques for our victory. Such is the disposition, in the Turkish population to start with, but also in the whole world of Islam in today's historical moment where the entire globe is burning with the greatest of all wars, in which for the first time in many centuries the whole of Islam has been called to fight its enemy.... The Sultan-Caliph has now declared Holy War against the enemies of Germany. The world of Islam and the Central Empires fight shoulder to shoulder for their very survival.[267]

Oppenheim vigorously insisted that for a successful implementation of the plan, "We must supply the Turks with personnel, money and equipment, and there, satisfactory results will only be attained if we apply very sizable resources. Half measures would be useless. The success we hope for is however worth a major effort." All assessments concur that the resources never met the requirements. Writes historian Fritz Fischer, "The actual commitment of resources and personnel in the Islamic world turned out to be… totally insufficient and the result attained nearly zero."[268] Wolfgang Schwanitz accepts that "[i]n the end, the execution of the jihad was disappointing for Max von Oppenheim" and that "it turned out that the majority of Muslims ignored the jihad, although the Germans spent a lot of money for the expeditions… and for Pan-Islamic propaganda printed in Berlin like the weekly *al-Jihad*." He nonetheless adds, quoting one of the leading German participants in the venture, the dragoman Karl Schabinger, that "the seeds of an uprising had been planted. One day there would be an accumulation of colonial people ready to turn against their rulers."[269] A leading historian of Pan-Islamism concurs that the proclamation of jihad was not a total failure: "It certainly did not generate any dramatic results, in terms of numbers" but, as a contemporary French military intelligence report he quotes analyzed: "Turkey, Tripolitania, the Libyan desert, and Darfur have risen for the Holy War, without any doubt.... One gets the impression that India has remained loyal, but we know that the Dutch Indies have known some effervescence. Iran has been gravely troubled, Afghanistan excited and Egypt trembling.... There is no doubt that the words 'Holy War' have been pronounced and exploited.... They failed, indeed, but they caused no end of trouble to the Allied powers."

In the long-range perspective of history, "[t]he qualitative gains of the [jihad] proclamation were not so insignificant as the quantitative ones. Quite a few brilliant and dedicated Muslims hurried to Istanbul to share in what they considered the war of Islam"[270] Here may be one of the most significant achievements indeed of the "Jihad Made in Germany:" while it helped the German Reich remarkably little, it helped jihad considerably. For the first time in many centuries the whole of Islam has been called to fight its enemy.[271] Seeds had been planted, and a global jihad had been declared. For the first time, rather than a local or regional Holy War, it was a worldwide jihad.

The Pan-Islamist jihadi propaganda had been spread all over the world of Islam in all of its major languages. Much—probably most—of the Pan-Islamist activity during the war years was carried out far from the limelight. The *Teskilat,* the Special Organization originally set up by Abdülhamid for clandestine work, carried out much of this activity. "Its agents continued to serve the [Young Turks], parallel with the agents of the Benevolent Islamic Society.... Indeed, propaganda was the main Pan-Islamic activity of the [Young Turks] (and the Germans) during World War I."[272]

But another, even less quantifiable type of work and of impact may be adjudicated as one of the most significant effects of the "Jihad Made in Germany:" it was the selection, training and development of a jihadi cadre force, clusters of individuals who, five, ten or twenty years later, would emerge as the local, regional, national or international leaders of jihad.

In the geostrategic conception that tended to prevail in the German Reich, Britain was the arch-enemy, the maritime power dead-set against Germany the continental power.[273] India was the keystone of the British Empire and Afghanistan was the gateway into India. The political and military mission sent by Berlin to Kabul early on in World War I was a tool of the policy to pull the Indian prop out from under the British Empire. It was bold in conception, but the resources assigned to the project were altogether insufficient. As an integral part of the German-Ottoman jihad, the Afghan project intended to leverage what its authors called "the fanaticism of Islam" against the British, throwing in Indian nationalism for good measure.

> By Sept. 3, 1914 the [German] Foreign Office had agreed that Germany would assist the Indian nationalists, and for the next few weeks, there were almost daily Indian-German meetings to discuss next steps. On September 9, two months before the jihad was proclaimed, the Kaiser declared that Muslims in Entente [Central Powers] arms would not be treated as belligerents but would be sent to the Caliph in Turkey when taken prisoners.[274]

Oppenheim, as reported *supra*, had assembled a core group of pro-German Indian revolutionaries, and more now flocked into Germany, so that in early 1915, the "Indian Independence Committee" was established at a meeting held in Charlottenburg, in Berlin. The Committee was subsidized on a regular basis by the Foreign Office. "Several prominent Hindu leaders left India in 1914 to campaign abroad for Indian freedom."

But distance was an insuperable obstacle for the planned Indian revolution. A forward base was needed closer to the planned theater. Imperial Germany hence threw itself into a new version of the "Great Game" Kipling had seen played out between England and Russia, with Afghanistan the centerpiece of the struggle. The country was the stepping stone into India, as it had always been in history: the Reich's strategists were pressing their Ottoman allies, their Persian friends, their hoped-for Afghan partners to follow in the footsteps of the Muslim conquerors of India, such as Mahmud of Ghazna or Babur, whose tomb General Hans von Seeckt, one of the designers of the anti-British jihadi plans, had reverently visited.

The German ambassador in Constantinople Baron Hans Freiherr von Wangenheim reported in August 1914 on a meeting with Ottoman members of parliament and Syrian notabilities: "In agreement with Enver Pasha" they had proposed "to support the revolutionary movement in [Egypt] and possibly Afghanistan," news that Oppenheim welcomed as a "godsend."[275] Accordingly, the diplomatic head of the Afghan mission, Werner Otto von Hentig, arrived in the Ottoman capital in April 1915 with an aristocratic and "charismatic" Indian political exile, Kumar Mahendra Pratap, who had been received with some luster by the Kaiser in Berlin in February.[276] Together, at Enver Pasha's behest, they were granted an audience by the Sultan who bestowed Allah's blessing on the expedition and its purpose.[277] They also spent six hours weaving plans with the former khedive of Egypt Abbas Hilmi, an indefatigable pro-German plotter whom the British had deposed. And off they were to Afghanistan with a group of Germans, Ottomans and Indians, with the Bavarian geographer and officer Oskar von Niedermayer as military head.

After grueling adventures through deserts and mountain ranges, hunted all the while by the British and their local auxiliaries, the mission arrived in Herat in August 1915 and that October in Kabul, where they were the honored guests of the King (amir) Habibullah, a crafty ruler accustomed to playing balancing games among tribes internally and between great powers externally. With an eye on military developments in Europe, the cool, calculating politician responded equivocally to the guests' insistent entreaties to sign a formal alliance with Germany. By December, however, his brother Nasrullah Khan was hinting that the king would be ready to sign the treaty, and by January 1916, the draft was indeed autographed by him and by the Germans. The latter were hopeful that the 80,000 men of the regular Afghan army, or at least the 43,000 whom they believed to be combat-ready, would now be dispatched into the Indian raj's North-West Province and thence into the north Indian valley. A large part of the [Afghan]ruling elite was pressing the king to do so. Shortly after the arrival of the expedition, the king's relative Mahmud Tarzi wrote in his newspaper: "Eat, *Aga*! So that you will not be eaten!"[278]

Military events thousands of miles away interfered: after the Russian Army took Erzurum from the Ottomans, the King' enthusiasm waned , and he went back on his word. The Germans found themselves empty-handed; soon most returned west. As the historian puts it, "The results of the Kabul sojourn… lied with long-term consequences, not in the unfulfilled immediate expectations." For one, the king was murdered twenty-one months after the German delegation's departure and replaced by a decidedly pro-German leader Amanullah, who proceeded in May 1919 to open hostilities against the British, in what became the Third Afghan War. As occurs often in history, the unanticipated consequences of human action override the plans and intents of the actors. Far more important indeed than Germany's absent gains were the developments set into motion by the German mission regarding India.

In Stockholm, whence the India Revolutionary Committee operated; in Berlin, where a number of Indian revolutionaries were active; in San Francisco, where many of the Indian revolutionaries arrived; in New York, where the Free Hindustan Movement was working with the Irish Fenians (both encouraged by German intelligence, with Major Franz von Papen as paymaster for the arms destined for India), an assault on the British Raj was being hatched. The Rajput prince Kumar Mahendra Pratap was an outspoken ally of Germany. As he had said in 1914, "I began to feel decisive sympathy for the Germans who were fighting this dirty British Empire."[279] The prince had been wined and dined by the German military and political elite in Berlin. Regarding the Indian revolutionaries, "it was not a mean achievement on their part to have acquired in Berlin the status of the representatives of a belligerent power, so as to enlist the support of the German government for India's struggle against British imperialism."[280] It was one of them who had recruited Mahendra Pratap.

As a member of the failed German mission to Afghanistan, Pratap had remained in Kabul where he was now joined by Muhamamad Barakatullah, or Barkat-Ullah (1859–1927), an *alim* who had met Afghani in 1883, a veteran Pan-Islam activist, publisher of Islamist journals in Japan, who was now the second in command of the Berlin-based Indian National Committee. The German Consulate in San Francisco had paid his transatlantic trip toward Berlin. In 1912, Barakatullah had said "There is really one man who holds the peace of the world in the hollow of his hand, and that man is Emperor William of Germany. In case of a European war, it is the duty of the Muslims to be united, to stand by the Khalif, and to side with Germany.... All that is required is a leader, and that leader will arise in Central Asia, probably in Afghanistan. The firing of an Afghan gun will give the signal for the rising of all Islam as soon as she [Afghanistan] is ready to open her gates for believers to fight under the green banner of the Prophet."[281]

On December 1, 1915, in Kabul, Mahendra Pratap proclaimed a Provisional Government of India in exile, with Barakatullah as prime minister; the former Sikh and Muslim convert Maulvi Obeidullah, a Deobandi figure and a future, lifelong Bolshevik fellow-traveler, as minister for home and foreign affairs; the Pan-Islamist figure Muhammad Ali as secretary; and Oskar von Niedermayer as minister of war.[282] This "government" would have been no more than a small historical footnote had it not intersected developments afoot in India, Russia and Germany. In India, the *Khilafat* movement was transforming the Muslim population; in Germany, ideas of a postwar *revanche* were stirring thoughts of warfare in the Orient against the British—but this time, with the help and cooperation of the new masters of Russia, the Bolsheviks.

The Khilafat Movement in India

Anti-British ferment had been on the rise in India for a long time, while the embers of the Sepoy Mutiny, a war that was largely a jihad, had never been extinguished. A first broad-based movement of support for the Caliph had developed in the years of the Russo-Ottoman war of 1877–1878. The Indian Muslim Sayyid Ameer Ali (1849–1928) so described the impact in India: "Few observers can have forgotten the extraordinary outburst of sympathy among the Mussulmans of India with the wrongs of Turkey and the afflictions to which their co-religionists were subjected in consequence of that war.... I am in a position to speak of the enthusiasm that prevailed amongst all classes to help the Ottoman nation and to relieve the universal suffering and distress among the stricken people of Turkey. Even women in the humbler walks of life sent their earrings, bracelets and anklets to be sold and the proceeds remitted to the Turkish Compassionate Fund… while many Mussulman soldiers offered their services to the Ottoman government."[283]

The momentum of the Pan-Islamist movement was quite irresistible. Far from remaining an elite ideology, "Pan-Islamic ideas filtered into the poorer populations."[284] At the same time, the British-led modernization led to greater and faster social differentiation; liberated from princely despotism and Muslim rule, though nationally oppressed, Indian middle classes, Muslim no less than Hindu, were becoming more assertive. Under the limited political freedoms extended by the British, a modicum of modern political life was developing which Mahatma Gandhi's political acumen was using to the full.

Originally, the All-India Muslim League, established by the great modernist Sir Sayyid Ahmad Khan (1817–1898), founder of the Aligarh College (the Anglo-Indian University) later led by the Ismaili chieftain the Aga Khan had been steered by both in a rather pro-British direction. It now veered sharply in the other direction: by century's end, it had joined the ranks of the proponents of Pan-Islam.

"Between 1908 and [1914], Pan-Islamism in India, which had been simmering steadily beneath the surface, erupted into active opposition to the British.… Under these circumstances, the ideas of Sayyid Jamal al-Din al-Afghani… became popular among sections of Indian Muslims. Of particular appeal were his call for Muslim unity, his stress on jihad against Western dominion." His protracted sojourn in India had focused and galvanized energies; some disciples he had recruited now emerged as leaders.

During and after World War I, Gandhi's non-cooperation movement, Bal Gangadhar Tilak's violent Hindu nationalism, and a spectrum of Muslim movements, were grasping for ways to throw off the yoke of British rule. "Resistance to British colonial rule had been growing in the Indian diaspora during the pre-war decade, not only among strident young Indians in Britain and South Africa… but also among more strident Indians in Japan and in anti-colonial circles in the United States."[285] On the Muslim side, the great event of the war had been the Sultan-Caliph's proclamation of jihad: the Muslim community of India had been the most attuned to and supportive of the Caliph's Pan-Islamist policies in the nineteenth century. A fever pitch was reached with World War I. Ottoman defeats and questions concerning the custodianship of the Holy Places in Mecca and Medina fanned the flames of Pan-Islamism. Logically, the focus was the question of the caliphate: by September 1919, the *Khilafat* movement was launched as an orthodox communal movement to protect the caliphate and save the Caliph's empire; by November, the national Conference for the Caliphate had been held. The movement's main leaders were Muhammad Ali, his brother Shawkat Ali and Maulana Abul Alam Azad. *Khilafat* conferences were organized in cities in northern India, regional and local committees were set up, a Central *Khilafat* committee was established in Bombay. In 1920, the Ali brothers produced the "Khilafat Manifesto." "The *Khilafat* was a genuine, powerful, all-India mass movement of Muslims.

The ulama were coming out of their political isolation and were participating in Pan-Islamist politics. "[E]very important move of the *Khilafat* was preceded by a fatwa and the ulama, *piris* and other religious dignitaries became political agents for recruiting support … a growing sentiment pervaded politically aware Muslims in India that ensuring Muslim power and government abroad was a guarantee for their own religious and national survival as a minority group; in other words, Pan-Islam assumed for them a nationalist significance." For India's Muslims, who had ruled the land and lorded over the Hindus for more than a half a millennium, the sinking feeling of having been reduced to the status of an impotent minority had needed to be allayed. "The *Khilafat* was rapidly being transformed from an agitational alliance into a religious-political mass movement."[286] The movement also had an international dimension: "In its heyday [it] had immense prestige among circles inclined toward Pan-Islam not only in India, but also abroad, chiefly in Turkey, in Egypt" and Afghanistan and the Dutch Indies (Indonesia).[287]

In India, the *Khilafat* originally held good and even cooperative relations with Gandhi's *satyagraha* movement. However, cooperation suffered major setbacks with the rise of the *Hijrat* movement. Some ulama ruled that India was not *dar al-Islam*, where Muslims lawfully are permitted live, but *dar al-Harb*, which Muslims must leave. As a result, between 18,000 and 30,000 Muslim peasants (by some accounts 50,000 to 100,000[288]), mostly from Sind and the North-West Province, sold their possessions and left India, marching westward in the hope of reaching Ottoman territory, a movement inspired by Prophet Muhammad's retreat from Mecca, *hijra*, and his establishment in Medina. Another nail in the coffin of Muslim-Hindu collaboration was the 1921 Moplah Rebellion in South India. Inspired by the *Khilafat* a jihad was proclaimed not only against the British, but also against Hindus, who were slaughtered in large numbers by Muslim rioters. One Mohommed Haji was proclaimed the caliph of the Moplah *Khilafat*, flags of the Islamic caliphate were flown, and Ernad and Walluvanad were declared *Khilafat* kingdoms.

Anti-British Pan-Islamist Indians themselves were not united.[289] There were *Khilafat* leaders with a "modernist" reputation, such as the Ali brothers, Muhammad and Shawkat. There were more radical disciples of Afghani such as Abul Kalam Azad, with his inflammatory Urdu-language journal *Al-Hilal*; Azad's circle founded many Pan-Islamist societies, including, in 1913, the *Jamiat-i Hizbollah*, which wanted to unite all Indian Muslims under one Imam, "to form an agreement with the Hindus and declare a jihad against the British." There was a group in Beirut, led by the Pan-Islamist brothers Abdal Jabbar Khairi and Abdal Sattar, that established an "Indian Muslim Committee" in Constantinople in 1915 with German and Ottoman support. Their newspaper *Akhuwat (Brotherhood)* appeared in Urdu and English. It urged Indian conscripts in the British Army to "shoot your English officers," and exhorted Muslims in India: "Murder Englishmen, set fire to their houses, destroy railway bridges and help [Germany] in all possible ways." The Kaiser declined to act on a proposal they conveyed to him during a visit to Constantinople in 1917 to the effect that the frontier tribes of Kashmir could be persuaded to declare war on the British if the Germans supplied arms and other assistance." Another group, the ulama of the *darululum* school at Deoband, was intent on returning to the "first principles" of Islam, on fighting for the independence of the Muslim world and the purification and renewal of

Islam. They took the lead in branding the Raj a *dar al-Harb*, which then, of necessity, was a land of jihad. Some ulama decided to leave India themselves and organize jihad from abroad. They joined the departing *Muhajirun*.

The war thus radicalized a diverse array of Islamist and Pan-Islamist groupings. As the Hindu revolutionary M.N. Roy wrote: "On the outbreak of the First World War in 1914, the Indian revolutionaries in exile looked towards Germany as the land of hope, and pushed there full of expectations. By the end of the year, the news reached us in India that the Indian Revolutionary Committee in Berlin had obtained from the German government the promise of arms and money required to declare the war of independence. The news spread like wildfire to affect the Indian soldiers of the British Army also. Revolution was around the corner… independence was within reach."[290]

Three events forced the revolutionaries to recast their expectations and their action: the defeat of both Germany and Turkey in 1918, the successful Bolshevik putsch in Russia in 1917, and the abolition of the caliphate in 1924. "The Muslims in India… had expressed Islamic solidarity long before World War I. However, it was the abolition of the Caliphate soon after the end of the war which served as a catalyst for their feelings and activities in activities in the cause of Pan-Islam. It ended the legitimacy of Pan-Islam and compelled Islamists to search for alternative loyalties."[291]

The *Khilafat* movement correspondingly petered out in the late 1920s. Political defeat, decline or dormancy, yet, has little bearing on the survival of ideological currents. Long periods of latency do not prevent ideas with great emotional pull from persisting. The movement died, but its ideas shaped generations of Muslim activists, journalists and theorists. A poem by Mohamed Iqbal (1873–1938), the intellectual leader of the Muslims of India from the 1920s until his death, spoke to hearts:

> *From the banks of the Nile*
> *To the soil of Kashgar*
> *The Muslims should be united*
> *For the protection of their sanctuary.*

The forces that had attached themselves to the *Khilafat* movement were now seeking new political outlets to bring their needs and their demands to bear. "with… the… defeat of Germany… their eyes turned to the Soviet Union for help."[292] After its protracted flirtation with pan-Germanism,

Pan-Islam now embarked on a tumultuous dalliance with Bolshevism. The Khairi brothers, prominent Indian Pan-Islamist leaders, whom we had left in Constantinople as cohorts of the German-Ottoman jihad, appeared in Moscow in front of the Central Committee of the Soviets on November 25, 1918, "and delivered a long message which echoed the radical changes in Muslim mood toward revolutionary Russia."[293]

Bolsheviks and Pan-Islamists

In the later decades, three external factors intertwined and shaped the destiny of modern jihad. The first was the renascent German ambitions of the early 1920s, formulated and led by General Hans von Seeckt. Although the importance of this element declined as Germany advanced toward National-Socialist rule, it was reinvigorated during World War II. The second was the pronounced Bolshevik attempt at leveraging Islam against the West, and against Britain in particular, leading to intensive interchange between them. The third was the Islamists' own acquisition of Bolshevik know-how, techniques and methods, by transfer, as it were.

In intellectual and political history, the study of the transfer of ideas is always delicate and difficult. In the material world, imported tools do not change once they cross a border. In the market of ideas, quantification is impossible. Tracing the immaterial can only be done by means of tracing the estimated effects of a cause. If in the "market" of ideologies, a certain technique offered only by one supplier appears in a given market segment and is acquired by a given purchaser, it is a reasonable assumption to infer that the transfer occurred from the known supplier to the known purchaser unless contrary evidence shows that some other pathways and suppliers were involved.

But "[i]deas—and particularly political ideas—on the other hand, seldom escape being significantly transformed when transmitted from one society to another, from one culture to another. Often, they are molded by the carrier, and by the time they reach their intended destination, much of their original plumage is gone and in its place are new markings which belong to the culture into which the ideas are being transmitted."

We will therefore study the multifarious ways in which critical Bolshevik "technologies" were transferred to the modern jihadi movement. No case is made that the "lines of communication"[294] identified here represent, even by far, the entire gamut of their transfer to the Muslim world; this will have to wait for countless monographs and studies that remain to be made. This survey merely attempts to identify the principal avenues and channels of the transfer, and its leading actors and institutions. It will also attempt to discern the ways in which the ideas and practices that were transferred were altered by their recipients

The Bolsheviks Buy the German Jihad

In the nineteenth century, backward and barbaric Russia had imported what the Russian intelligentsia believed was Marxism, while in reality it was a simplistic, pared down version of the German ideologue's canon.[295] This ideology, christened "Marxism-Leninism," was a communistic doctrine recombined with the Gnostic heresies inherent to Russia's national religion and ideology.[296] Soviet Russia's role turned out to be the re-exporter of this bowdlerized version of Marxism to other areas of the world, especially the extra-European parts. The Russians had absorbed, digested and broken down the doctrine into bite-size notions of infinite elasticity. One of the dark shadows of modernity, the Marxian revolt against "capitalism" was elastic enough to fit the innumerable variations of the anti-modern revolt, especially in traditional societies turned inside out by brutal contact with the West.[297] The Bolshevik ideologues, Lenin, Stalin and the epigones, were the *terribles simplificateurs*[298] who fed a new rhetoric, new intellectual constructs, but also a new know-how, new techniques of agitation, propaganda and organization, and the practice of terror as a chief instrument of politics to the "revolutions" of the so-called "Third World," in particular the world of Islam. A preponderance of the know-how and technologies acquired by Russia had been German, including the intellectual and political imports. The world of Islam duly acquired the Russian version of German items, including the "Jihad Made in Germany."

Germany's war strategy had been twofold, to fight her enemies frontally in Europe and to "revolutionize," or destabilize them, as today's language goes, especially in their colonial possessions, by means of political warfare. The Russian component of the indirect strategy was the most important and the most successful of all the attempts made in the war.

The Germans had woven far-flung networks of agents and successfully enabled a revolution, but the Russian revolutionaries rapidly escaped the control of their Berlin Svengali. In order to bring about Lenin's success, the Germans had developed a rich set of connections in the Russian Socialist movement.[299] In this diplomatic demi-monde, ideologues mixed with adventurers, cranks with killers, crooks with activists, spooks with financiers. The pivot of the entire project was Lenin's feared and envied arch-rival, the picaresque Alexander Helphand, a.k.a. Parvus (the little one), a Russian socialist who had been Trotsky's master and mentor and was the smartest theorist of the entire Russian Left—its *enfant terrible*. Helphand had lived for years in Germany, moving to Constantinople in 1910. There he developed a trading company dealing in Russian wheat and German machinery, and exploited his wide set of acquaintances in Russia, the Balkans and Central Europe quite mysteriously to rise in record time from rags to riches. He was also apparently involved in selling German weapons to the Ottoman Empire, and was rapidly emerging as an influential economic analyst and financial adviser to the Young Turks. By 1912, the newly minted millionaire had been appointed to a semi-official position as economic editor of the Young Turk daily newspaper *Turk Yurdu*, "[making] him one of the most influential financial advisers of the Young Turks."[300] His direct connections to the regime included the triumvirs, Enver, Talaat, and Cemal, and the finance minister, Djavid Bey.

Parvus was neither the first nor the only Russian socialist approached by the Germans with a view to destabilizing Russia.[301] But he was the gateway to the most radical elements of the ultra-left, including Lenin, and his millions allowed him to employ large numbers of ragged Russian émigrés in his political machinery. As the German gold flowed into Helphand's operation, the latter was busy establishing organizations, recruiting Mensheviks and Bolsheviks, publishing journals and newspapers to further the project. The nerve center of his venture, located in Copenhagen, was the "Research Institute on the Social Consequences of the War." Through it, Helphand funneled large amounts of money into the Bolshevik coffers and employed or influenced a veritable Who's Who of the Bolshevik leadership, including, most importantly—and most topically—Karl Radek, the future secretary of the Komintern (Communist International) and future herald of the Bolshevik jihad.

Karl Radek was a professional revolutionary and a renowned socialist journalist, equally at ease in Russia, Poland and Germany. On account of his plasticity, he also had been nicknamed a "revolutionary Harlequin" and "the court jester of Communism." He was a great admirer of Helphand but also a close confederate of Lenin's. In the spring of 1917, as German money flows to the Bolsheviks went from drip to flood, Radek was one of the chief players, having had one last, decisive meeting with Helphand to plan the directing of the flood for Lenin's benefit. Radek was on board the famous train that the German military used to bring Lenin and his entourage from Zurich to St. Petersburg over German and German-controlled territory. On April 17, 1917, the station chief of German military intelligence in Stockholm could send a cable to Berlin: "Lenin successfully arrived in Russia. Is working exactly as we wish."[302] When the Bolsheviks took power, Radek became a member of the party's Central Committee, and was sent to Berlin at the end of 1918 to "advise" (control) the German Communist Party (KPD), also known as the Spartacus League.

Spartacus launched an insurrection on January 5–6 that was put down by the government within a week. The revolutionaries were hunted down, with many killed, including the top leaders Rosa Luxemburg and Karl Liebknecht. On February 12, Radek was nabbed. The German military command did not inflict the same fate on him, however, and Radek was not summarily executed. Instead, he was interned at the Moabit prison in Berlin and "treated as a respected interlocutor."[303] The Bolshevik leader's opposite number—his negotiating partner—was none other than General Hans von Seeckt, now the head of the Reichswehr and the grand strategist of the German revanche.[304] Out of talks then held between Radek and the German military, political, diplomatic and business elite grew the anti-Western alliance between the Soviet Union and the Reich, the April 1922 Treaty of Rapallo. Out of these talks also grew the Bolshevik jihad.

For the key to the Bolshevik leader's cell was in Seeckt's hand. "Amongst Radek's first visitors in his Moabit jail cell were two old acquaintances: Enver Pasha and Talaat Pasha. The Young Turk leaders had fled [Istanbul] in November 1918 to Odessa and Nikolaev, whence they reached Germany. They had sought asylum in Berlin. Radek knew Talaat Pasha from [the 1918 German-Soviet peace negotiations at] Brest-Litovsk, where the latter had sat on the winners' side.... As a revolutionary he offered Radek the collaboration of the Young Turks refugees: in alliance with the Bolsheviks, the Islamic masses of the East would be liberated from enslavement to the Western powers."[305]

Talaat—until just yesterday one of the leaders of a mighty empire, and one still liable to return to power—was offering Radek, and through him, Lenin, a strategic partnership that inverted the fronts of World War I: Russia would this time fight alongside the Germans and the Turks. Radek liked what he heard, and he invited the Turks to Moscow. "Radek's willingness to bid the Turkish refugees to Moscow was not the tactical gamble of a jailed revolutionary; he acted out of a global strategic concept, which was compatible with Seeckt's aims, interests and instruments." Enver and Talaat were not acting unbeknownst to their German hosts, but at their very urging: "Cooperation with Soviet Russia, based strictly on geopolitical and strategic interests, was to shake the British Empire's foundations and bring about revision of the Treaty of Versailles. The underpinning of these clandestine networks derived from contacts and concepts established during the First World War, particularly the idea of the 'Holy War'— 'Jihad'—against the West."[306]

Late in the war, Seeckt and other Germans had proposed to the Ottoman triumvirs that they should shift the center of gravity of their war effort from the futile, or secondary aim of fighting in Palestine and Mesopotamia, to the more substantial and promising theater of the Caucasus and Central Asia. Rather than focusing on the Arabs, who had betrayed the Turks, the "Turanian" perspective should be emphasized. Together with his brother Nuri Pasha, Enver led Turkish troops—renamed the "Army of God"—into the Caucasus. They took Baku in September 1918; the huge oil resources of the Caspian Sea were now theirs. To Seeckt, this meant that those regions could be made into springboards for an attack on "key British positions in the Persian Gulf and India" through Iran.[307] Although the ultimate failure of this "last gasp of Turkish military energy" (Seeckt) sealed the fate of the triumvirs, defeat damped down neither their geopolitical ambitions nor Seeckt's.

The latter's geostrategic design had three pillars: an unremitting hostility to the "Anglo-Saxon" powers, Britain and the United States; a permanent alliance with Russia—a "continental alliance" against the "maritime powers;" and the formation of an "indirect empire" dominated by Germany. This latter, new-style Reich was to be based on trade treaties and a customs union rather than on territorial conquests. An "indirect power projection" would make Berlin the hub of a great Eurasian empire able in the long run to challenge Anglo-Saxon power. "This is why the way to Asia must be free…. We need to be the supreme power [*Herrschaftsgebiet*] from the Atlantic Ocean to Persia … [as] the coalition of interested states that are disposed to be in such a union."[308] This scheme necessitated an entente with Russia. As a senior military commander, Seeckt had disagreed with the policy of destabilizing of the tsar and fragmenting his empire. Now the functional equivalent of the commander-in-chief, Seeckt hastened to collect the threads of a Russian alliance: "Germany's hopes of regaining her position as a world power position can only be fulfilled by means of a firm confederation to Russia," he wrote in 1920.[309] "The staggering colossus will eventually roll over on its side and England will feel its weight in Central and East Asia."

Seeckt had served as chief of general staff of the Ottoman Army. A number of German officers who had served under him there informally constituted what may be deemed a "Turkish mafia," an old boys' network that worked for him at least as long as he was the unchallengeable man in charge of the Reichswehr, until 1926. In September 1919, this "mafia" formally incorporated itself as the *Bund der Asienkämpfer*, Union of the Asian Fighters. This would be the human infrastructure for Seeckt's new chapter of Germany's *Orientpolitik*,[310] its purpose being to collect and analyze political and military intelligence regarding the regions where the Germans had been fighting the British. One of the leitmotivs in their activities was to prepare an attack on British India.

In order to get there, Enver had to move to Moscow and work directly with the Soviet and Red Army leadership. Without his Pan-Islamist networks, an assault on the Raj was inconceivable and unpractical. In the very testimony of M.N. Roy, who loathed Enver with a passion, "Enver Pasha was the idol of the anti-Imperialist and Pan-Islamist movement in the Middle East and India."[311] In short, the German strategist arranged for Lenin's envoy to send the Ottoman triumvir to Moscow, in order to organize the jihad among Oriental Muslims.

A first attempt to smuggle Enver into Soviet Russia ended in failure, when inclement weather forced his German military plane to land at Kaunas Airport in Lithuania. One of Seeckt's "Turkish mafia" officers stationed there saved the day by preventing the secret from leaking. Another member of the network, Ernst Kostring, later German military attaché in Moscow, successfully ferried Enver over in a second attempt in the summer of 1920. He delivered Enver to General Tukhachevsky's Red Army then advancing into Poland, and thence to Moscow. By August 25, Enver was able to write a first report to Seeckt. One faction in the Bolshevik leadership, he reported, was focused on a European revolution, but another advocated an attack on British positions in the East. The option to strike a blow against world capitalism in India, its perceived weaker spot, coincided with Seeckt's own geopolitical intents.[312] Enver also asked his friend in Berlin to forward to him an 1883 book by Lord Roberts, *Is An Invasion of India Possible?*

With Enver's help, the threads between Berlin, Moscow and Kabul were tightened."[313] The CUP front organization, the "League of Islamic Revolutionary Societies," which received significant Soviet financial support, moved to Moscow. The League was described as "the foreign policy arm of the Committee." Its last meeting held in Moscow gathered a dozen participants around Enver.[314]

Enver, M.N. Roy reports, "approached the Russians with the offer to cooperate in the plan of inciting the Muslim peoples of the Middle East to revolt against British imperialism. He would establish contact particularly with the *Khilafat* in India through the cooperation of the Muslim tribes along the Indo-Afghan frontier. He was sure to enlist the support of king Amanullah of Afghanistan and before long take up his headquarters at Kabul. In response to his call, backed up by military operations based on the North-West Frontier tribal territories, India would rise up in a mighty revolt and drive the British rulers out in no time."[315]

In his second Moscow letter to Seeckt, Enver reported having met Efraim Skliansky, War Commissar Leon Trotsky's deputy, who had spoken very favorably about the alliance with Germany. Three hours later, Enver was meeting the president of the Communist International, Grigory Zinoviev, on board a train that was taking them both to Baku, to the "Congress of the People of the East," also known as the "Congress of the Toilers of the East." As a disappointed Roy testified, "The Russians appeared to be taken in by Enver Pasha's diplomacy."[316]

Lenin craftily kept several separate lines of approach to the Muslim world. Besides the Baku crowd, one of the aces in his sleeve was Narendra Nath Bhattacharya, an Indian revolutionary better known under his lifelong alias of M.N. Roy (1887–1954). Roy's role in conveying Bolshevism and Bolshevik knowhow to the Muslim world was "crucial."[317] Even though he was born a Hindu of the Brahmin caste and his father's family were hereditary priests of Shakti, Roy exhibited a "radical rejection of India's so-called 'spiritual heritage' and viewed Hinduism as "an ideology of slavery."[318] His *Historical Role of Islam: An Essay on Islamic Culture* is an embarrassing piece of Muslim apologetics. The following offers a taste of Roy's unbridled Islamophilia:

> Mohammad assumed the role of the singular Prophet spreading his Message of Peace…. Every prophet establishes his pretension by the performance of miracles. On that token, Mohammad must be recognized as by far the greatest of

all prophets, before or after him. The expansion of Islam is the most miraculous of all miracles.... The phenomenal success of Islam was primarily due to its revolutionary significance and its ability to lead the masses out of the hopeless situation created by the decay of antique civilizations ... a tremendously dynamic historical phenomenon. The miraculous performance of the "Army of God" usually dazzles the vision, the nobility of character, purity of purpose and piety of spirit. Their devoutness might have been fortified by superstition, but was not stained by hypocrisy. Their fanaticism was softened by generosity and sound common-sense. Their ambition was remarkably free from selfishness. Godliness, for them, was not a veil for greediness.[319]

An activist of violent leanings from his teens, Roy was a seasoned militant cadre when World War I broke out. The clandestine movements he was working with "planned to arrange armed insurrection all over India.... The revolutionary organizations were extended to [the] Far East, West [Coast] America, and Germany, where [the] Indian revolutionary committee was formed."[320] Contacts with German intelligence were advanced enough that by the end of 1914, Roy headed to Java to rendezvous with German agents, including the consul general there, who gave him large amounts of money though no arms. Roy then met the German ambassador to China, Admiral von Hintze,[321] who strongly recommended that he meet the German Consulate staff in San Francisco and the Mexican revolutionaries in Mexico, and then go to Berlin. "Since I was to go to Berlin on the advice of the German Ambassador, his subordinates and other influential countrymen were helpful in arranging my trip," Roy recounts.[322] By the summer of 1916, Roy arrived in San Francisco. In Mexico, high-level German emissaries came to see him: he was now secretary general of the Mexican Socialist Party and an influential adviser to president Venustiano Carranza.[323]

In keeping with this spooky world of underground intrigue, Lenin's emissary Mikhail Borodin now arrived in Mexico City and conveyed Lenin's personal invitation to Roy to visit Moscow. After more contacts with German military intelligence, Roy arrived in Berlin late in 1919, where he made the acquaintance of the leadership of the Left-Socialists and the KPD. The interpenetration between Bolsheviks and German military and intelligence officers went deep, as the development of the ideology of national bolshevism shows. Karl Radek was the key exponent of this intersection of extreme, radical nationalism and militarism on the one side and bolshevism on the other.

National bolshevism was an ideological vehicle for German military officers especially to effect a rapprochement with Soviet Russia—on the basis of a shared hatred for Western liberalism and modernity.[324]

The Indian radical was following in the footsteps of his fellow Indian revolutionists in Berlin. Champakraman Pillai, for instance, was close to Graf zu Reventlow, the "Red Baron," a Prussian aristocrat who championed not only an alliance with Russia, but also some form of national-communist regime in Germany.

Borodin planned Roy's trip to Moscow with the help of national-Bolshevik German officers in the Seeckt network.[325] When Roy finally arrived, it was mid-July 1920 and time for the Second World Congress of the Communist International. "Everybody knew that I was 'the wise man from the East' who had come from the New World on Lenin's special invitation." Roy was instantly co-opted into the Commission on the National and Colonial Question chaired by Lenin. The latter needed people like Roy: "the oppressed and exploited masses of Asia have to be mobilized in a gigantic revolutionary movement… [Roy] in practice had anticipated the theory of revolutionary strategy in colonial and semi-colonial countries."

At Lenin's emphatic insistence, his and Roy's own theses on colonial revolutions were jointly presented to the congress (they involved some ideological hair splitting with respect to Marxian theory).[326] The repeated defeats of pro-Bolshevik uprisings in western and central Europe were lending even greater emphasis to extra-European areas for the realization of the Utopia: "The drooping spirit of the Bolsheviks was bucked up by Lenin's declaration that Europe was not all of the world; that London and New York might fall on the Ganges and the Yangtze. The Asiatic provinces of the fallen tsarist empire were still to be brought under the jurisdiction of the Soviet Republic."[327] A kernel of Roy's "Supplementary Theses" was to become the stock in trade of most radical third-worldist movements in the twentieth century, singularly in the Muslim world. This was the doctrine of grievance and victimhood ascribing all of the ills of the extra-European countries to "imperialist" and "colonialist exploitation and plunder." The theses assert that the entire strength of European capitalism comes from "superprofits" derived from the looting and enslavement of the third world. Later speeches on the issue by a Gamal Abdel Nasser, or an Osama bin Laden, for that matter, offer very little that is not already present in Roy's and Lenin's doctrine.[328]

Germany, therefore, and the rest of Europe, were losing their priority status in the eyes of the Bolsheviks. "Revolution should have easy victories in the neighboring Muslim countries which, inspired by the message of the liberation of Central Asia, would rise against European imperialism.... [The example of Turkey] was bound to inflame the entire Islamic world. A faint echo of the *khilafat* movement reached Moscow to encourage the view that Pan-Islamism was a revolutionary force and, as such, should be welcomed and supported as an ally of the proletarian world revolution."[329]

Concrete consequences followed. Roy recounts: "I did some hard thinking. The result was a plan for opening the second front of the world revolution," and, from Kabul to India, to "raise an army from the frontier tribes which would be strong enough not only to raid British territory, but to seize certain parts of it and hold them as the base for operations for advancing further."[330]

Roy's "hard thinking" consisted purely and simply in appropriating, lock, stock and barrel, the plans developed by Max von Oppenheim, Oskar von Niedermayer, Hans von Seeckt and Enver Pasha! Given Roy's persistent association with German military intelligence, and the Germans' osmosis with the Bolsheviks, this was not surprising.

Deputy Soviet foreign minister Lev Karakhan approved of the plan, Deputy War Minister Skliansky liked it and Lenin supported it. As a result, "the strategy of revolution in Asia was given a prominent place in the agenda of the 'Small Bureau' [of the Communist International]," and two decisions were taken: a Central Asiatic Bureau of the Communist International run by Roy would be set up in Tashkent; and a "Congress of the Oppressed People of the East" would be held in Baku.

The affair was Zinoviev's own idea, although Karl Radek, by now secretary of the Communist International, "was very enthusiastic." Of course Radek would have been enthused, as he most likely originated the idea, together with his bosom friend Enver Pasha. The Congress was meant to celebrate in grand style the official alliance between the Bolsheviks and the Pan-Islamists. To achieve this kind of marital bliss, however, Enver, who was despised by any number of Central Asia leftists, nationalists and Islamists, had to be given a certificate of revolutionary virginity signed by the Bolshevik experts. In the end, Enver's past was amnestied, the Bolsheviks gained a powerful ally, and Enver joined Zinoviev and Radek on the train to Baku.

Lenin's Jihad

In words dripping with demagogy, the Second Congress of the Communist International issued a summons inviting the "enslaved popular masses of Persia, Armenia and Turkey" and of Mesopotamia, Syria, Arabia, and more, to gather in Baku. "Spare no effort to ensure that as many as possible may be present on Sept 1 [1920] in Baku. Formerly you traveled across deserts to reach the holy places—now make your way over mountains and rivers, through forests and deserts...." This was a new *hajj*, it was hinted. The "peasants and workers of Persia," appealed to in the name of sharia, were told that they were being "robbed and exploited" by local reactionaries "who have sold [out] to Britain the rich oilfields of South Persia, thereby cooperating in the plundering of your country." The "peasants of Mesopotamia" were told: "80,000 British soldiers stand upon your soil, robbing and killing you and violating your women." The "peasants of Anatolia" were told that Allied powers "dictated their alien laws" and had "made the Sultan prisoner and forced him to agree to the partition of purely Turkish territory." Every sectional, national or ethnic group was addressed in the same way,[331] setting the tone. The Bolsheviks were ready to go very far indeed to meet the world of Islam, whatever they themselves were doing domestically to "their" Muslims.

During the first session of the congress Zinoviev gave a speech that called five times for a "Holy War." He argued for it as an attack on "the policy which conferred the colonies syphilis, opium and a debauched caste of officers, the policy which turned these countries into the bourgeoisie's rubbish dump and which plundered them relentlessly." The Bolsheviks "respect the religious feelings of the masses," Zinoviev proclaimed, though they "must educate the masses of the East to hate and to want to fight against the rich in general—Russian, Jewish, German, French." What was Zinoviev suggesting? "We are now faced with the task of kindling a real holy war against the British and French capitalists.... Comrades, you... for the first time assembled in a congress of peoples of the East, must here proclaim a real holy war against the robbers and oppressors.... The time has come when you can act about organizing a true people's holy war, in the first place against British imperialism!" At this point the stenographic report notes: "Tumultuous applause, prolonged shouts of 'Hurrah!' Members of the congress stand up, brandishing their weapons. The speaker is unable to continue for some time. All the delegates stand up and applaud! Shouts of 'We swear it!'"[332] The congress was attended by 1,891 participants, two-thirds Bolshevik party members. The largest contingents were from Turkey (235), Persia (192), Armenia (157), Russia (104), Georgia (100) and Chechnya (82). Other attendees included 61 Tadzhiks, 47 Kirghiz, 41 Jews, 35 Turkmens, 33 Kumyks, 25 Lesgians, 14 Indians, a few Arabs, some Kurds and some Hazaras (from Afghanistan).[333] In time-tested Bolshevik manner, the "delegates" were self-appointed and delegated by nobody in particular. Still, from what is known of the biography of a number of them, they commanded the allegiance of, or were members of, significant groups, networks and associations.

At the next session of this highly choreographed congress, the main speech came from Communist International secretary Karl Radek, whose presence was not due to any particular knowledge of or acquaintance with the East—he was a quintessential *Mitteleuropa* intellectual—but rather his close connection to Enver Pasha. Radek's speech sounded like an ideologized, and less lyrical, version of the famous 1918 poem "Scythians," by Russian writer Aleksandr Blok, which had been a Russian declaration of hatred against the West:

> You are millions. We are hordes and hordes and hordes.
>   Try and take us on!
> Yes, we are Scythians! Yes, we are Asians –
>   With slanted and greedy eyes! …
>
> We, like obedient slaves,
> Held up a shield between two enemy races –
>   The Tatars and Europe! …
>
> For hundreds of years you gazed at the East,
>   Storing up and melting down our jewels,
> And, jeering, you merely counted the days
>   Until your cannons you could point at us!
>
> The time is come. Trouble beats its wings –
>   And every day our grudges grow,
> And the day will come when every trace
>   Of your Paestums may vanish!

O, old world! While you still survive,
    While you still suffer your sweet torture,
Come to a halt, sage as Oedipus,
    Before the ancient riddle of the Sphinx! ….

Russia is a Sphinx. Rejoicing, grieving,
    And drenched in black blood,
It gazes, gazes, gazes at you,
    With hatred and with love! …

It has been ages since you've loved
    As our blood still loves!
You have forgotten that there is a love
    That can destroy and burn! …

We love the flesh—its flavor and its color,
    And the stifling, mortal scent of flesh…
Is it our fault if your skeleton cracks
    In our heavy, tender paws?

When pulling back on the reins
    Of playful, high-spirited horses,
It is our custom to break their heavy backs
    And tame the stubborn slave girls.…

Come to us! Leave the horrors of war,
    And come to our peaceful embrace!
Before it's too late—sheathe your old sword,
    Comrades! We shall be brothers!

But if not—we have nothing to lose,
    And we are not above treachery!
For ages and ages you will be cursed
    By your sickly, belated offspring!

> Throughout the woods and thickets
>   In front of pretty Europe
> We will spread out! We'll turn to you
>   With our Asian muzzles....
>
> We will not lift a finger when the cruel Huns
>   Rummage the pockets of corpses,
> Burn cities, drive cattle into churches,
>   And roast the meat of our white brothers!....
>
> Come to your senses for the last time, old world!
>   Our barbaric lyre is calling you
> One final time, to a joyous brotherly feast
>   To a brotherly feast of labor and of peace!

Radek the Bolshevik offered the same kind of brotherly love as Blok the poet, who had welcomed the Bolshevik revolution as the apocalypse. The Muslim East was being taught by its new teachers a new rhetoric as well as new concepts, such as "imperialism," "colonialism," "plundering" of their countries, etc.[334] The occasion was "historic," Radek told the congress, because

> [T]he representatives of the [laboring] masses [of the East] here present, all moved by the same emotion, rose and swore an oath to wage holy war... against the oppressors of the world of labor.... We appeal, comrades, to the warlike feelings which once inspired the people of the East when these peoples, led by their great conquerors advanced upon Europe. We know, comrades, that our enemies will say that we are appealing to the memory of Genghis Khan and to the mercy of the great conquering Caliphs of Islam. But we are convinced that yesterday you drew your daggers and your revolvers not for aims of conquest... long live the Red East, which together with the workers of Europe will create a new civilization under the banner of Communism."[335]

The principal problem the Bolsheviks had to tackle to gain control over the Muslims was the latter's mistrust of Russian imperial designs. The suspicions transpired quickly. At the third session, one Narbutabekov flatly stated, "The Muslims will not abandon the Soviet power, but this on condition that the peculiarities of the Eastern peoples be recognized.... We need a special yardstick in [the] case of [the 400 million Muslims]." He suggested that "only the paying of close attention to the life of the Eastern peoples..." would allow the Bolsheviks to acquire and keep influence, and he reminded them of the terms of the November 1917 Council of People's Commissars' "Appeal to All the Toiling Muslims of Russia and the East:" "Henceforward your beliefs and customs, your national and cultural institutions are declared free and inviolable. Build your national life freely and without hindrance."[336] The contradiction between Islam and Bolshevism as ideologies was real, and would continue to haunt both Islamists and Bolsheviks. There was enough kinship between the two groups for cooperation and limited osmosis, but too much difference for a full merger. The dalliance would forever be conflict-laden.

After Radek finished speaking, Comrade Korkmasov was happy to inform the crowd that "Assembled in their own congress a month ago, the [Caucasus] Highland poor, and even the ulama, issued a call for a *ghazawat*, a holy war, against all the oppressors of the East."

The next day, at the fourth session, came the crux of the congress. Zinoviev announced: "Next, comrades, two prominent Turkish leaders, not delegates to our congress, who are here in Baku [quite a bold lie by omission since he and Enver had traveled thither together!] have sent the Presidium a statement in writing, and as these statements are of great political importance, the presidium has decided to make them public, both from this tribune and in the press. One of these statements is by Enver Pasha."[337] Enver's declaration read to the congress was a virtuoso piece of mendacity, wherein he complained that "German imperialism used us for its bandit aims"—a tall story from a man who only days before had been writing intelligence reports to Hans von Seeckt! "But our desire was only to safeguard our independence. Comrades, the sentiment which caused us to leave a calm, refuge-seeking life for the burning deserts of Tripoli and the poor tents of the Bedouin and forced us to spend there the most difficult time of our life, was no sentiment of imperialism.... Comrades, during the world war I occupied a very important post. I assure you that I regret that we were obliged to fight on the side of German imperialism. I hate and curse German imperialists as much as I hate and curse British imperialism and the British imperialists." Completing this piece of Oriental farce, Enver announced: "Comrades, I declare to you that the Union of revolutionary organizations of Morocco, Algeria, Tunisia, Tripoli, Egypt, Arabia and India, which has sent me here as its representative, is in full solidarity with you in this respect." By this, Enver meant his once-powerful personal intelligence network, the *Teshkilat-i Mahsusa*.[338]

After this fine show, the Hungarian Communist leader Bela Kun "propose[d] to [Enver and his friends] that they prove in deeds that they are now ready to serve the toiling people and make amends for their false steps of the past." Uproar followed, since many participants were still upset by Enver's association with Kaiser Wilhelm. In a fine display of Bolshevik manipulation, the presidium then drowned these voices by proposing an immediate vote, with Zinoviev screaming, "holy war!"

The Bolshevik jihad continued to be elaborated on. Comrade Utushev, in his praise of Islam, this "colossal ideological stock of spiritual culture," quoted a poem by Bolshevik writer Sergei Gorodetsky: "This is why, when the black coffee bubbles with a golden glint in the porcelain cup, there rises to the brain a wave of desire for violent actions, and the heart suddenly yearns for catastrophe. Blow up Europe! Sweep away with fierce will the evil shamelessness of buying and selling!"[339] The apocalyptic messianists of Russia held out their arms to their Muslim counterparts. Both recognized one another because they partook in similar Gnostic belief-structures, with similar political consequences. Both exuded a seething hatred for the "materialist West;" the diverse ideological conceits used to drape the hatred mattered less than the driving emotion itself. Thus, Zinoviev concluded, "that moment... when the assembled representatives of the peoples of the East swore to begin a Holy War, that moment will be preserved in our hearts as a sacred experience.... Yes, a Holy War against the plunderers and capitalists."[340]

Accordingly, the "Manifesto of the Congress of the Peoples of the East" stated:

> Peoples of the East! You have often heard the call to holy war from your governments, you have marched under the green banner of the Prophet, but all these holy wars were fraudulent, serving only the interests of your self-serving rulers, and you, the peasants and workers, remained in slavery and want after these wars.... Now we summon you to the first real holy war under the red banner of the Communist International. We summon you to a holy war for your own wellbeing, for your own freedom, for your own life!

No less that fifteen times the Manifesto contained the call for a Holy War:

> [W]e—representatives of the toiling masses of all the peoples of the East ...united in unbreakable union among ourselves and we revolutionary

workers of the West—summon our peoples to a holy war.... Go forward as one man into a holy war against the British conquerors! High waves the banner of the holy war!... This is a holy war for the liberation of the peoples of the East ...into the holy war...! Into the holy war for the liberation of all mankind from the yoke of capitalist and imperialist slavery, for the ending of all forms of oppression of one people by another and all forms of exploitation of man by man! Into the holy war against the last citadel of imperialism in Europe, against the nest of pirates and bandits by sea and land, against the age-old oppression of all the peoples of the East, against imperialist Britain! Into the holy war for freedom.... Peoples of the East! In this holy war all the revolutionary workers and all the oppressed peasants of the East will be with you.... May the holy war of the peoples of the East and the toilers of the whole world against imperial Britain burn with unquenchable fire![341]

One other part of the Manifesto deserves special mention in view of later events—the early injection of Communist anti-Semitism into the Muslim East, and the supplying by the former to the latter of rhetorical and propaganda themes that were to have a singular fortune in decades to come: "Peoples of the East!... What has Britain done to Palestine? There, at first, acting for the benefit of Anglo-Jewish capitalists, it drove Arabs from the land in order to give the latter to Jewish settlers. Then, trying to appease the discontent of the Arabs, it incited them against these same Jewish settlers...." This sanctimonious analysis was music to the ears of such leaders of the Palestinian movement as Amin Husayni, whom the British governor-general had just appointed to be Grand Mufti of Jerusalem. As later events proved, this was not to remain the only case of anti-Jewish collaboration between Communists and Islamic radicals.

The congress—or its Bolshevik masterminds—decided to set up a "permanent executive committee of the Congress of the People of the East" under the name of "Council for Propaganda of the People of the East." The council included a close associate of Roy's, a prominent Tatar Islamic revolutionary, two of Joseph Stalin's close cohorts, a Persian Muslim, and a few others lesser lights. A decision was also made to publish a journal, *Narody Vostoka* (*Nations of the East*), and to establish a "university of the social sciences for activists in the East," which took the form of the Communist University of the Peoples of the East (*Kommunisticheskii universitiet trudiashchikhsya vostoka*).

The congress had struck a powerful blow for the Bolsheviks. Their crude but effective anti-imperialist rhetoric and the blending of the Islamic concept of jihad with their own design could now be spread far and wide. The homeward-bound participants were armed with new rhetorical, conceptual, agitational and organizational instruments unknown in their lands of origin.

Unsurprisingly, in Germany, the journal of the Union of Asian Fighters was all praise for Baku and the Bolsheviks: "Lenin and [Soviet foreign minister Georgy] Chicherin have identified Britain's weak spot—India (…) The Congress of Baku must be considered as the prelude of the fight to the death [with Britain]."[342] Enver Pasha returned to Berlin in mid-October 1920. There, in a safe-house kept by a member of Seeckt's group, Enver received a large number of "officers, professors and diplomats," including the Soviet "trade" representative in Berlin, Viktor Kopp, a man very close to Trotsky's War Commissariat.

In great secrecy, Seeckt was creating the high-powered "*Sondergruppe R*" (where "R" stood for Russia) that brought together all the threads of the secret collaboration between the Reichswehr and the Red Army. As Oskar von Niedermayer had written, action against the British in their Muslim sphere of influence "can only be carried out under the leadership of Moscow."[343] And, as he was to write later, "Afghanistan is the intersection of Russian expansion and Indian revolution."[344] In mid-January 1921, having conferred with Seeckt, Enver left Berlin to return to Moscow. In February, Seeckt secretly asked his loyal aide Niedermayer to present a paper at a private—secret—"assessment of military geographic conditions of an attack on India." Seeckt attended his subordinate's presentation. "We will wait for the opportunity, and the opportunity must arise, when Britain must fight to save her position of power in the world takes on the most violent forms," and "she will pay for [a situation] where a people of 50 million fools itself that it can lord it over and plunder 400 million of the people of the world.… When continents awake, Island-empires collapse," Niedermayer concluded.[345]

Enver helped further tighten the connections between Berlin, Moscow and Kabul. He soon announced to Seeckt the forthcoming visit of General Mehmed Veli Khan, a senior Afghan military figure, who was tasked with developing military cooperation. The Afghan mission arrived in Berlin in April, and was received by no lesser figures than the Foreign Minister Walter Simon and German president Friedrich Ebert. Enver continued to send visitors, all in the framework of the planned operation in India. A member of Seeckt's group, Günther Voigt, was also sent, with the help of the Soviet trade delegation in Berlin, to Kabul via Moscow to dispose the Afghan government favorably toward Moscow. In Moscow, Voigt met with Foreign Minister Chicherin,

Trotsky became directly involved with "*Special Group R*," and Niedermayer was assigned as a permanent delegate to Moscow. Among those attending the first meetings he held there were Radek, Trotsky and Lenin!

"The best laid schemes o' Mice an' Men, /Gang aft agley," Robert Burns wrote in his "Ode to a Mouse." So went this multi-fangled scheme. By the summer, Enver Pasha had determined that there was a greater empire for him to carve out by working with the Afghans against the Soviets than by working with Moscow. He was drifting away from the deal of mutual instrumentalization he had made with the Bolsheviks. Initially, in the first months of 1922, with the support of the Afghan army, Enver scored successes against the Red Army—to the great annoyance of his old German friends. By May 1922 Enver had conquered Ashkhabad, but on August 4, he was killed on the battlefield. As Seeckt put it, "Que voulez-vous, c'est la fin d'un révolutionnaire."[346] The Indian operation was stillborn, but in the intervening time the Germans and the Soviets had signed the Rapallo Treaty. With respect to the Muslim world, Enver had been Lenin's joker card. Yet Lenin still held some aces, as Baku had shown, and as M.N. Roy was about to show.

Red Jihad, Green Jihad

Out of loathing for, and personal rivalry with, Enver Pasha, whom he called "the dangerous Turk," M.N. Roy had disagreed with the idea of the Baku congress, which he derisively called "Zinoviev's Circus." Although Roy himself ostentatiously refused to attend, he sent at least one of his trusted lieutenants, Acharya, who was included among the new organization's leadership. His self-serving protests to the contrary, Roy was at one with the Bolshevik like of using Pan-Islamist jihad as the mainstay of their strategy in the Muslim world.

The Communist International duly established a Central Asia Bureau (CAB) in Tashkent, immediately tasked to foster revolution in the vast region of "Turkestan," including the Emirates of Bokhara and Shiva, earlier protectorates of the tsar. The CAB was led by the prominent Bolshevik Fyodor Raskolnikov, the commander of the Red Army in Central Asia and chairman of the Turkestan Committee of the Soviet government; Georgi Safarov, "a passionate believer in the revolutionary significance of the colonial nationalist movement, particularly of the Islamic countries;" M.N. Roy himself; the Latvian leader of the Cheka, the Bolshevik terror police, Jakob Peters; the administrator Lazar Kaganovich; and the president of the Turkestan Soviet, a Tajik named Abduqadir Rahimbaev.

On the strength of Enver Pasha's plan to attack the British in India, Raskolnikov was appointed ambassador to Kabul. Roy reports that Raskolnikov was of the belief that the *Khilafat* movement was going to overthrow the Raj. "The breakdown of British rule in India would open the floodgates of revolution.... That was my old idea, which still fascinated me," Roy adds, naively claiming authorship of the Oppenheim-Seeckt strategy. Further, "I submitted the plan for Lenin's consideration and approval.... He was interested."[347] The plan to raise an "Army of Liberation" then suddenly received a fillip—the Muslims who had left India in the framework of the *hijrat* movement. "A new factor had appeared on the scene.... Reports had reached Moscow that, responding to the call of the *Khilafat* Committee, thousands of Muslims, including many educated young men, were leaving India for Turkey.... It was a religious Pan-Islamist movement, but it gave me an opportunity to contact a large number of possible recruits for an army to fight for the liberation of India instead of a lost cause."[348] Roy describes his intent as consisting less in enlisting the "religious fanaticism" of the "ignorant masses" than the

> politically motivated educated youth ...the educated amongst the Indian *Mujaheers* might realize the pointlessness of a pilgrimage to Turkey to fight for the cause of secular nationalism. My plan was to raise, equip and train such an army of liberation. Using the [Indo-Afghan] frontier territories as the base of the operation and with the mercenary support of the tribesmen, the liberation army would march into India and occupy some territory where a civil government should be established as soon as possible.... It would call upon the people to rise in the rear of the enemy, so that the liberation army could advance further and further into the country. The requirements for implementing the plan were obvious: a sufficiently large quantity of arms, field equipment, training personnel and plenty of money. The last item was sanctioned by the Council of People's Commissars on the recommendation of the Communist Party."[349]

The German jihad plan had been recast as a Bolshevik enterprise, but the underlying jihad remained. "Who will guard the guardians?" the wise Romans asked. "Manipulator, beware being manipulated" would be the challenge for the modern sorcerer's apprentices of jihad.

Ill-treated by the Afghan amir, a large number of *Muhajirun* walked the whole distance across Afghanistan, joined along the way by Indian deserters from the British Army. "The position of the Indian muhajirun was transformed by the Russian Revolution."[350] Some had made their way to the Baku congress. Turkmen tribesmen had taken a large number of them prisoner. Bolshevik authorities in turn arranged for the release of this promising prey that they could work over. Roy was also counting on the support of a number of prominent Pan-Islamists turned pro-Bolsheviks. Maulana Barakatullah, for one, already a character in the cast of the pro-German Indians in Berlin, and the "prime minister" of the provisional Indian government proclaimed in 1915 in Kabul, "though a staunch Muslim throughout his life … was permanently involved in developing the new relationship with the Bolsheviks…. Though he never claimed to be a Bolshevik … his views on most temporal matters became almost identical with those of the Bolsheviks." Barakatullah's book *Bolshevism and the Islamic Body Politick*, appearing in several languages, appealed to the Muslims of the world "to understand the noble principles of Russian Socialism and to embrace it seriously and enthusiastically…. O Muhameddans, listen to this divine cry. Respond to the call of liberty, equality and brotherhood which comrade Lenin and the Soviet Government of Russia are offering to you."[351]

By March 1919, Barakatullah was the ambassador extraordinary of Afghan king Amanullah to Soviet Russia, "and for the rest of his life, he worked closely with the Soviet Union in the struggle for Indian freedom." With him at first was Abd al-Rab Peshawari, who then moved with Roy from Moscow to Tashkent, where he joined the Oriental Propaganda Bureau along with other Indian revolutionaries. Peshawari, M.P.B.T. Acharya—of the Baku Congress secretariat—and others created the *Inqilabiun-i Hind*, the Indian revolutionary association. Acharya also moved to Tashkent, where, with lavish funding from the Bolsheviks, he published a newspaper, *Zamindar*, and recruited support from wealthy Indian merchants plying their trade in Central Asia.

One of the most significant figures connecting the Bolsheviks and the *Khilafat* was Maulana Ubaidullah, or Obeidullah. The Maulana was a prominent Deobandi—quite a jump from the Deobandi school to Bolshevism, as M.N. Roy put it, "a respected Muslim divine," with whom he collaborated closely.[352] Ubaidullah Sindhi (1872–1944) was a Sikh convert who had been trained at the highly politicized school in Deoband *Dar-ul Uloom*. There he had reinterpreted the traditional Deobandi creed in a radical way and given it a revolutionary content.[353] In 1913, he had set up a madrasa, the *Nizarat al-Marif*, in

New Delhi that aspired "to mobilize India's Pan-Islamists to take up jihad against the British." The *sheikh al-Hind* Mahmud al-Hassan, the principal of the Deobandi *Dar-ul Uloom*, however, instructed Ubaidullah to enter clandestine political activity as a more effective way to struggle for Pan-Islamist goals. Hence Ubaidullah's plan of action, which was the plan of action of the Deobandi leadership: to seek revolution abroad. He, al-Hassan, would go to Hijaz, the stronghold of the Wahhabi, while Ubaidullah would go to Kabul with the purpose of persuading the King of Afghanistan to declare war on Britain, while a Muslim insurrection would be started in the tribal belt to spill over into India proper. In September 1915, Ubaidullah set out to Kabul with a retinue of followers as an advisory group. In the Afghan capital, he met of course with Barakatullah and the other pro-German revolutionists.[354] From there, he called for the unification of the Muslim world in the form of a hierarchical league: "This is a special Islamic society based on military principles. Its first object is to create an alliance among Islamic kingdoms." This was to be called *Jund al-Rabbaniyya*, the Army of God.[355]

The welcoming committee for the *Muhajirun* was in place. "The general strategy of the Bolsheviks toward the *Muhajirun* recognized the very considerable power of Pan-Islamism."[356] At Tashkent, Roy established a military school (*Induskii kurs*) to start training one hundred of the *Muhajirun*. As the Bolshevik schooling proceeded, an emotional transfer of identity occurred. At first, "[t]hey understood the world only in Pan-Islamist terms" but were impressed with the efficiency of the Bolsheviks' anti-British power. The product of the confluence of Islam and Bolshevism was a novelty. According to Roy, "Islamic ideas were so strongly entrenched in the minds in the minds of the *Mujahirun* that even when some of them adopted Socialist ideas, it did not mean that they totally rejected their identification with Islam. 'Islam preaches equality, so does Communism, that is why I am a Communist,'" one of them said.[357] By the end of 1920, a number of them had become convinced Communists. "I was very much surprised to find that a few of the educated youth were more fanatical than the emigrant mass.... My preliminary efforts with the educated minority produced greater results than I expected and wanted. Most of them transferred their fanatical allegiance from Islam to Communism."[358] For two species to be able to cross and hybridize, they must have enough in common—that they did.

Roy had successfully transformed his raw material, or a part of it. He established "the first international brigade of the Red Army," which was used to harass British troops on the Ashkhabad-Meshed road connecting to Persia.

The Red Army soon elevated a number of Indians to officer rank, which had an "incalculable" effect on morale, notably that of prompting Indian soldiers and non-commissioned officers to desert from the British Army. "The international brigade soon became an effective auxiliary of the Red Army. In less than a year, the Indo-British Army evacuated Meshed and the entire Persian province of Khorasan was cleared of British influence."[359] No wonder that the Bolsheviks "believed that Pan-Islamism could be a powerful anti-British movement, provided its reactionary leaders were isolated by clever diplomacy and devious political maneuvers."[360]

The Bolshevik leader explains: "I made a careful study of the Quran and other classics of Islamic theology. In public meetings I could justify the Revolution on scriptural authority."[361] The convergence was deep. As Roy himself stated, "The Soviet Republic was not a national state." It was like the *umma*, an ideology embodied in a polity.[362]

Roy returned to Moscow to take charge of the Eastern Section of the Communist International. "I conceived the idea of establishing in Moscow a center for the political training of revolutionaries from various Asiatic countries," he writes with some exaggeration—since a number of other Bolsheviks had come up with the same idea, including at the Baku Congress. "Lenin enthusiastically approved the idea and advised me to consult Stalin about its execution."[363] Roy then had his first meeting with Stalin, the crafty Georgian who knew about Muslims in a way none of his Europe-oriented Bolshevik colleagues did. Stalin's opener was brutal: "So you do not see the revolutionary significance of Pan-Islamism?"[364] The People's Commissar for Nationalities outlined a fully-formed strategy: "Not only the national bourgeoisie in less backward colonial countries like India and China, but even the feudal landlords, *ulama* and mullahs in the Islamic countries must also be helped."[365]

Social-political movements in the Muslim and "colonial" world "must be strengthened by a well-trained revolutionary cadre," Stalin continued, a perspective with which Lenin agreed. The Communist University of the Toilers of the East was to be founded to serve that purpose. Indeed, KUTVa was launched in April 1921 and effectively opened for business in September. It was "[t]he most important center for transmission of these ideas" and "remained an extremely active and influential forum" for years[366] as the cadre school for high-level Bolshevik operatives in the Orient. At various points, the student body included, among others, Ho Chi-Minh; Deng Xiaoping; Liu Shaoqi; Tan Malaka, founder of the Communist Party of Indonesia; Japan's Sen

Katayama; the Turkish Communist leader and poet Nazim Hikmet; Khalid Bagdash, decades-long head of the Syrian Communist Party; and "Fahd," head of the Iraqi Communist Party. Courses included the theory of historical materialism, the history of class struggle and the Western labor movement, the program [of the Party] and tactics of the Communist Party, a history of India and Russia, problems of nationalism, the history of the French Revolution, and the evolution of modern capitalism. Until its dissolution in the 1930s during the great Soviet purges, KUTVa trained hundreds of Muslim cadre for the holy war—red jihad, green jihad, but mostly jihad.

Sultan Galiev, the Hybrid

Muslims could very well become Bolsheviks, and many in Russia did. But Muslim Bolsheviks could with equal ease shuttle back to their roots. In such adventures, however, the mind of the traveler is not static; the journey changes him. Consciously or not, willingly or not, selectively if not in every respect, he absorbed much of the air he breathed along the way. We have seen Muslims embrace Bolshevism, and acquire Bolshevik "technologies" of power. We will now see Bolshevized Muslims turn away from their recent Communist faith and shift to a form of political Islam, but bringing with them what they have imbibed in the process. In the case of the Soviet Muslims, the hybrid at one point received the name of "national communism." "Sultangalievism," as the Soviet state called this movement, proved to be a critical conveyor belt for transferring the new Bolshevik "technologies" to the world of Islam.

How significant was the turn to Bolshevism of the Muslims of the Russian Empire? In the first place, it was an essential element in the victory of Soviet arms in the vicious civil war that bloodied the country starting in 1918, and from which the Bolsheviks emerged as the unlikely winners. Almost fifty percent of the 6th Red Army, which held the Siberian front, one of the main fronts in the war, consisted of Muslim soldiers and officers. "At the time when the Civil War was at its peak on the Eastern and Turkestan fronts, the proportion of Tatar combatants in the Red Army exceeded fifty per cent of the total… and in certain units (for example the 5th Army) even reached up to seventy or seventy-five percent…. The courses for [Muslim] military leaders … trained thousands of Red Tatar military leaders."[367] By July 1918, the 6th Army had enrolled 50,000 Tatar and Bashkir fighters, and by early 1919, the number of Muslims fighting in the ranks of the Red Army totaled 225,000 to 250,000, "virtually all under the command of Muslim officers." They fell under the control of the Central *Muskom*, Muslim Central Committee and the Muslim military Collegium. Muslim troops were indeed the decisive factor that tilted victory in the direction of the Bolsheviks.

The surprising alliance grew out of the racial and religious chauvinism of the "White" leadership, which utterly alienated the Muslims of the empire. The strategic obtuseness and "supercilious attitude" of Admiral Aleksandr Kolchak and General Anton Denikin "pushed [the Muslims] into the arms of the Bolsheviks."[368] To the contrary, Lenin, and especially Stalin, took great care in offering a "new deal" to the Muslims. On November 17, 1917—two weeks, that is, after the Bolshevik putsch—the new authorities issued an "Appeal to All Toiling Muslims of Russia and the Orient:" "We declare that from now your beliefs, your traditions, your national and cultural ways will be freely exercised and inalienable. Arrange your national life as you intend and decide. This is your right. You must be the masters of your own countries. You yourselves must organize your life in your own way and desires."[369] As befits Bolshevik statecraft, the intent, as summed up by one of the Bolsheviks' prominent expert handlers of the Muslims, was one of instrumentalizing the new friends: "In the East, [Muslim] nationalism is in full development. We must not try to stop this natural movement, but we must try to canalize it," wrote S. Dimanshtein.[370] With some exaggeration, but not wholly out of step with reality, the same depicted the situation in the vast Muslim communities of the empire: "Even the most hardened clericals and reactionaries were transformed into socialists."[371]

The Russian Revolution, by obliterating the age-old institutions of Russia, had released all inhabitants of the empire from their traditional allegiances. It created a classic situation of *anomie*, where the components that have been let loose by the dissolution of old bonds seek new identities, new loyalties, and new institutions as pegs on which to hang these.

The Bolsheviks faced two constraints: they needed to mobilize the Muslims, without whom they would not able to maintain themselves in power, but at the same time guard against their indispensable ally's possible wish to set themselves free, or even to constitute an autonomous power. This explains why Soviet policy toward "domestic" Muslims went through two distinct phases. At first, as with all other layers of the population courted by Lenin, all was sweet pleasantness. This "policy of meeting the minorities half-way [was] instituted by Lenin and expressed itself in using the Muslim… groups on the basis of cooperation and promises allowing them… complete freedom of religion and education. Some of this propaganda was couched in evident Pan-Islamist phraseology."[372] Another testimony states: "The Communist Party proceeded only with caution toward Islam…. A Central Committee circular letter dated Feb. 24, 1920, advises to behave cautiously regarding the [religious] beliefs of the masses."[373] For Lenin, and for Stalin who had built his Commissariat for Nationalities (*Narkomnats*) into a powerful network of power within the Soviet structures, one major task of the Muslim organizations and leaders was to Bolshevize the Muslim masses; they were "genuine schools of Marxism."[374] More immediately, Stalin "understood that to win the allegiance or neutrality of the non-Russians was to take a giant step toward winning the Civil War…. Stalin succeeded in securing the participation of a number of prominent Muslim leaders. Typically, they were former nationalists who viewed this new Soviet institution as the stage on which they could act out their national demands."[375]

The Muslim leaders made their flocks available to the Red revolution for their own reasons. As Hanafi Muzaffar, a prominent Volga Tatar radical intellectual, put it: "[A] considerable number of Muslims viewed the revolution in Russia—and hence the Bolshevik cause—as the first step toward the liberation of Islam from European and Russian encroachments."[376] The Muslim "national socialists" were aware of the anti-religious character of their Bolshevik partners, but "rationalized that an alliance with the Russian proletariat was possible because the Communism of the latter was in fact compatible with Islam." Explaining how they could have believed that, Muzaffar wrote: "Muslim people will ally themselves to Communism. Like Communism, Islam rejects narrow nationalism. Islam is international and recognizes only the brotherhood and the unity of all nations under the banner of Islam."[377] A Kazakh leader, Ahmed Baytursun, believed that the Kazakhs "will accept Communism even before all other peoples, because its traditional way of life is already close to Communism."

In a book that was the Muslim national Communists' breviary, Hanafi Muazzar proffered a broad outline of the Muslims' complex motivations:

> The essential point for us is the survival of our nation, and even more broadly, the survival of all Muslim peoples and all colonial peoples who are oppressed and threatened by European imperialism. But as long as Europe can use its might to maintain its imperialistic policy [in the East] our situation will remain hopeless…. It would be a great mistake for us people oppressed by Europe to fail to recognize that Marxism is fighting imperialism. As the Communist

Party is fighting the same imperialism in Russia and abroad, we must accept the anti-religious character of the dictatorship of the proletariat because the alliance between the Russian proletariat and the Muslims could deal a death blow to Europe.[378]

The last clause is fundamental: The Muslim leaders were fully aware of the Bolsheviks' hostile attitude to all religions, but for tactical purposes, *Paris vaut bien une messe*. Marxism looked powerful, viable, conquering. Bolshevism was a formidable energizer; it was the guiding ideological force behind the battlefield victories. "These tangible manifestations of power and success reinforced in the mind of the native radicals the belief that Marxism was action as well as ideas. All other ideologies appeared bankrupt in comparison."[379] In the calculus of profit and loss made by the Muslim leaders, the ability of Bolshevism to destroy the "European" order exceeded the damage it was able to inflict on Islam. Islam would gain in the bargain. Musa Jarulallah, "then the greatest living leader of Russian Islam, not only lauded this potential alliance but envisaged Communism as a springboard for a deeper penetration of Islam in Asia. 'A great revolution has triumphed in Russia, giving birth to a regime of justice and equality instead of the former tyrannical regime. There Muslims enjoy equality, unity and peace.... We must take advantage of this situation to promote the Quranic Unity of Believers.'"[380]

As a result, "the Red Army was for the non-Russian, non-Proletarian peoples their first school of political action.... For them, the psychological impact of this army in motion was overwhelming. Massive numbers of them rushed to join its ranks, and, subsequently, the ranks of the Russian Communist Party.... [T]he Socialist army [was] as [a] political machine."[381] Even by the gruesome standards of civil war the world over, the Russian Civil War was exceptionally callous and brutish. The Bolshevik school of "politics" was a school of terror, mass murder, countless summary executions, mutilations and torture. Those were the techniques of war, and what recruits and officers were trained and encouraged to do. As a school for political action, the Bolsheviks' Red Army taught that untrammeled violence was the supreme power. As Benningsen and Wimbush persuasively argue: "Submerged in revolution and civil war, the Russian Empire.... Soviets experienced the unleashing of forces which had been suppressed and repressed for many decades. It was as if Dostoyevsky had created his Grand Inquisitor and his most famous dictum for this one Russian Apocalypse that he could not foretell: 'God is dead; all things are permitted.'" For

Russia's many Muslim cadres, officers and soldiers, the Red Army was a school of terror, and a school of government by violence and terror.

Lessons so learned were overlaid on the earlier layers of jihad. In the Caucasus, for example, the tradition was the anti-Russian jihad of Sheikh Shamil and his *murids*. More broadly among the Muslims, "the fighting heritage of the Sufi *tariqa* [brotherhoods] was renewed and revitalized.... By a curious paradox some brotherhoods adopted revolutionary and even Socialist ideas. This was especially true of the Naqshbandi *tariqa*, which had a long and violent history of opposition to Russian power. In Socialism, some adepts found new arguments to buttress their traditional holy war against infidels." The convergence, or congruence, was not limited to technical aspects. Marx's historical materialism, with its predetermined course of history, was in some way akin to *kismet*, fate. Supranational communism was embodied in a "Soviet Union" that was not a nation-state, and was therefore analogous to the *über*-national *umma*. Hanafi Muazzar had written in this respect that "in the national question [w]e can point by point be at one with then Marxists, for from the viewpoint of Islam nationalism does not exist. In Islamic doctrine, the national question as it is understood today has no standing. In Islamic doctrine, there is but one *Islamiyyat*, only one brotherhood, with unity of all nationalities under the banner of Islam."[382] The similarity extended to a pseudo-history that pitted European "imperialism" against all other nations, that ascribed the origin of Western wealth to the "exploitation" of the others, and reconciled this newfangled theory of imperialism with the past, Islamic and non-Islamic, of Central Asia: "The invasions of Europe by Tamerlane, Dzhingis Khan, and the other Mongol princes, in all the cruelty of their devastating strength, pale before what the Europeans have done," wrote the leading figure of Muslim bolshevism, Mir-Said Sultan Galiev. From Marx and Engels' assertion that "all recorded history is the history of class struggle" to Iran's Islamo-Marxist hero Ali Shariati's hagiographic rewriting of history, the line is one.[383] Bolshevik ideas were "nationalized," or, to give it its proper name, Islamicized.

Mir-Said Sultan Galiev (1880–1939) joined the Bolshevik Party in November 1917. Thanks to his exceptional gifts as an organizer, he rapidly became the highest-ranking Muslim in the party hierarchy—a member of the Central Muslim Committee, chairman of the Muslim military collegium, member of the Little Collective of the *Narkomnats* (Commissariat of Nationalities), editor of the *Zhin Natsionalnostei* (*The Life of Nationalities*), the official organ of the *Narkomnats*, and member of the Central Executive Committee of the Tatar Republic.[384] Even more important, however, was Sultan Galiev's gradual evolution of the doctrine of "national communism," which transformed Bolshevik Muslims into modern Islamists. As such, Galiev was the forerunner of the new species of Islamo-Bolshevik jihadis.

Stalin and the Bolsheviks started to rein in the Muslims as early as they could. The party was already trying to bring under control the Communist political organizations of the Muslims by the end of 1918, and was doing the same inside the Red Army. In turn, the Nationalist Communists (Muslims) became radicalized. In the period between 1919 and 1923, Sultan Galiev elaborated his "Eastern Strategy" and lay the foundations of a "Colonial International" which was to be based in a projected "Republic of Turan," thus reviving Ender Pasha's dream kingdom with the same Pan-Islamist outlook. By the spring of 1920, Sultan Galiev and his cohorts were meeting secretly and establishing clandestine organizations—which they called *Ittihad ve tarakki,* Union and Progress, just like the Young Turks' own secret organization!

As the exile Turkmen leader Mustafa Chokay-Oglu wrote in 1935, "There was a time when we were ready to believe what the Moscow Bolsheviks were telling us, and we did believe them. The author of these lines defended Lenin, Trotsky and Stalin against their own Turkmen agents, who were plundering and murdering the Turkestani natives...."[385] As the devastations perpetrated by the Bolsheviks in the Muslim areas spread and worsened, and as state repression increased, the disillusionment accelerated. The revolt of the Basmachis—a Sufi-led popular insurrection against Soviet power—was one of the most powerful manifestations of the break between Muslims and Soviets. At the 12th Congress of the Bolshevik Party in April 1923, a general campaign was launched against Sultan Galiev and his ideas. "Sultan Galiev was thoroughly vilified, accused of deviations and treason, and ejected from the Communist Party." He was arrested in May, but released in June; Moscow could not go too far yet in confronting the Muslims. But a new category of crime had appeared—that of "Sultangalievism."[386] In 1928 Sultan Galiev was accused of plotting to carve a "Turanian Empire" out of the Muslim and Turkic territories of the Soviet Union (Tatarstan, Bashkiria, Kazakhstan, Kirghistan, Uzbekistan, Turkmenistan, Tadzhikistan, the Volga Tatar territories).[387] He was arrested again, summarily received a ten-year sentence and was deported to the Arctic Circle sub-zero Solovki Island death camp. It is presumed that he died around 1939.

Sultan Galiev's doctrine, which started as the quite improperly named National communism, rapidly developed as a hybrid between Bolshevism and Pan-Islamism. "Nonproletarian nations can bypass the capitalist stage of development and leap directly from precapitalism to socialism," he wrote. Since this was exactly the argument Lenin had used, in subversion of orthodox Marxism, to justify the Bolshevik Revolution, this carried an irony the Russians failed to notice, or appreciate. Some of Lenin's self-justificatory bickering was particularly appealing, in particular the notion that backwardness, once a stumbling block to Socialist development, now was an asset. "All Muslim colonized people are proletarian peoples and as almost all classes in Muslim society have been oppressed by the colonialists, all the classes have the right to be called 'proletarian.'... Muslim peoples are proletarian peoples.... [I]t is legitimate to say that the liberation movement in Muslim countries has the character of a Socialist revolution."[388] According to his cohort Veli Iskhakov, "The Tatars objectively are more revolutionary than the Russians, because they have been more heavily oppressed by Czarism than the Russians."[389] This was a remarkable anticipation of the cluster of ideas that were to develop fully in the form of "Castroism," "Guevarism," "thirdworldism" and "Arab Socialism," or the Mao-Lin Biao doctrine of the encirclement of the cities by the countryside as well as the doctrine of "the oppressed" and victimhood expressed later by Iranian Islamo-Marxist Ali Shariati and Ayatollah Khomeini himself. Or, rather than an anticipation, was this not the influence of the forerunners?

"If a revolution succeeds in England, Sultan Galiev wrote, the proletariat will continue oppressing the colonies and pursuing the policy of existing bourgeois governments.... In order to prevent the oppression of the toiler of the East, we must unite the Muslim masses in a communist movement that will be our own and autonomous."[390] Under the veneer of Marxian phraseology, Sultan Galiev had returned to the antinomy of *dar al-Islam* versus *dar al-Kufr*, or rather he recombined both to create the new doctrine. He went even further: his *neo-umma* would have to extend to the entire world. "Soviet Russia is a transitory phenomenon. The hegemony of the Russian people over other nations necessarily must be replaced by the dictatorship of those same nations over the Russians" in a first stage.[391] Further, as Benningsen and Wimbush stress, the movement "charted a theoretical course which, if successful in practice, would guarantee them supremacy not only over the Russians, but over the whole industrial world. What emerged was an 'Eastern strategy.' The thrust was ... that the revolution should be exported beyond the borders of the former czarist empire, incorporating into the National Communist universe millions of oppressed peoples—mostly Asian Muslims."[392] According to their Bolshevik opponents, they "acted as the standard-bearers not only of Tatar nationalism but also of Pan-Islamic democracy."[393] Sultan Galiev was rapidly developing his doctrine of a "Colonial International" and the ambitions it carried. "The sovietization of Azerbaijan is a highly important step in the evolution of Communism in the Near East. Just as Red Turkestan is playing the role of the revolutionary lighthouse for Chinese Turkestan, Tibet, Afghanistan, India, Bukhara, and Khiva, Soviet Azerbaijan with its old and experienced proletariat and its party—the *Hümmet* Party [of Azerbaijan] will become the Red lighthouse for Persia, Arabia and Turkey."[394]

Collaborators of Sultan Galiev who controlled the government of the Tatar Republic in 1922 created within the Commissariat of Justice a special *sharia* commission, entrusted with the task of reconciling and coordinating Soviet and Quranic law! The integration of Islam into a form of Bolshevism, or vice-versa, was working apace. Sultan Galiev and his comrades were not traditional Pan-Islamists, but hybrids representing the new species of Pan-Islam in the Era of Terror and Revolution. Stalin's interventions in 1923 to liquidate them politically show how dangerous they were considered to be. As their biographies, or their obituaries, testify, many of the Muslim National Communists were purged in the late 1920s and executed in the Great Purges of the 1930s.

"After the liquidation of the NCs, their ideas ... muted in the Soviet Union, lived on, and while the Republic of Turan was not realized in their lifetimes ... their ideas found other springboards to the underdeveloped world, leaving them a legacy."[395] The legacy was "a body of ideas or disconnected notions about the past which float through the collective memory of society." Further, one can only concur with Benningsen and Wimbush's conclusion that the ideas developed by the Soviet Muslims "about the synthesis of Nationalism and Communism, about the complementary nature of Marxism and Islam, about Asia's role as the progenitor of revolution and about the division of the world into oppressed and oppressors in one variant or another has penetrated into virtually every corner of the Third World. It is impossible to say with certainty that in each instance these ideas were carried beyond Soviet borders by intimate personal contacts with the Muslim Communist leaders themselves."[396] But the transmission occurred—organically, as it were, through KUTVa, most of whose teachers were of that persuasion, including the leading Muslim figures of the Bolshevik Party; through the KUTVa alumni who returned to their own countries; through the Communist Parties that continued to preach more orthodox forms of the doctrine; through Muslims who left the USSR and settled elsewhere. KUTVa leaders and professors, such as the Dutchman Hj.F.M.

Sneevliet (Maring), M.N. Roy, the Persian Sultan Zade, and others—many of whom, like Roy, subsequently broke with Stalin and communism—spread those ideas farther after their disillusionment with Soviet communism.

The ambiguity of the hybrid ideology was captured in an article authored by Sultan Galiev in 1921 entitled "The Methods of Antireligious Propaganda among the Muslims." His definition of Islam was light-years away from the accepted Marxist-Leninist canon, and fell foul of the Bolsheviks' League of the Godless' unceasing outpour of atheist propaganda:

> The essential factor which determines the position of Islam is its youthfulness. Of all the "great religions" of the world, Islam is the youngest and therefore the most solid and the strongest as far as influence is concerned.... Islam has best preserved social and political elements, whereas other religions emphasize above all ethnic and religious elements. [Regarding] Muslim law—the *shariat*— ... many of its prescriptions have a clear-cut, positive character.... Islam penetrates the spirit of the believer more deeply than other religions; it is therefore a more difficult and delicate task to combat its influence. The best proof of that lies in the personal position of Muslim clergymen, which is much more solid than that of representatives of other religions.... The Russian priest, appointed by superior authorities, certainly has a lesser authority over his flock than does the Tatar mullah or the Uzbek [*alim*].... The latter consider themselves to be "servants of the people" and lend an attentive ear to their wishes. They are more democratic and closer to the people and exert a greater influence on them than does the village priest over the Russian muzhik."[397]

Along with this pseudo-sociology went a pseudo-history of anti-imperialist victimhood according to which:

> [D]uring the course of the last century the whole of the Muslim world was exploited by European imperialism and served as the material base for its economy. The fact has profoundly marked the religion of the Muslims. The expansion of Western imperialism manifested itself first in the form of the Crusades and later by economic conquest. But the majority of Muslims always felt this battle to be a political conflict, that is to say a battle against Islam as a whole. Moreover, the reverse would have been impossible, for in the eyes of the Muslims, the Muslim world forms an indivisible whole, without distinction, nationality or tribe. Because of this, Islam was and still is, at least in the

eyes of Muslims, an oppressed religion forced to be on the defensive. In other words, the historical evolution of Islam fosters a feeling of solidarity among the diverse groups of the faithful and lands.... These conditions make the anti-Islam campaign a difficult one.... We must repeat that Islam is different from other religions in substance."[398]

Was this the plea of an atheist to the Bolsheviks to go soft on Islam for tactical reasons, or an Islamist's manipulation of the Bolsheviks' tactical need to go soft on Islam? Of course, the reality of the Bolshevik attitude toward religion—and non-Russian peoples—was far removed from their sanctimonious rhetoric. Regarding the principle of national self-determination which Lenin had fought teeth and nail throughout the history of the party, his disciple Nikolai Bukharin had said in a somewhat unguarded moment: "If we accept [the principle] and proclaim it regarding all the colonies, all these Hottentots, Bushmen, Blacks and Hindus and all the rest, we will lose nothing at all. To the contrary, we will gain, for all these national masses in motion will go against foreign imperialism and their struggle will merge with the general struggle against imperialism. Thus, as resolutely nationalist a movement as that of the Hindus only brings grist to our mill inasmuch as it applies to the destruction of British imperialism." The leading Bolshevik intellectual Riazanov chimed in: to him the salvation of Soviet power lay with "unleashing the hunting pack of the oppressed nations against the imperialist wolves."[399]

In the end, it was not the intent but the result that mattered. For many years, the party leadership gave Sultan Galiev and his friends a rather unrestricted mandate to do as they saw fit, to expound their "mutated Marxism" in party theoretical and political journals, and to train more cadre in this spirit. The arguments used, at any rate, were standard talking points of Muslim apologetics; there is little new in the grand historical narrative proffered by a Sayyid Qutb, a Maududi, a Shariati or a bin Laden compared to this Manichean travesty of history, an ahistorical morality tale of self-justification.

What the National Communist experience of the Soviet Muslims established was that on the Muslim side, it was necessary to espouse the whole of Bolshevism—"dialectical materialism," "historical materialism," and the philosophical mumbo-jumbo that go with them—to acquire what was most essential to that creed: the techniques of power through terror, of the management and manipulation of masses, of politically organizing people. Bolshevism and Islam may make strange bedfellows—but at bottom, it was not unreasonable of French sociologist Jules Monnerot to describe communism as the "Islam of the 20th century."[400] Had he lived longer, he could have added that Islam was the communism of the twenty-first century.

Ideological Infectors: Communist Parties in the Middle East

If "Sultangalievist" heterodoxy was ruthlessly crushed within the borders of the Soviet Union, Soviet power found milder forms of the virus to be of high value for export. It was admittedly never an easy thing for the Bolsheviks to do so, even in their Stalinist incarnation. For any form of "national" communism carried with it the threat of a "nationalist deviation," meaning a loss of Moscow's direct control over the local Communist forces. On the other hand, the ability to mimic, chameleon-like, local nationalisms and to leverage religion-based discontent and rebellion was too precious a political instrument to be neglected altogether.

In practice, this meant extremely sharp zig-zags in Moscow's marching orders to local Communists, oscillations between "united front" tactics with native peoples and organizations, and sectarian retrenchment on a Moscow-only party line. Still, as time went on, and especially as a result of the 7th World Congress of the Communist International in 1935 and its emphasis on "Popular Fronts," Sultangalievism-for-export gained currency, notably in the Middle East.

Politics in the region was a very fluid and inconstant concept. Ideologies tended to be factional markers, or flags, rather than coherently embraced world outlooks, as in the case of European political parties.[401] An adviser to President Anwar Sadat once said that states in the Middle East, save Egypt, are tribes draped in national flags. The same could be said for parties that very rarely transcended the boundaries of a given religious or ethnic affiliation. As usual in the region, family, clan and tribe trumped other considerations. "Left" and "right" were alien vestments that uneasily fitted the body politic of the region. One could jump without much compunction from being a socialist to a fascist, a Nazi to a Communist; nobody cried wolf! And the jump was not that big—feathers changed, but not the body.

Most Middle Eastern politics, though, were possessed of a few common denominators. The peoples there "want[ed] their own government—not good government;"[402] "'Anti-imperialism' … more often than not, cover[ed] an *impérialisme manqué*;" and "the climate of opinion in the Middle East in the late 1930s was vaguely pro-Fascist as it now [in 1956] vaguely pro-Communist. This does not mean that all the main tenets of totalitarian ideology were or are accepted by most of the people. But there was and is a conviction that Fascism (and Communism), apart from certain excesses, ha[d] somehow a good kernel, that it fill[ed] people with enthusiasm and rejuvenates nations, that it gets things done, and that, in short, the future belongs to the dynamic movements."[403]

Communist Parties in the Middle East never assumed power; when they took part in government, they merely were the junior partners of stronger, and better armed, forces. More often than not, their allies cast them out as soon as they were dispensable. They often were kept in a tame state, as interfaces with either some part of the local population that had to be co-opted, or as interfaces with the Soviet Union. The only exception, a party that was a genuine mass party and came closer to political power, was the Tudeh in Iran, of which more will be said later. But the role assigned by Soviet Russia to the Middle Eastern Communist Parties was not primarily to be contenders for power. They were Moscow's conveyor belts, and they conveyed crucial Soviet ideas and practices, which were avidly lapped up by the target audiences.

In this context, whether Middle Eastern Communist Parties bought Moscow much or little influence matters little. The question here is whether—and if so, how much of—their messages and behaviors were assimilated through various channels by the socio-ideological forces on which modern jihad has rested.

On the one hand, "Communist leaders [in the Middle East] have pointed out ever since the period of the Popular Front in the mid-1930s that early Islam was indeed communistic (or at least democratic)." On the other hand, "Attempts to find Socialist or Communist parallels in the Quran have been made by the left wing of the Muslim Brotherhood in Egypt and Syria."[404] A common hatred toward the West and a deep-seated ideological kinship explain the convergences; the claim by both to be the exclusive owner of absolute truth accounts for their bitter enmity. Historian Walter Laqueur made a very revealing observation: "Communism and extreme nationalism, frequently without a clear dividing line, [were] the two main forces among academic youth in the Arab countries. Members of orthodox Muslim organizations and right-wing extremists collaborated closely with the Communists under the framework of various 'fronts' [because] a radical change [could] be effected only by means of an authoritarian regime, a dictatorship."[405]

The great ideologist of the Muslim Brotherhood Sayyid Qutb wrote in 1952: "I have demanded liberty for the Communists under the same conditions as for all others who fight against tyranny. I have claimed this liberty for them, considering them honest men who are to be met with arguments, not bullets."[406] Considering Qutb's penchant to recommend sending hails of bullets toward all *jahili* forces, the compliment was significant. Cooperation was a pattern. "The Middle East has been a successful experimental field for Communist front organizations of various kinds.... Communist collaboration with other political parties and movements began in the late 1920s when the party line was to collaborate with the left wing of national movements," the course Stalin and M.N. Roy had defined.[407] Partnership with Muslim extremists and Arab nationalists went far beyond the left. The Grand Mufti of Jerusalem Amin al-Husayni, who is often better known as a Nazi collaborator, was the object of assiduous courting from the Communist International over a period of time spanning several decades. The case of the Palestinian leader affords us a window into this underlying pattern of Soviet-Muslim collaboration. The role Moscow ascribed to the Communist Party of Palestine had profound, long-term and largely unanticipated consequences on the Arab and Muslim world.

Lenin had carried out virulent polemics against all attempts by oppressed minorities within the Tsar's empire to constitute their own parties. One of the principal targets of his venom had been the organization of Jewish socialist workers, the *Bund*, ever treated as a "splintering" proletarian force. Nations were *passé*, nationalism was reactionary. Animus against Zionists was ever greater, for theirs was a bourgeois, or petit-bourgeois ideology. If Lenin was not particularly anti-Semitic, Stalin was devoured by the passion. The Communist International's Middle Eastern policy bore witness to the legacy of both.

The Communist Party of Palestine (CPP) had been tasked with "Arabization." "Out of the Jewish ghetto!" Karl Radek proclaimed—a slogan that remained in force for many years.[408] Success depended on the party becoming an Arab mass party. In November 1924, Bedouins and fellaheen violently attacked Jewish settlers arriving in the valley of Jezreel. The CPP had called on the Arabs to fight the Jews on the eve of their settlement, charging that they intended "to colonize the country of the ruins of the fellaheen village." Although no villager had been displaced by the Jewish National Fund's land purchase—Afula was considered an uninhabitable swamp—"the Communists claimed that the Arabs were the rightful owners of the country, that the Jews were imperialists, and that the fight against them was part of the general anti-imperialist struggle in the colonies. The Afula pattern returned frequently during the late 1920s and 1930s."[409]

While the CP called on its members to support the extremist wing of the Arab national movement, the latter's leaders Musa Kasim and Amin al-Husayni, did not initially reciprocate. The CP nonetheless persisted. In 1928, addressing the "7th Arab Conference," Communist Party leaders stated, "The homeland of a Jew is wherever he happens to be born, while Palestine belongs to the Arabs.... It is our sacred duty to fight side by side with the Arabs and to arouse the people of the world against the Zionist danger." The CP was ever trying "to give additional impetus to the Arab demonstrations and [armed] attacks as 'a link in the chain of peasant uprisings against imperialist colonization in all colonial countries.'" The Arabic-language periodicals of the CP "called on every patriotic Arab to go out and fight to save his honor and country against the invaders."[410]

In 1929, Amin al-Husayni set off bloody riots against the Jewish communities of Palestine, during which 133 were killed and 300 wounded, mostly in Hebron and Safed. For the German Communist daily *Rote Fahne*, "the anti-Jewish concomitant of the [Arab] revolt was a natural development that should not be regretted." In a programmatic document, the CP of Palestine stated: "In a country like Palestine a revolutionary movement without pogrom is inevitable." Leaflets called on Arabs to rise against their Zionist and British oppressors. In later "self-criticism" the party blamed itself for having been insufficiently bloody-minded: "The party has forgotten that the fellaheen and bedouin waited for leadership and wanted to be shown what to do with their knives and revolvers." As Laqueur concludes, "The CP had, in fact, become a part of the most extreme wing of the Arab national movement." It was actively inciting pogroms and killings. "But the day is near when the Arab peasant will rise again and no imperialist force, no Jewish fascist cohort, will be able to prevent this explosion," a Communist paper wrote in 1930. The party even criticized Amin al-Husayni for being too moderate. It called on the Arabs to march on Tel Aviv and to use force against the "Nazi Histadrut" (the Jewish labor union).

The CP worked closely with the newly formed *Istiqlal* [independence] party and especially its left wing, led by Hamdi Husayni from Gaza, who had visited Russia in the early 1930s. The party overall was led by members of the mufti's Arab Higher Committee, in particular religious aides of the Mufti such as Sheikh Muzafir. Together, they violently opposed the inflow of German Jews fleeing the Third Reich. In 1934, the latter were branded a "Zionist-Imperialist-fascist army." Communist literature heavily insisted on "the remarkable identity between Nazism and Zionism." The next year, the CP announced a new "Arab Revolt" and denounced the "Zionist Fascists and chauvinists for waging war on the Arab people and killing fellaheen." The Jewish self-defense force, the *Haganah*, ought to be outlawed and disbanded, the party said. On the eve of the major riots that then broke out and started the bloody Arab Revolt (1935–1937), "representatives of the party met the [Grand] Mufti in order to hammer out a working agreement." This occurred after the party executive had decreed that "the Arab Communists should actively participate in destroying Zionism and imperialism, while the Jewish members should do their share by weakening the [Jewish side] from within." Two Communists were attached to the general staff planning and coordinating the revolt, one as the intelligence chief of the Arab militias and another as a field commander.

"The Jewish minority in Palestine is a colonizing minority by its very nature," the party insisted. It sent members to commit terror acts against the "Zionist and imperialist" camp on behalf of the "progressive Arab" side. By the mid-summer of 1937, the party press denounced the "mad, chauvinist, militarist incitement of the Zionists." The party's support for the Arab leadership, the Grand Mufti, "reached the stage of full identification," even as al-Husayni by then was receiving substantial support from Fascist Italy and Nazi Germany. When the British authorities deported him, the party organized protests. Even after World War II, when Amin al-Husayni "escaped" from Paris with the help of various Western intelligence services intent on employing his valued services, and found shelter in Cairo, the Communists kept in close contact with him. "The Arab people, which has remained faithful to its leaders, celebrates … throughout the country."

In sum, starting in the 1920s and 1930s, the Palestinian Communist Party was the great instructor of the Pan-Islamist nationalist movement led by the Grand Mufti Amin al-Husayni in the fine arts of Communist *agit-prop*, the conveyor of crucial Marxist-Leninist concepts, such as "imperialism" and "colonialism." It pioneered the application of European political categories to the Middle Eastern scene in general, and the Jewish-Arab conflict in particular. Most of the ugly repertoire of modern Arab and Muslim anti-Semitism came from the Soviet Union (with only the racial-biological component added by the Nazis). The PCP taught the Arab extremists the use of Bolshevik rhetorical devices previously unknown. The "anti-imperialism" so imported by the Communists was remarkably ingested by the Muslim extremists, to the point of becoming integral to their conceptions and expression. It merged with traditional jihadi views that animated the Arabs of the region. In the amalgamation of bolshevism with jihad that turned out to be so crucial to modern jihad, this was crucial to training the Arabs in Soviet-style politics.

Communist cadres and promising leaders had been sent to Moscow for training. Starting in 1927 groups of Arab Communist students went there for a prolonged course at the Communist International academy. Between 1929 and 1935, over 30 such cadres went to the USSR, some for three years—the duration of the course for future party leaders at the International Lenin School. Among them were all leaders of the party in the 1930s. A study of their biographies, which historians should undertake, would trace more precisely than may be done here the precise pathways of the transfer of ideology, know-how and practices. Many Communist leaders and cadres left the party and found themselves new political homes. Their training did not go to waste, but spread farther afield into those new homes, whether these were those of pan-Arab nationalist or Muslim extremist movements.

Communist "united front" tactics had already advanced this kind of osmotic relationship. Laqueur, writing in 1956, reported: "The political allies which the Communists have found in recent years came from different quarters: the extreme-right wing and fanatical religious camp, such as the Muslim Brotherhood and Ahmad Husain's 'Socialist' party in Egypt, the *Istiqlal* in Iraq, and other groups elsewhere. Each particular tie of this kind could probably be explained as a freak, an interesting phenomenon but nevertheless atypical. But the fact that such collaboration has not been restricted to one particular country but has taken place everywhere in the Middle East makes generalization and the drawing of certain conclusions imperative. It cannot be mere coincidence that the main proponents of fascism in Egypt, Syria and Iraq cooperate nowadays with the Communists in the framework of sundry national, anti-imperialist and 'peace' fronts."[411] The pattern, as the adventures of the *Khilafat* movement have shown, was not incidental, but rather systematic. Whatever the very real ultimate differences in ideologies, cooperation and interpenetration were rife.

Likewise, in Egypt, in the last years of King Faruq's rule, Communists and Muslim Brothers shared prison cells, giving the latter their first opportunity to meet the former in the flesh. It is in "the internment camps at Huckstep and Abukir ... that the foundations for the 'National Front' of 1951-52 were laid through which the Communists achieved their greatest successes in the history of their movement." Already in 1950, the other Communist front organization,

"Partisans of Peace" ("Peace Movement" in Europe), collected 12,000 signatures for the "Stockholm Appeal," and a year later another 100,000 for successor appeals. Leaders of the semi-fascist right Ahmad Husain and Fathi Ridwan attended "Peace" congresses, while the secretary-general of the "Peace" organization was Yusuf Hilmi, earlier of the pro-fascist wing of the Nationalist Party. The *Mouvement démocratique de libération nationale*," a Communist front, began a period of intense collaboration with Ahmad Husain and the Muslim Brotherhood, and in 1953 reached an agreement for joint action with them against the military regime. The Egyptian quasi-fascists became "neutralists." The "progressive" wing of the Muslim Brothers affirmed the necessity of collaborating with the Communists against imperialism. By July 1954, Sayyid Qutb and the other Brotherhood leaders were cooperating with the Communist Party against Nasser, and a common political platform was ironed out. "Not a few mem--bers of the *Ikhwan* [Brotherhood] went over to the Communists."[412] The Communists' allies also included the already mentioned Fathi Ridwan and Ahmad Husain, once leader of *Misr al-Fatah* (Young Egypt), or "Green Shirts," a paramilitary organization directly modeled on Nazi and fascist movements. Husain had asserted: "We are infinitely closer to Rome and Berlin than to Paris and London." His movement continued its violent activities during the war. By 1945, though, articles favorable to the Soviet Union and communism started appearing in the movement's press. By 1949, "Socialism" was a staple notion. Fathi Ridwan was now minister for propaganda—and an honored member of the Peace Movement. By 1951 fascistic Yusuf Hilmi had progressed to be the president of the Egyptian Partisans of Peace and Ahmad Husain the publisher of the journal *Ishtirakiyya*, "Socialism," which according to Laqueur could be "compared only with the early writings of Adolf Hitler in the *Völkischer Beobachter* of 1921 and 1922. Incitement to kill all foreigners, together with anti-feudal slogans, an anti-Jewish hate campaign, threats against the Western 'plutocrats,' demands for agrarian reform, and defense of religion and the interest of the Holy Fatherland."[413]

The same scenario transpired in Syria. The "Islamic Socialist Front" "offered interesting parallels to both the Muslim Brotherhood and Ahmad Husain's 'socialism,'" and it was the local front for the Muslim Brotherhood. Its leader Sheikh Mustafa al-Sibai demanded that Syria "adopt an Eastern [pro-Soviet] orientation," as he orated at a mass demonstration held in 1950 to honor Joseph Stalin. "We shall fight the West regardless whether its pressure continues or not; we shall cooperate with the Russians and ask them for help." Front leader Muhammad Mubarak averred: "We shall welcome the idea of Islamistan on condition that it is not directed against the Soviet Union." And to crown the whole affair, another leader of the Islamic Socialist Front stated: "The I.S.F. is a Marxist drink in a Muslim cup." The leader in question was Maaruf Dawalibi, an old associate of Amin al-Husayni, the Nazi mufti, who had spent the Second World War churning out pro-Nazi propaganda in Berlin while political secretary to al-Husayni. He was now "the leading exponent of a pro-Soviet orientation."[414] "The Arab countries would prefer to become a Soviet Republic rather than a Jewish state," he said, and Israel was "tantamount to establishing an American colony in the Middle East." No wonder that the Soviet front organization the Partisans of Peace was such a hit in Syria: 60,000 signed the first Stockholm "Peace Appeal," in 1950, and 265,000 a successor the next year. This included a majority of the members of parliament and large numbers of prominent divines. A wide network of Communist front organizations was spawned, for students, artists, lawyers, youth. One of the leading Damascus *ulama* was Sheikh Muhammad al-Ashman, a former gang leader in the Palestinian revolt of 1936–1939. He had gone to Moscow and returned to head the Peace Movement.

Alongside the Syrian party, the Communist Party of Lebanon was the strongest and best organized of all CPs in the Middle East. It operated as "a sort of foster-parent to the other [Communist] parties in the Arab world."[415] Relations between both parties were especially close, both having been part of the French Mandate in the interwar years. Khalid Bakdash and a group of cadre had spent several months in Moscow, taken part in the 7th World Congress of the Communist International, and underwent training in Marxism-Leninism, agitation and propaganda. The "Anti-Fascist League," established in 1938 by party honcho Antun Thabit, held its first congress in 1939. As the war went on, "Everyone in the Levant was in favor of friendship with Russia so soon as it became clear who was going to win the war.... Communist progress in Lebanon was spectacular, notably in the intelligentsia." At the time, the CP ruled the streets of Beirut: "The Communists had almost no competition in street demonstrations because in Lebanon, as in the other Arab countries, political parties in the Western sense did not exist… [and did] not maintain a party apparatus capable of competing with the Communists."

The Party and its front organization made the "struggle for peace" their prime aim. Many of the great names in Lebanese life, the heads of the *grandes familles* who were the lead notabilities under the Ottomans and the political leaders thereafter, affixed their names to the Stockholm Appeal—former president Alfred Naccache, Sami al-Sulh, Hamid Franjieh, Pierre Gemayel, the

Maronite patriarch, the Greek Orthodox bishop, the Mufti. Laqueur underlines that "the leaders of the Syrian and Lebanese Communist Parties have shown a larger measure of political acumen than their colleagues at the helm of other Middle East parties.... [T]hey have shown much adaptability to national exigencies and traditions. They have quoted the Quran and the *hadith* and made a wide use of Arab history and tradition."[416]

In Iraq, the Communist Party was close to the "great national movement" of the pro-Nazi regime of Rashid Ali Gailani. Indeed, when Gailani and his backers, the Nazi "Four Colonels," took power in 1941, the Soviet Union was the first country in the world—before the Third Reich!—to extend the new government diplomatic recognition. Palestinian Communist leader Fuad Nasir, later first secretary of the Communist Party of Jordan, belonged to the entourage of the Grand Mufti al-Husayni, who had resided in Baghdad since October 1939 and was an important leader of the putschists' coalition. The Mufti declared jihad against Britain. Several leading Iraqi Communists worked in the regime's Department of Propaganda, led by the fascist leader Sadiq Shinshil—who ten years later again collaborated with the Communists as head of the *Istiqlal* Party. That party was the reincarnation of the Iraqi fascists' prewar and wartime movement, but from 1951 on was working directly with the Communist Party. Saddam Hussein's own family bore witness to this fluid cooperation. He was raised by his uncle, pro-fascist Khairullah Tulfah; joined the Baath Party, which was an eclectic mix of Nazi and Communist themes; and built a regime that was a favorite partner of Moscow's.

Communism was often a transitional faith, a temporary substitute. As Fouad Ajami in particular has shown, secular ideologies among the Arabs kept their religious substratum, which allowed many of the *pro tempore* Marxists and the transient Communists to return to Islam after some years spent immersed in pro-Moscow or other Communist organizations.[417] Once again, they did not return to the fold as if nothing had happened. They had been steeped in Soviet ideas concerning the nature of politics, the manner in which propaganda and agitation should be carried out, the way in which people should be organized—Marxist-Leninist concepts of imperialism, colonialism, exploitation, front organizations, the practice of the united front, the acceptability of terror and mass murder as legitimate tools, the overriding importance of the secret police, contempt for the Rule of Law and other "formal liberties" which only "bourgeois prejudice" respected, the notion that masses are only malleable dolts in the hands of the self-proclaimed vanguard—in brief, all the governing shibboleths of Leninist-Stalinist Communism. "A Marxist drink in a Muslim cup," Dawalibi had said. Yet that Syrian figure, first and foremost a radical Islamist who in turn found himself happily working with Nazis, and then Communists, testifies to the contamination of the cup by the drink.

In his overall assessment of the impact of the Young Turks on the entire region once ruled by the Ottomans, Bernard Lewis wrote: "The brutalization of public life by violence, repression and terror; the intrusion of the army into politics, leading to the twin evils of a militarized government and a politicized command …[a] wretched cycle of plot and counterplot, repression and sedition, tyranny, humiliation, and defeat."[418] Elie Kedourie showed how the brutalization played itself into modern Iraq by way of Ottoman-trained Arab military officers and the political role they played.[419] The next wave, or the next cycle, of brutalization, of internalization of terror as the principal tool of politics in general and of government in particular, came from the Soviet contributor. An additional donor brought components as toxic as those thrown in by the Soviets: National-Socialism was no less than bolshevism present at creation in the genesis of modern jihad.

The Nazi Contribution

As both Eric Voegelin and Hannah Arendt have variously shown, Soviet communism and National-Socialism are kin. Both are utopian enterprises that aim at radically reshaping human nature and the world, and propelling them into a final state of perfection inhabited by their respective version of the "New Man." The principle espoused excludes and supersedes any other consideration. Those who know the Principle are the Elect, and the stupendous import of their cosmic mission gives them exorbitant rights. They are the law unto themselves, while the rest is chattel, liable to be used or exterminated at will. As the first volume of this study examined, both communism and National-Socialism in turn were the echoes in modern European society of the ancient Gnostic creeds, and of the collective Gnosis mass movement that had wreaked havoc for centuries in Medieval Europe.

As the world of Islam forcibly became aware of European doctrines and practices, some interest was directed at the Liberal tradition—on and off during the *Tanzimat* period of the Ottoman Empire, as well as in the remarkable efforts of Sir Sayyed Ahmad Khan in the Indian *Raj*. But whereas guns were readily assimilated into military forces, parliamentary democracy was not, and in the Arab world, the consideration of democracy was fleeting at best. As Albert Hourani and Bernard Lewis, among other authorities, have shown, what borrowing took place almost exclusively concerned the authoritarian, dictatorial and totalitarian ideologies.[420]

Antagonism toward the West, itself identified with Liberalism, played a role. My enemy's enemy is my friend; my friend's ideology is the enemy of my enemy's ideology. The apparent "efficiency" of the totalitarian model to mobilize society's resources also had an impact: if it was possible for many in Western society, with its experience of democracy, to believe that the totalitarian regimes "worked better" than liberal democracy, it was all the more so in regions which had no experience of it at all. But the assimilation of ideas and practices went beyond mere fashion or misreading. There was enough of an essential similarity between donor and recipient to allow the ready acquisition of many components of the donor's worldview and modus operandi. Besides bolshevism, the other principal twentieth century influence on modern jihad, accordingly, was German National-Socialism two ideologies that competed for the same turf while sharing many of their core tenets.

The intellectual influence of the Romantic-reactionary form of German nationalism in the Middle East, from Fichte to the ideologues of Wilhelminian Germany, has been abundantly documented. We have also examined the political story of "jihad made in Germany" in the period leading to World War I and thereafter. Germany's direct intervention in the Middle East, however, receded in step with the relative stabilization of Germany in the 1920s. When Hans von Seeckt was forced to retire from his command of the *Reichswehr* in 1926 (and seek new adventures as Chiang Kai-shek's senior military adviser), the Weimar Republic's geopolitical interest in the region vanished altogether. For the Middle East, Germany was merely an important trade partner: "[T]he Germans were attractive partners especially for Middle Eastern nationalists who looked for alternative suppliers."[421]

Hitler's policy toward the Middle East originally resembled Bismarck's. He fully accepted the British Empire, thought colonial outposts to be "nothing but trouble," and he was happy for his ally Benito Mussolini to have his way in the eastern Mediterranean, Africa and the Arab world. Additionally, his racially conditioned views of the Arabs and of Islam were not flattering. He referred to them as "painted half-apes, who want to feel the whip."[422] He had only a jaundiced view of the use the Reich could have for the Muslims: "The 'Holy War' can produce in our German muttonheads the pleasant thrill that now others are ready to shed their blood for us, because that cowardly speculation has, to speak bluntly, been the silent father of all such hopes—but in reality it will meet a ghastly end under the fire of English machine guns and the hail of explosive bombs."[423] Accordingly, the Middle East occupied but a secondary place in Hitler's geopolitical schemes, far second to what he foremost coveted—the Russian *Lebensraum*. "An examination of German Middle Eastern policy under Hitler confirms that the region was of no concern to him."[424] It was only if and when the region became a major war theater that it would matter: "German planners were interested in French and British-influenced territories and immediate neighbors of Russia such as Afghanistan and Turkey." The Middle East would thus be a drain on British resources in manpower and material and a potential staging area for attacks on the USSR. "Just for this eventuality, Jihad made in Germany became important again." The by-now-ancient Max von Oppenheim even updated his World War I plan and memorandum for the benefit of the German Foreign Office. The Reich was however hampered by its Italian ally's own designs. Hitler's *Order #32* called for German Middle East plans to pave the way for later battles against the British. There too, he would inflict an "uncompromising war against the Jews." Thank to the new friends of the Reich, "the Arabs will liquidate them," went Berlin opinion in 1937.[425] As a result, "The formation of a Jewish state … under British mandate is not in Germany's interest, since a Palestinian state … would create an additional position of power for international Jewry.… Germany therefore has an interest in strengthening the Arab world as a counterweight against such a possible increase in power for world Jewry," an instruction from Foreign Minister Konstantin von Neurath read.[426]

Accordingly, as early as 1937, the "half-apes" were promoted by the *Völkischer Beobachter* to proto-Aryans, thanks to Armenian and Circassian blood. Nazism became a highly attractive and fashionable ideology.[427] Radical pan-Arab and Pan-Islamist Arabs, Michel Aflaq and a small group of the founders of the *Baath*, Antun Saada of the Syrian National Socialist Party, Ahmad Husayn, Young Egypt and its Green Shirts, to name but a few, were enthralled. "One party, one state, one leadership," the latter proclaimed. "Their ideology and form of organization and activity [were] thoroughly Nazi, including such devices as fascist salutes, torchlight parades, leader worship…" and "most characteristically, their use of gangs of toughs to terrorize and silence their political opponents."[428]

Still, financial aid to Arab rebels led by Amin al-Husayni against the British and the Jews was still "small and irregular." But radio broadcasts in Arabic were begun in the summer of 1938, "and proved immensely effective.... Supplemented by other forms of propaganda ... they evoked a powerful response...."[429] In 1934, "when the anti-Jewish Nuremberg Laws were promulgated, telegrams of congratulation were sent to the Führer from all over the Arab and Islamic worlds."[430]

There were of course old networks of sympathy, acquaintance and agentry to supply an infrastructure. German intelligence had developed an extensive network of agents in the Arab world. According to a CIA report declassified in 1976, in Egypt, a close friend of Muslim Brotherhood Supreme Guide Hasan al-Banna, General Aziz Ali al-Masri (who also was a close associate of Ahmad Hasan of Young Egypt fame), a "prestigious Arab nationalist,"[431] "formed and led an espionage ring to work for German intelligence."[432] A number of these officers seem to have had connections with Young Egypt. The ex-Khedive Abbas Hilmi, already active in Oppenheim's World War I network of jihad, was of their number. Werner Otto von Hentig, another veteran of German operations in the Great War, was posted at the German embassy in Constantinople and maintained an impressive network of contacts. Al-Azhar University professor Sheikh Ali Hasan Abdelqader was to chair the Central Islamic Institute in Berlin in 1939. Al-Azhar leader Sheikh a-Maraghi was more sympathizer than agent. Dr. Mustafa al-Wakil, a.k.a. Kurt Hoffmann, was to be the Grand Mufti's personal secretary in Berlin, and had been a leader of the Green Shirts.[433]

According to the same source, several of the top advisers of Saudi King Abdulazziz ibn Saud were agents. These included Khalid Abulwalid al-Hud, who visited Hitler on the king's behalf; Fuad Hamza, wartime envoy to Vichy France; Sheikh al-Ardh Midhat; and Sheikh Yusuf Yasim, the king's personal secretary.[434] Iraq "was the Arab nation in which the German intelligence service [GIS] expended the most efforts and met with the most willing response.... [H]elped by ties which had been developed during World War I, the GIS began building up contact there in the early 1930s. Since 1939, Iraq was the epicenter of the Pan-Arab nationalist movement, not only because Iraqis themselves were ardent supporters of the Movement, but also because many radical Arab nationalists had fled there."[435] In Baghdad, senior members of the military and the bureaucracy were members of a "semi-secret Iraqi Nazi organization," including the same Dr. Sami Shawqat, director-general of the Ministry of Education who but a few years earlier had exalted "the manufacture of death" as the paramount objective to be pursued. The Grand Mufti's secretary Osman Kamal Hadded, a.k.a. Max Müller, worked for the GIS in Baghdad, with the assistance of the chief of Iraqi military intelligence, Col. Hamid Rafat.[436] Palestinians and Jordanians, including the Grand Mufti's nephew Sawfat al-Husayni and other family members, were part of the political intelligence and spy network. In Syria, Maarouf Dawalibi, Muslim Brother, future Communist fellow-traveller, spent part of the war as a radio-propagandist operating from Zossen, outside Berlin.[437] There also was the ubiquitous Sheikh Shakib Arslan (b. 1869) from a prominent Syria Druze family. This soulmate of the Grand Mufti had been a friend of Enver Pasha before World War I, a member of the Young Turk Committee Union and Progress, and an envoy of Enver's to Berlin. In 1921 he went to Moscow with Enver, returned to Germany and then settled in Geneva. This restless agitator worked for Abbas Hilmi, was a close friend of Karl Radek's own national-Bolshevik friend Count Ernst von Reventlow, became a regular acquaintance of Benito Mussolini as early as 1922, and, in 1930, established the periodical *La Nation arabe*.[438] Publication continued as long as the flow of Italian and German funding continued—he was a fully paid agent of the *Abwehr*.[439] The periodical's tone was "extremely violent, it aimed at galvanizing the readership." At the request of Rashid Rida, this "*mujahid of the quill*" wrote several pamphlets on the causes of the backwardness of the Arab world, and presented Mussolini as the example for Muslims to follow. He also whitewashed Mussolini of any imperial designs over the Arabs, pushing mendacity into unexplored regions. Sheikh Arslan's influence was great in Algeria, where the leading anti-French *ulama* were under his spell. He is credited with having turned the most important pro-independence figure, Messali Haj, away from communism and into the embrace of Muslim Pan-Islamism.[440] "At the beginning of the war, Shakib Arslan received specific marching orders from Germany." He went to Berlin in September 1939 "as a technical adviser to the Reich's propaganda to Arab countries." *Reichspropagandaminister* Joseph Goebbels moved the German government to make him an *Ehrenarier*, Honorary Aryan, and citizen of the Reich. Arslan had met Amin al-Husayni in 1934; the two men struck a lifelong association.

"[Amin] Al-Husayni was regarded by the Axis as one of their top-level assets"[441] even though until 1941, "Arab nationalists like the Grand Mufti Amin al-Husayni of Jerusalem were more interested in [Hitler] than vice versa."[442] Al-Husayni had been working for the Abwehr since before the war.[443] He maintained "close ties" with Fritz Grobba, the *Auswärtiges Amt*'s pioneer spy-diplomat-agitator in the region,[444] who was orchestrating action. "[I]n cooperation with influential natives like Shakib Arslan of Greater Syria, [Grobba would] organize the uprisings that would weaken British positions in Egypt and India. A government under the leadership of Amin al-Husayni should be established in Palestine, and only the Jews who had lived there before the First World War should be allowed to stay."[445] The Mufti had taken up contact with the authorities of the Reich in 1933, shortly after Hitler's seizure of power. The alliance he sought had not only political and geopolitical aims, but also ideological ones. His purpose was "conceived not so much in pan-Arab as in Pan-Islamic terms, for a Holy War of Islam in alliance with Germany against world Jewry, to accomplish the final solution to the Jewish problem everywhere."[446]

Haj Amin al-Husayni (1897–1974) concentrated in his own person, action and legacy the conscious adhesion of Muslim Arab elites to the totalitarian extremism that arose on European and East European soil in the twentieth century. We have observed him in cahoots with the Communist International. We shall now watch him in league with Nazism and Italian fascism, remaining all the while the chief of the Muslim Brotherhood's Palestinian operations. Husayni had enjoyed "personal ties" with leaders of the *Khilafat* movement of India, the Ali Brothers, themselves successively pro-German and pro-Bolshevik. He had organized the pogroms and risings in Palestine, and, in the 1936–1939 "Arab Revolt" in Palestine, the systematic assassination of thousands of Palestinians inclined to compromise with the Jews. The Palestinian Arab Party he established in 1935 was "inspired by German Nazism." Its youth group for a time called itself the "Nazi Scouts."[447]

Husayni had been instrumental in organizing several "World" Islamic conferences in the 1930s. The 1931 Congress was a great success, as it attracted prominent Muslim figures such as Rashid Rida; Abdal Rahman Azzam, future head of the Arab League; the Syrian Riyad al-Sulh; later prime minister and future president Shuqri al-Kuwwatli; the prestigious figure of Sir Muhammad Iqbal; the former Iranian prime minister Ziya al-Din Tabatabai; and even a noted Twelver Shiite cleric, Sheikh al-Ghita.[448]

In the course of their "Congresses of Collaboration," "the disciples of Afghani and heirs of Rashid Rida cast their lots with the rising forces of totalitarianism, in the conviction that it would rid the Muslim worlds of two seemingly greater evils, colonialism and imperialism."[449] In the summer of 1940, Husayni organized an inter-Arab mission to travel to Berlin "to establish direct contact with the German government at the highest level. [It] included government-appointed representatives" from independent Arab states, such as Iraq and Saudi Arabia, and national committees from Allied-controlled ones.[450] Husayni moved his operations from Palestine to Lebanon and, in October 1939, to Iraq. In Baghdad Prime Minister Nuri al-Said received him well, and added to the subsidies he was receiving from Rome and Berlin. "Germany enjoyed a degree of confidence among the Muslims seldom manifested toward unbelievers," wrote General Hellmuth Felmy, who was in charge of training Arab and Muslim warriors fighting the German Army.[451]

Husayni promptly proceeded to plot against his pro-British host, in tandem with the German Legation. The Grand Mufti was one of the prime movers in the pro-Nazi coup led in April 1941 by Rashid Ali al Gailani, who was trying to extend the Germans' influence to other Arab countries, starting with Syria. Gailani, though he was less a Nazi than sympathetic to the Nazis, had been an *Abwehr* agent prior to the war, while the "Four Colonels," who were the power behind the throne, were ideologically committed. The Grand Mufti "helped the Germans by declaring a jihad against the allies in broadcasts to the Middle East."[452] Having failed to kill all the Jews of Palestine, the Grand Mufti took his revenge by organizing the bloody pogrom of June 1 and 2 in Baghdad: 600 Jews were killed, official sources reported; many more, said unofficial ones. "The massacre was carried out by troops, police, and other elements incited by the fallen Rashid Ali regime and seeking vengeance for its regime."[453]

After the British reclaimed control of Iraq, Husayni fled to Iran, was sheltered there by Axis embassies, in October 1941 went to Rome, where he was hosted by the regime, and at the end of the year arrived in Germany. In Rome Mussolini himself greeted him.[454] Claiming to be the head of a secret Arab nationalist organization with branches in all Arab countries, Husayni volunteered it to join the Axis war against Britain "on the sole condition that they recognize in principle the unity, independence, and sovereignty of an Arab state of a Fascist nature, including Iraq, Syria, Palestine and Trans-Jordan."[455] On October 27, 1941, the *Duce* met the Mufti, and a draft agreement with the Axis was prepared. On November 6, Husayni arrived in Berlin, where he met Ernst von Weizsäcker, Ribbentrop's second in command at the Foreign Office. But the declaration ended up being "no more than a bland statement of general principles." The only concrete clause was Axis agreement to the elimination of the Jewish National Home in Palestine.[456] Still, the way was opened to future parleys—which started soon: on November 28, 1941, the Mufti was to meet with Hitler.

The Mufti needed Hitler more than Hitler needed him. Hitler gave him generalities. The issuance of the Axis declaration on the Middle East was postponed. What agreement was finally made was limited and was to be kept secret. The Mufti nonetheless stuck to his guns and continued to work on behalf of the Axis, notably through the "Arab Bureau" in Berlin. Various training programs for Arab and Muslim fighters, guerrillas and spies were begun. In September 1942, the Mufti proposed the formation of Arab irregulars for sabotage, and regular Arab military units to assist Axis military operations."[457] In the following years, he and Rashid Ali shuttled between Rome and Berlin. Fritz Grobba "released weekly talks for Arabic broadcasts from Germany to the Middle East and coached Grand Mufti Amin al-Husayni in declaring Holy War against the Allies. Thus Grobba uncorked a magic bottle of warfare under cover of religion."[458] Radio Zossein, broadcasting from a suburb of Berlin, tried its best to inflame the Muslim world.

If Hitler had dampened down the Mufti's great hopes—Husayni considered himself nothing short of the voice of worldwide Islam and its leader—"Amin al-Husayni made a far deeper impression upon the *SS-Hauptamt* and the *Ostministerium*," the fiefs of Heinrich Himmler and Arthur Rosenberg, the race theorist respectively. "Both were responsible for the political mobilization and military recruitment of Muslims in German-occupied territories, and offered Amin al-Husayni another opportunity to fill the role of Muslim spiritual leader. It was on behalf of the *SS-Hauptamt* that he embarked upon a recruitment campaign among Bosnian Muslims in 1943, a success which owed much to ties forged in earlier Muslim congresses with leaders of the Bosnian Muslim community." As a result of Husayni's entreaties, Turkic POWs joined the SS in large numbers. The Mufti also helped found a school for SS Muslim chaplains in Dresden, which opened in April 1944—Husayini delivered the inaugural address.[459] Beginning in the summer of 1943, "the SS leadership discovered the Muslim Arab and Turanian fount of manpower." Himmler and al-Husayni met in Berlin in July 1943 "for a long, detailed exchange that ended with mutual assurances of covert cooperation. In late July, there followed concrete negotiations between the Mufti and the chief of the SS Main Office, Gottlob Berger." The battalion Imams "under al-Husayni's close supervision during frequent visits, developed into the backbone of the Muslim units of the *Waffen-SS*."[460] At the Nuremberg Trial, SS Dieter Wisliceny, an aide to Adolf Eichmann, Hitler's executive manager for the extermination of Europe's Jewry, declared to the Court that "the Mufti was a friend of Eichmann and had in his company gone incognito to visit the gas chamber at Auschwitz."[461] As Bernard Lewis wrote, Husayini "made his own not insignificant contribution to the destruction of European Jewry."[462]

In his dying days Hitler rued his strategic mistake of underutilizing the Arabs and the Muslims: "We had a great chance of pursuing a splendid policy with regard to Islam. But we missed the bus.... Alone Germany could have aroused the enthusiasm of the whole of Islam."[463] "A bold policy of friendship with Islam had still been possible until 1941."[464]

After the defeat of the Reich, the French interned the Mufti, who, after all, had continuously incited their Muslim populations to revolt against their masters. Yet since he was anti-British, the French let him go in the form of being given the slip. U.S. Secretary of State Dean Acheson explained, or explained away, "We cannot indict him." In both cases, it was clearly more convenient to use the war criminal than to prosecute him. Instead the Mufti was welcomed raptly by King Faruq into Egypt, where he was able to resume control of his "Army of Salvation" paramilitary organization. After the defeat of the Arab onslaught against Israel in 1948, the Mufti set up a "government of all [Mandatory] Palestine" under Egyptian auspices. In 1951, it was one of his agents who murdered the Jordanian King Abdallah in Jerusalem, inside the Al-Aqsa Mosque.[465]

But the Mufti was not only a megalomaniac and a fanatic. He was a man with a plan, and a substantial network of influence. When he claimed, as others have before and after him, that the entire Muslim world, or merely the whole Arab world, was supporting him to a man, he was delusional. But his secret network, the *Al-Umma'l Arabiyya* was real. Originally established in 1911 as *al-Fatat* and at first not anti-British, it seems to have been a club and coordination committee at elite level. Amir Hussein of Mecca, the Hashemite, was a founder; Nuri Said of Iraq was a member as well as King Faisal of Iraq. During the early stages of the Palestine War of 1936–1939, al-Umma radicalized in an anti-British direction and its Anglophile elements purged. "By the end of 1936, *al-Umma* had become wholeheartedly anti-British,"[466] Husayni told *SS Obergruppenführer* Erwin Ettel who was debriefing him in Rome. According to his inflated report, *al-Umma* had members in all Arab countries; each country had an Executive Committee whose members were also members of the Supreme Committee. He, the Mufti, had been a member of *al-Fatat* since World War I, and chosen as successor at the insistence of King Feisal of Iraq. Ertl wrote in his report: "*Al-Umma* ... was a compelling force behind every

Arab move for unity and independence. It directed the Palestine War in 1936–39, and engaged the 1941 Iraqi coup by first gaining direct control of the Iraqi army and through the Muslim church [sic], the tribal leaders and the youth movement." Membership required lifelong loyalty, based on an oath on the Quran. It is difficult to know whether the Mufti was merely embellishing the picture of his personal associates, grandly shaping them into a huge Pan-Islamic organization able to move mountains, taking ex post facto credit for events, and ascribing his own action to the power of said organization, or whether it really existed as such. Unraveling this riddle requires more archives to surface—notably the Mufti's personal archives, which the CIA has kept under wraps for decades for reasons unstated and rather unspeakable.

Members of the Supreme Committee included Rashid Ali al-Gailani (between al-Husayni and whom developed an increasingly tense rivalry); Nadji Shawqat the Iraqi Nazi; the Palestinian Ishaq Derwish, a leader in the 1936–1939 Palestinian insurgency and a member of the extended Husayni family; other leaders of the insurgency recycled in Egypt and elsewhere; as well as King ibn Saud's advisers al-Qarqani, Yusuf Yasim, Sheikh Shakib Arslan, his brother Amir Adil Arslan, and Sami al-Sulh.[467]

The Grand Mufti attended the great anti-imperialist conference of the Third World held in Bandung, Indonesia, in 1955. In the early years of the regime of Gamal Abdel Nasser, "the Nazi sympathies of the new rulers of Egypt were undisguised."[468]

The legacy lived on through the modern Palestinian movement, as well as the senior places where one found Iraqi Nazis, pro-Nazi Egyptians and Muslim Brothers in general. The coordinator of information about German propaganda in the Muslim world at the Office of Strategic Services (OSS) wrote toward the end of 1941:

> The Arabs are united on one general purpose, to free their world from the domination of French and British masters. Some Arabs are blinded to Italian imperialism and to German domination of Europe by their anxiety to get rid of the foreign control. This arises not only from a desire to play all European powers off against each other but from a naïveté which assures that any one who is against their masters is a friend of the Muslims. They fail to realize that, in case of a British defeat, there would be a substitution of Axis for the British or the French domination.[469]

The Soviets were replacing the Germans—again! The pattern had not changed.

On October 23, 1970, the following ad appeared in a European newspaper: "Wanted! Courageous comrades to join us for a tour or several months in the Middle East as war correspondents to study the WAR OF LIBERATION of Palestinian refugees to reconquer their homeland. If you have tank experience, apply at once. Money is no obstacle. What matters is a comradely spirit and personal courage. Information on the PLO free on request." What was remarkable was where the ad appeared: It was in the *Deutsche Nationalzeitung*, the unequivocally neo-Nazi weekly newspaper. The text was replete with code words appealing to the SS spirit.[470] In killing Jews, "the radical right [had been] there first. Europe's Black International had not only discovered the anti-Zionist cause a good quarter century earlier; it worked side by side with the same slogans, promising the same services, dealing with the same Palestinian agents."

The *Nouvel Ordre Européen* which operated out of Paris—and organized a secret meeting between the fascist "Black Prince" Valerio Borghese and Giangiacomo Feltrinelli, a senior KGB coordinator of terrorist networks that spanned Cuba, Latin America, eastern and Western Europe, and the Middle East—held a summit meeting on the Palestinians' behalf in Barcelona on April 2, 1969. "The Barcelona meeting dealt with several of Fatah's requests. The delegates talked about raising money, organizing efficient arms traffic, providing ex-Nazi military instructors to help the guerrillas get started, recruiting White Caucasian youths to beef up Fatah's forces in the Middle East, and collecting elements disposed to collaborate in acts of sabotage in Europe. They also discussed a propaganda campaign outlining all-purpose slogans—'Long live the glorious Palestinian fighters against Imperialism!'—with anti-Semitic classics like the *Protocols of the Elders of Zion* and a volume about Israel called *The Enemy of Man*." There were several Black Summits for the Palestinians after that, in Paris in 1970, in Munich in 1972—ten days after the Palestinian outrage at the Olympic Games. The 600 delegates cheered Black September and also praised Sirhan Sirhan, the assassin of Robert F. Kennedy. Another summit took placed in Rome in 1974. Ironically, the cream of the Red International rushed to Palestinian camps for training, while Palestinians flocked to Black International camps in the mountains of Spain and Italy. "The ultra-Left sponsored a huge rally for Arafat in Milan, and Italy's most flamboyant neo-Nazi, Franco Freda, held one to honor Arafat's Fatah in Padua."[471]

What Bernard Lewis wrote about the borrowings made by the Young Egypt movement holds for the radical Islamist movement as a whole, "its racism and anti-Semitism. This included support for Nazi philosophy, viciously anti-Jewish propaganda in the party press."[472] Islamic extremists acquired the perverse modern form of racism, biological racism and racial theory. Nasser himself told the *Deutsche Nationalzeitung*, "[D]uring the Second World War, our sympathies were with the Germans.... [T]he lie of the six million murdered Jews is not taken seriously by anybody."[473]

The Mutated Virus: "Islamic Revolution"

A further reason for my hatred of National Socialism and other ideologies is quite a primitive one. I have an aversion to killing people for the fun of it. What the fun is, I did not quite understand at the time, but in the intervening years the ample exploration of revolutionary consciousness has cast some light on this matter. The fun consists in gaining a pseudo-identity through asserting one's power, optimally by killing somebody—a pseudo-identity that serves as a substitute for the human self that has been lost.

ERIC VOEGELIN [474]

Stealthy Borrowing

Prior to the twentieth century, the term *revolution* had never been applied to Islam or things Islamic. The juridical and theological framework of Islam radically preclude any notion of "revolution."

Islam conceives of itself as the perfect political system, since it flows from a perfect revelation. It derives its entire body of law from God's *expressis verbis* prescription. There is no conceivable change in a system of that kind. As Ayatollah Khomeini famously said, "You have no need for new legislation; simply put into effect that which has already been legislated for you. This will save you a good deal of time and effort.... Everything, praise be to God, is ready-made for use"[475] Either a polity is ruled by God's law, *sharia*, in which case it is Muslim, or it is an infidel, pagan, a *jahili* society. If *sharia* is not being followed, this is a *prima facie* case of *fitna*, sedition, disorder, troubles, a highly-charged term describing an appalling situation, the normal course of things must urgently be re-established.

In a situation where un-Islamic accretions have disfigured "genuine" (original) Islam, allowance is made for the *mujaddid*, the renovator said to appear every century to cleanse the body of Islam. The notion is based on a particular *hadith*: "Surely, Allah will send for this *Umma* at the advent of every hundred years a person (or persons) who will renovate its religion for it."[476] This "renovation" makes it "as new," it does not renew it. The distinction is fundamental: after the advent of the seal of the prophets, Muhammad, no adjunction is licit or even possible; the renovation, *tajdid*, restores the original beliefs and practices. The *mujaddid* is not like the prophet or the Messenger. He is the one who recreates and demarcates the authentic *Sunna* from the counterfeit *bida*. Islam makes provision for is what it terms "reform," a radical return to its postulated roots, the "ready-made" Islam.

Given this, "revolution" in the Islamic polity is a theoretical impossibility. There may be vicissitudes of fortune for the ruler, or the wheel of fate may favor some other leader; there may be rebellion or insurrection; but there will be no revolution.[477]

In the European sense that spread to the rest of the world and was adopted by it, "revolution" is opposed to mere rebellion, or rising, or disorder. It implies a radical change and a radical transformation. The *jacqueries* of yore were revolts; the French Revolution intended and partially succeeded in changing the order of things. But in turn, revolution was vested by history with two vastly different meanings. The French Revolution intended to change human nature (Robespierre's "dictatorship of virtue") whereas England's Glorious Revolution of 1688 and the American Revolution intended to bring the political order into conformity with the natural rights of man, and took full account of human nature to compose the new institutional arrangements.[478] Thenceforward, revolutions in the West and elsewhere were either of the one or the other type. The Anglo-Saxon "liberal" model intended to create equality of opportunity, the French model, equality of outcomes.[479] The former built on tradition, the latter intended a *tabula rasa*.[480]

In the political language of Islam, "there was no positive term for the violent replacement of one regime by another until modern times, when the influence of the French Revolution, and of other European revolutions that followed it, percolated into Muslim political thought and language," Bernard Lewis wrote. The word *thawra*—"rising," "excitement," "rebellion"—ended up as "the universal Arabic term for good or approved revolution," he adds.[481]

Still, the Shiite Islamists who triumphed in Tehran in 1979 spoke of it as their "Islamic Revolution." In a far-reaching statement of intent, the Ayatollah Khomeini had written: "Both the Shariah and common sense dictate that we do not let the existing governments persist in their [wrong] ways... They have suspended the Shariah of God. For this reason it is the duty of all Muslims of the world, wherever they may happen to be, to rise up for the Islamic Revolution."[482] Moderate Islamist Ibrahim Yazdi concurred: "Our revolution is Islamic. Let no one be in error about that."[483] Article 2.5 of the Constitution of the Islamic Republic of Iran clearly refers to the unorthodox notion of the "revolution of Islam" as follows, "continuous leadership (imamah) and perpetual guidance, and its fundamental role in ensuring the uninterrupted process of the revolution of Islam."[484]

Abul Ala al-Maududi, one of the most significant and influential figures of Sunni radicalism in the twentieth century, incessantly spoke of the need for an "Islamic Revolution." "There is no doubt that all the Prophets of Allah, without exception, were Revolutionary Leaders, and the illustrious Prophet Muhammad (SAAS) was the greatest Revolutionary Leader of all. But there is something which distinguishes these Revolutionary Leaders who worshipped Allah alone, from the general, run-of-the-mill, worldly revolutionaries: these worldly revolutionaries, however honest and sincere their intentions may be, can never attain to a perfect level of justice and moderation," he wrote in 1939. He added: "'Muslims' is the title of that 'International Revolutionary Party' organized by Islam to carry out its revolutionary program. 'Jihad' refers to that revolutionary struggle and utmost exertion which the Islamic Nation/Party brings into play in order to achieve this objective."[485]

The same was true for his Egyptian friend and counterpart Sayyid Qutb, the ideologue of the Muslim Brotherhood. "No God but God is a revolution against the worldly authority that usurps the first characteristics of divinity," writes Qutb, using the word *thawra*. Revolution to him is "the only credible instrument of attaining social justice and of applying the *sharia*."[486] He insists on "the necessity of revolution as the only proper remedy for decaying societies. *Zalzalah* (shaking) or revolution is the word used to describe the first step in the process of building a new society." Prophet Muhammad led the greatest revolution, Qutb insists, and this should be repeated. He calls for "the comprehensive revolution in the government of man in all its forms, shapes, systems and situations, and the complete rebellion against every situation [contrary to the principles of Islam] on the whole earth."[487]

To say the least, the convergence of such eminent authorities of radical Islam, both Sunni and Shia, on an un-Islamic concept emanating from the West, is paradoxical. Coming from axiomatic haters of everything Western, the choice may not be simply ascribed to a desire to imitate, or to Islamic leaders and thinkers taking a leaf from the "secular nationalists" of the Arab world, whom they spent lifetimes insulting and combating when not slaughtering or being slaughtered by them—the Nassers, Assads and Saddam Husseins. Their choice of word, for sure, betrayed intent to signal how radical the change they intended to wreak was, and seized on a word the twentieth century *Zeitgeist* propagated everywhere. Still, Islamists eager to eradicate any *bida*, any innovation and accretion on the holy body of Islam posterior to the Golden Age, should not have been hobnobbing with the *Zeitgeist*. Yet hobnobbing they were.

In inter-cultural exchanges, the first elements adopted and absorbed by a culture from another one are those easiest to perceive and assimilate. In turn, those elements that are easiest to perceive and to assimilate are those most similar to the adopting culture. The greater the cultural distance, the greater the difficulty in assimilating. Facing European culture, it turned out that the Muslim and especially the Arab Middle East did not assimilate liberalism, democracy, constitutionalism, pluralism or federalism but hastily discarded them all as inefficient.[488] When the world stage was dominated by the rivalry between the "Anglo-Saxon" culture of pluralist democracy, and Prussian-inspired authoritarianism, the heart of the Arab elites went to the latter. When this was vanquished, its tyrannical successors, Soviet bolshevism, Italian fascism and German National-Socialism became the rage of the Arab and much of the Muslim world—in succession or simultaneously.

Muslims were attracted to those elements they recognized. Political pluralism was inconceivable in the cultural and intellectual terms of reference of the Muslim Middle East: power there has ever been one, centralized and indivisible. Muslim culture is a culture of the One—*tawhid*, the unity of God, is reflected by unity on earth. The *umma* is and must be one; the Caliph is "God's shadow on earth," and thus sole ruler; all political relationships converge on a center.

Totalitarianism had an appeal based not only on the efficacy ascribed to the totalitarian regimes; it also was culturally far easier to understand. *Ein Reich, ein Volk, ein Führer* had more allure than parliamentary debates, as had Stalin's

Five-Year Plan and NKVD, Mussolini's *stato totale* and the cries of *Duce! Duce!* That oneness was akin to something well understood in Islam, *tawhid*. As Maxime Rodinson, a French Marxist with strong feelings of sympathy for Islam, analyzed:

> Islam has been totalitarian to an extreme. Indeed, in principle, it dominated every act and every thought of the faithful. This domination was symbolized, for instance, by the reciting of the *basmala* [*bismillah*] during even the most trivial actions, and by the hadith's universal relevance. All actions, even those arising out of the most elementary biological needs, such as excretion and coition, were regulated by the ideological system. Even social actions of the kind which other cultures considered outside the realm of religion, be they technical, economic or artistic, were integrated into the system and interpreted in terms of it.... This totalitarian aspect of Muslim ideology persisted for a considerable time.[489]

As the partial osmosis between Europe and the Middle East proceeded, the transfers concerned in priority those elements in European political culture that appeared compatible.

How did revolution come to the jihadis? What else did they borrow? What mixture came out of the witches' cauldron where the new ingredients were mixed with the jihad of old? These are the questions we will now try to answer by looking at Sayyid Abul Ala Maududi, founder of Pakistan's *Jamaat-i Islami*, the intellectual godfather of the modern radical Islamist movement, the correspondent of Sayyid Qutb and Ruhollah Khomeini, and the original standard-bearer of the "Islamic Revolution."

Maududi, the Terrible Simplificateur

In the Islamic universe Maududi is the purest modern embodiment of Medieval Europe's millenarian *propheta*. His person and work concentrate almost all the characteristics of the Gnostic ideologue and leader described in Norman Cohn's *Pursuit of the Millenium*. Maududi, like the *prophetae* of old, was largely self-taught, and "never felt himself tied to any school of theological thought as are the *ulama* who graduate from the great traditional establishments of Deoband or Lucknow."[490] He was a *déclassé*, whose aristocratic lineage and family intimacy with the Moghol court had given way to lean times; he had to leave school at 15 to earn his keep. The self-developed intellectual undertook "to reconstruct the religious thought of Islam" on grounds he alone selected.[491] Unshackled by obeisance to tradition, conceiving of himself as a self-created, "born-again" Muslim. ("In reality, I am a new Muslim."[492]) Maududi practices his own *ijtihad* without being acknowledged by the Sunni world as worthy of this rare badge. He "overthrew the authorized interpreters of the Law."[493] He acted and thought like a prophet, and, as we will see, as a quasi-Mahdi—another trait in common with the countless pseudo-Messiahs that litter the history of the Christian world. The dimension of his mission was unlimited: "Now the only way open for reform and resuscitation is to rejuvenate Islam as a movement and to revive the meaning of the word Muslim anew," Maududi wrote.[494]

His undertaking was based on a novel consideration, namely that "Islam is one rational whole." This he did by "reconstructing the entire history and thought of Islam in order to make it a rational whole. His presentation may seem to be simplistic and highly logical. He isolates the… cornerstone ideas of Islamic thought and orders them in a clear synthesis."[495] Like the *propheta*, he needs to rebuild the entire edifice of his belief-structure in ways that uniquely suit him:

> Islam is not merely a religious creed or compound name for a few forms of worship, but a comprehensive system which envisages to annihilate all tyrannical and evil systems in the world and enforces its own program of reform which it deems best for the well-being of mankind. Islam addresses its call for effecting this program of destruction and reconstruction, revolution and reform not to just one nation, but to all humanity.[496]

His construct was an abstract-logical reconstruction that excluded considerations of facts. It was, as H.A.R. Gibb put it, a "shocking method of argument and treatment of facts… [and] writing to a predetermined conclusion."[497] *Islam and the World*, Maududi's well-known *magnum opus*, is a strange compendium of bite-size tidbits of knowledge, mythographic pseudo-history, Quranic quotes and peremptory assertions, all designed to prove his overarching point. In order to do that, Maududi needed to "erase thirteen centuries of history with all the social and political arrangements that intervened in that period.… Between his doctrine and the traditional sources of law [*fiqh*] and theology, there is nothing:

no school of thought, no mystical tradition, nothing, save Maududi himself."[498]

Maududi does away with the depth of history between the Prophetic Age of Muhammad and the "well-guided caliphs," and his "break with the past allows the irruption of modern and innovative aspects…."[499] But in order to do so, the charismatic leader of the *Jamiaat Islami* had to make himself into a *mujaddid*, the renovator of Islam for a century. In his words, which amount to a self-portrait:

> Though a *mujaddid* is not a prophet, yet in spirit he comes very close to prophethood. He is characterized by a clear mind, penetrating vision, unbiased straight thinking, special ability to see the right path, clear of all extremes, and keep balance, power to think independently of the contemporary and centuries-old social and other prejudices, courage to fight against the evils of the time, inherent ability to lead and guide, and an unusual competency to undertake *ijtihad* and the work of reconstruction.[500]

For a Muslim, a claim of "coming very close to prophethood" comes perilously close to blasphemy, since Muhammad is "the seal of the prophets." This was one the reasons why the Deobandi school ultimately pronounced the *takfir* against their former favorite, declaring Maududi to be a *kafr*, an unbeliever.[501] Yet Maududi went even further. He insisted that "[t]he ideal *mujaddid* (or *Imam al-Mahdi*) can be a true successor to Prophethood" and added: "If the expectation that Islam eventually will dominate the world of thought, culture, and politics is genuine, then the coming of a Great Leader under whose comprehensive and forceful leadership such Revolution is to come about is also certain." This millenarian self-appointment as quasi-prophet and great leader has no limits. "In my opinion the Coming One [the Mahdi] will be a most modern Leader of his age possessing an unusually deep insights in all the current branches of knowledge, and all the major problems of life.… Most probably he will not be aware of his being the promised Mahdi. People, however, will recognize him after his death to be the one who was to establish 'Caliphate after the pattern or Prophethood' as mentioned in the prophecies." Maududi's personal role was of messianic proportions. "With extensive study and practice one can develop a power and can intuitively sense the wishes and desires of the Holy Prophet.… Thus … on seeing a *hadith*, I can tell whether the Holy Prophet could or could not have said it."[502] This extraordinary claim turned Maududi into the pinnacle and center of the world, the decisive historical figure of the age, which in turn gave him unlimited rights. He "was" Islam. His Islam was "a universal ideology."[503] His party is the party of God (*Hizb Allah*). The party was so tasked: "We must … create out of nothing a minority of pure upright and educated men, in the image of the first Companions of the Prophet. In short, people who, like Muhammad himself … will rebuild from top to bottom the edifice of the State.… There must exist an upright community devoted to the principle of truth, and whose sole goal in the world is to establish, to safeguard and to realize correctly the system of Truth."[504]

Let us sum up: a *déclassé* semi-intellectual with a powerful, charismatic personality sets himself up as a figure of Messianic qualities whose cosmic mission is to establish perfection on Earth on behalf and according to the prescriptions of God. He is the quasi-peer of the great prophetic figures, and is possessed of extraordinary abilities. He is also possessed of a complete knowledge of how to move the world from its present, desolate *nadir* to the zenith of perfection: he is a Man with a Plan. He expounds that plan, which encompasses all aspects of life. He will radically transform the entire order of the world and replace the destroyed old order by a new one according to the Plan. His total knowledge allows him to pay no heed to traditions and their present bearers, since he is clearly vested by God with this stupendous mission. He is in charge of the immense bloodshed God requires for the Plan to be implemented. A population group is selected as representing Satan, and liable to be destroyed. Norman Cohn has left a definitive portrayal of the Gnostic hero who was Maududi's distant ancestor. But he also had more recent templates.

In 1941, Maududi created the *Jamiaat-i Islam* to implement the plan outlined above. In his conception, "[R]evolution did not involve society as a whole, it was *inqilab-i Imamat*, revolution in leadership." Also: "[S]ocieties are built, structured, and continued from the top down by conscious manipulation of those in power."[505] For all practical purposes, his party was established on a Leninist-Stalinist model. The *Jamiaat* was a highly centralized party led by an *amir*, with a consultative council (central committee) and an executive committee (politburo). It had central departments for finances, propaganda, welfare, education and research, and parliamentary affairs, and parallel professional organizations for students, youth, labor, peasants and *ulama*. The party's nucleus was a core of professional revolutionaries, with a first circle of committed sympathizers and a second circle of more loosely connected supporters. The party recruited in the first place lower middle class semi-intellectuals who had not yet made it in the "modern" (English-speaking) sector of the economy. "In sum, most of the members of the *Jamiaat-i Islam* came from layers of society that had a veneer of education but little means and little success."[506]

The resemblance to the Soviet model was not limited to organizational similarities, as Maududi repeatedly expressed his admiration for totalitarian movements and parties, communist and fascist alike. His ambition was no less universal than theirs: "Islam has prescribed that through a systematic effort (*jihad*)—if necessary by means of war and bloodshed—all these [corrupt] governments should be wiped out. In their stead must be erected a just and equitable government based on the fear of God and established on the basis of the canons He ordained."[507] "In short, not only was 'Revolution' ... an axis around which Maududi conducted his debate," but he "appropriat[ed] the myth of revolution" to apply it to "a utopian sociopolitical order," a biographer writes.[508] "Revolution" was not just a semantic loanword. In his *Jihad in Islam*, Maududi waxes endless on the subject:

> Islam is not the name of a "religion," nor is "Muslim" the title of a "Nation." In reality, Islam is a revolutionary ideology and program which seeks to alter the social order of the whole world and rebuild it in conformity with its own tenets and ideals. "Muslim" is the title of the revolutionary party organized by Islam to carry into effect its revolutionary program and "jihad" refers to that revolutionary struggle and utmost exertion which the Islamic party brings into play to achieve this objective.[509]

Revolutionary jihad is defined:

> Like all revolutionary ideologies, Islam shuns the use of current vocabulary and adapts a terminology of its own, so that its own revolutionary ideals may be distinguished from common ideals. The word "jihad" belongs to this particular terminology of Islam. Islam purposely rejected the word *harb* and other Arabic word bearing the same meaning of "war" and used the word "jihad" which is synonymous with "struggle." ... The sole intent of Islam is the welfare of mankind. Islam has its own particular ideological standpoint and practical program to carry out reforms for the welfare of mankind. Islam wishes to destroy all states and governments on the face of the earth which are opposed to the ideology and program of Islam regardless of the country or the nation that rules it.[510]

Never one to spare emphasis, Maududi adds, "Islam requires the earth—not just a portion, but the whole planet." A "mental revolution" is needed; "a revolution in the system of life." Islam is a "revolutionary creed:"

> [It] was the call for a universal and complete revolution.... [T]he call of the Prophet was never a metaphysical proposition; it was a charter of social revolution.... There is no doubt that all the Prophets of God without exception were Revolutionary leaders, and the illustrious Prophet Muhammad ... was the greatest revolutionary leader.[511]

Maududi politicizes religion. If Lenin and Hitler replaced God with a secular religion, Maududi turns religion into a political cause. "These men who propagate religion are not mere preachers and missionaries, but the functionaries of God (so that they may be witnesses for the people), and it is their duty to wipe out oppression, mischief, strife, immorality, high-handedness and unlawful exploitation from the world by the force of arms." What the Communist utopia desired—the classless society, the liberation from the realm of necessity and the advent of the realm of freedom; what Nazism wanted—the unimpeded rule of the Race; Maududi's Islam equally calls forth. All evils shall disappear, harmony will prevail, all troubles will vanish. God's kingdom will be realized on earth.

What is so distinctive about Maududi and his co-thinkers, Sayyid Qutb, Ruhollah Khomeini, etc., is the central role they award the State in their overall scheme. Islam does not separate "Mosque and State" in the sense that the same Law, *sharia*, applies to the public and the private realm, and the State is tasked first and foremost to ensure the implementation of *sharia*. Islam is not a *theo*cracy but a *logo*cracy. And Quran, *hadith* and *sharia* are the only law.[512] But there has long been a pragmatic separation between the affairs of the State, the preserve of dynasts, and the affairs of religion, the realm of the *ulama*. The latter have traditionally shunned the affairs of state, the only condition being that the Caliph, or any ruler for that matter, must not go against divine law. Even an impious scoundrel will legitimately be recognized as Caliph, provided he does not try to hinder *sharia*, says Sunni orthodoxy. It is a political quietism. As the great codifier of that orthodoxy al-Ghazali had it, any revolt was illegitimate, even against an oppressive and evil ruler, since it would likely generate anarchy and chaos—the greatest evil being *fitna*, the seditious splintering of the *umma*. The radicals decisively broke with that hallowed doctrine, and made the conquest of the state the central objective of their political action, as if Lenin's *The State and Revolution* had become their bedtime reading.

So Maududi's claim: "Hence this party [of God] is left with no other choice except to capture state authority."[513] Why is this so? "Apart from reforming the world it becomes impossible for the party itself to act upon its ideals under an alien state system. No party which believes in the validity and righteousness of its own ideology can live according to its precepts under the rule of a system different form its own:" the absolutist claim of ideology to have unlimited writ. The example Maududi chooses to illustrate his assertion is noteworthy: "A man who believes in Communism cannot order his life on the principles of Communism while in England or in America, for the capitalistic state system will bear down on him with all its power and it will be quite impossible for him to escape the retribution of the ruling authority," he writes, not without some semantic legerdemain. He adds: "Likewise, it is impossible for a Muslim to succeed in his intention of observing the Islamic pattern of life under the authority of a non-Islamic system of government. All rules which he considers wrong; and taxes that he deems unlawful; all matters which he believes to be evil. The civilization and way of life which, in his view, are wicked; the education system which seems to him as fatal—all these will be so inexorably imposed on him, his home and his children that evasion will become impossible. Hence a person nor a group of persons are compelled by the innate demand of their faith...." As a result of all this, "the acid test of the true devotion" of the believer is that he commits himself to world revolution.[514]

Maududi the Leninist elaborates on his concept of "World Revolution," which he sees as synonymous with "jihad:"

> [T]he objective of the Islamic 'jihad' is to eliminate the rule of an un-Islamic system and establish in its stead an Islamic system of state rule. Islam does not intend to confine this revolution to a single state or a few countries: the aim of Islam is to bring about a universal revolution. Although in the initial stages it is incumbent upon the members of the party of Islam to carry out a revolution in the state system of the countries to which they belong, buttheir ultimate objective is no other than to effect a world revolution. No revolutionary ideology which champions the principles of the welfare of humanity as a whole instead of upholding national interests can restrict its aims and objectives to the limits of a country or a nation. The goal of such an all-embracing doctrine is naturally bound to be world revolution.[515]

This was vintage Lenin, with a strong whiff of Trotsky added. As a biographer noted, "Maududi's program did indeed sound revolutionary in intent and possibly Marxist in origin when he wrote in *The Process of Revolution* 'Islam is a revolutionary ideology with a revolutionary practice, which aims at destroying the social order of the world totally and rebuilding it from scratch… and jihad denotes the revolutionary struggle.'"[516]

Maududi appropriated the image and concept of "Revolution," this potent myth of the twentieth century, in the sense the French radical anarcho-socialist Georges Sorel gave to the word in his *Réflexions sur la violence* (1906): Given the violent and irrational motivations of social and economic conduct, a deliberately-conceived "myth" must be concocted to sway masses into concerted action.

> [The revolutionary mobilization of the masses] could not be produced in a very certain manner by the use of ordinary language; use must be made of a body of image which, by intuition alone, before any considered analyses are made, is capable of evoking as an undivided whole the mass sentiments which correspond to the different manifestations of the war undertaken by socialist agitation against modern society. This problem [is solved] perfectly by concentrating the whole of socialism in the drama of the general strike; there is no longer place for the reconciliation of contraries in the equivocations of the professors; everything is clearly mapped out, so that only one interpretation of Socialism is possible. The method has all the advantages which the "integral" knowledge has over analysis.[517]

For Sorel, the shibboleth was "the general strike;" for his disciple Mussolini, it was "the total State;" for Lenin, "communism" and "The Revolution;" for Hitler, the "Aryan Race;" and for Maududi, "The Islamic world revolution." Different creeds, same structure: the myth is the actualization of redemption in the here and now. All were Manicheans and Gnostics. All cultivated the drama that overwhelmed analysis and placed the mass under the sway of the *propheta*. Based on his sociopolitical reading of the Quran, Maududi redefined Islam from faith to ideology, and converted religion into a mass movement fostering the drama of world Islamic revolution.

More study is required to identify precisely the channels and lines of communication through which Leninist thought came to Maududi, beyond the mere fact that it was "in the air," or in the *Zeitgeist*. Some traces may be identified which are as many clues. The starting point is Maududi's active membership in the *Khilafat* movement at the very early age of 16. "From the *Khilafat* activists he learned about the West and about politics; he learned the value of social mobilization and political propaganda, as well as the utility of putting Islamic slogans and symbols to communalist and political use. Many of the ideas of the *Khilafat* movement, such as its anti-imperialism, its effort to unite the various expressions of Islam in India, its appeal to Pan-Islamist sentiment, and its belief in the viability and desirability of resuscitating the institution of the Caliphate remained hallmarks of Maududi's political thought."[518] In turn, we have seen how leading figures in the *Khilafat* movement were mesmerized by and attracted to Bolshevism, and how at the same time the Deobandi school drew close to Moscow. The conclusion, if needing to be fleshed out, is: however inescapable it was that the multifarious Bolshevik influence we have charted found potent ways to shape Maududi's thinking, as it did many other Muslim leaders and intellectuals, at the hand of this *terrible simplificateur*, jihad and world revolution became one.

Sayyid Qutb, the chief ideologist for the Muslim Brotherhood in Egypt, whose contribution we studied in the first volume of this study, was Maududi's disciple. He in turn made Maududi's absolute dichotomy between Islam and un-Islam into the cornerstone of his revolutionary Islamist ideology.

Gnostic Mullahs and Smaller Satan

"The nationalism of the Arab-Muslim peoples [has a] double profile. On the one hand, it presents itself as a nationalistic movement of the conventional European style, based on a sense of racial kinship, and with certain general claims that are justified on historical grounds. On the other, it is a thinly disguised Mahdist movement aimed at forcible purification of Islam and at the revival of the traditionally demanded imperialism of the Umma. The interlocking of those two activistic drives gives [the movement] its strength."

G.E. von Grunebaum[519]

Jihadis of all stripes in the modern age share the same highly toxic mix of messianism, revolution and the cult of blood and violence. Modern jihad is the tapestry resulting from the weaving together of different warps and woofs: Pan-Islamism and Bolshevism, Nazi and fascist ideology and practices, Gnostic-Manichean beliefs within Islam. Originally distinct and distant threads have been woven together by artisans. We have so far described the German, Ottoman, Russian, Indian and some Arab craftsmen of the weaving. We will now examine the Iranian woof, and how it came about.

Khomeini and the militant clerics aimed at establishing an Islamic state by means of an Islamic revolution: "[T]he proponents of Islamic traditionalism had appropriated the most potent myth of modern politics, the myth of the revolution."[520] In their ability to access the masses—an ability largely lost by the Iranian clergy—they had to learn from the Iranian Communist Party, the *Tudeh* ("Masses"). In bringing about a fusion of Marxism and the Gnostic tradition of Shia Islam, they received the invaluable input of Ali Shariati and Navab Safavi. Safavi showed them how to make terror a principal instrument of politics, much of which he had learned from Hasan al-Banna and Sayyid Qutb. Ayatollah Motahhari synthesized the lesson from his friend Shariati and the legacy of his friend Navab Safavi. With stupendous cunning, Ayatollah Khomeini used them all to develop his revolutionary Mahdism, a doctrine he had in part learned form his correspondent Abul Alam Maududi.

The militant clerics led by Khomeini were avid readers of the writings of

Sayyid Qutb and of Maulana Abul Ala Maududi, both in Arabic and in Persian translation. "Their influence is unmistakable in the revolutionary slogans and pamphleteering" in Iran.[521] In his preface to *Social Justice in Islam*, Qutb's clerical translator praised the author for having established "a living and invaluable ideology."[522] The Iranian Islamists readily acknowledged their intellectual debt to the Sunni revolutionaries. Had Navab-Safavi, Khomeini's old terrorist acolyte, not consorted with the Muslim Brothers in Cairo as early as the 1940s? "Maududi ... had met the chiefs of the Muslim Brotherhood.... The Iranian *fedaiyan-e Islam* had serious relations with the Muslim Brothers of Egypt, Syria [and] Jordan.... Khomeini's 'Islamic Revolution' is a resurgence of that of the defunct *fedaiyan* movement. Ali Shariati's ideas, which are explicitly claimed by the heroes of the Iranian Islamic revolution… they are close to Sayyid Qutb's."[523]

Back in the 1930s, Muslim Brotherhood founder Hasan al-Banna, "[a]s soon as he was sure he could stand on his own feet … began to advertise his admiration for the Italian fascist dictator Benito Mussolini and, later, for Adolf Hitler." The Muslim Brothers apparently circulated the rumor that Mussolini was an Egyptian Muslim, that his real name was Musa Nili ("of the Nile"), and that Hitler too had converted to Islam and bore the name of Hayder, "the brave one."[524]

Navvab Safavi, Iran's First Modern *Propheta*

Muhammad Navvab Safavi, *née* Sayyid Mujtaba Mir-Lowhi (b. Tehran 1924) was the purveyor of Banna's brand of fascistic Islamism to Iran. This "young and not very well educated cleric," who had spent two years at the Najaf Seminary, established the *Jamiyat-e Fedaiyan-e Eslam*—those who sacrifice their lives for Islam—in 1945. The movement rapidly attracted a large membership of lower class and urban poor, and the religious middle class, and acquired powerful protectors among wealthy bazaar merchants and influential clerics. At its peak, the organization of the charismatic Navvab Safavi boasted 7,000 members.[525] It was an assassins' army, as its very name implied. It quickly emulated the Muslim Brotherhood's terror campaigns and murders of "corrupt," pro-Western political figures. All the atrocities perpetrated by his group were blessed by prominent clerics. Ayatollah Murtaza Mutahhari, a student, disciple and trusted lieutenant of Ruhollah Khomeini, was a close friend and associate of Navvab Safavi. The first killing was of the modernizer Ahmad Kasravi, an author whose 1946 assassination was signed off on by Khomeini himself, by Ayatollah Abdol Hoseyn Amini, who issued a *fatwa* calling for the elimination of the "Satanic" writer, by cleric Mohammad-Hasan Taleqani, who provided the money, and by the most prominent political leader of the Iranian clergy of the time, Ayatollah Kashani, speaker of the *Majlis*, the Iranian Parliament, who was to make extensive use of Navvab Safavi's murderous services in years to come.[526] Clerical pressure forced the government to let the killer go with but a slap on the wrist.[527]

Kashani gave the upstart plebian cleric a serious religious cover, and in return acquired the support of an organization able to mobilize activists. After a failed assassination of the Shah, the top clerics again protected the fugitive Navvab Safavi, who hid at the house of Ayatollah Mahmud Taleqani, while the young killer of Kasravi now killed the minister of the court. The *fedaiyan*'s rampage went on undisturbed. The prime minister, the tough General Ali Razmara, fell victim to one of their assassins, who again was protected by Kashani. The organizer of the targeted assassinations, Navvab Safavi was now a celebrity, granting menacing interviews and meeting Arab heads of states in the course of a late 1953–early 1954 tour of the Middle East. He was feted in Cairo by the Muslim Brothers and treated as a guest of honor by the Egyptian government.[528] When he returned to Iran, the Shah tried to co-opt him, even as the *fedaiyan* openly called for the Shah's death: "[T]he Shah was a usurper of Islamic rule and the government was illegitimate; the usurper of Islamic rule must be killed and the illegitimate government banished."[529]

Navvab Safavi now published a Manifesto that foreshadowed the Islamic state that arose in Iran after 1979. Bearing some resemblance to Italian fascist and German National-Socialist propaganda, it was a curious jumble of reactionary-romantic nostalgia for an idealized past, violent rejections of anything modern or Western, panicked fear of female sexuality, statist and redistributionist economic and social views, radical demands for clerical executive power. Society was to be placed under "the university of the Quran" and "the barracks of Islam." The Manifesto described an idyllic Islamic state, "where the government would be the father of the people, where nobody would fear the state's representative nor the thieves, where stores and houses had no more locks and keys. Sexual passions are released in marriage,"—though temporary marriage must be promoted—"there is no more unreason, no alcohol, no binges. Truly it would be a paradise."[530] Of course, the pathway to paradise was brutal: "Reform can only be achieved under the shadow of force; force is sacrifice, and sacrifice is but under the shadow of Islamic education. Hence, we, children of Islam, with God's help, we can achieve these reforms through our own sacrifice." War was necessary and beautiful: "Human wars come from ignorance, and Islam's wars come from God's command." With this creed, Safavi recruited very young men—was Ayatollah Khomeini later not to say that "people over 20 were already contaminated by Satanic civilization"?[531] These candidates for martyrdom were "processed" by Navvab Safavi himself, in a functional equivalent of brainwashing, a technique that was later refined for mass use by the regime.[532]

The charismatic Navvab Safavi was finally executed in 1956. He "left a deep imprint on the religious opposition to the regime."[533] He was the first incarnation of the Gnostic *propheta* in contemporary Iran, but by no means the last. In 1963, barely seven years after his death, three activist religious groups which he had deeply influenced coalesced to form the *Heyat-e Motafeleh-ye Eslami*. Composed of bazaar people and youngsters, it was led by a four- or five-man clerical committee appointed by Ayatollah Khomeini, including Ayatollahs Beheshti and Mutahhari, and able to deploy about 500 activists. The clerics issued guidelines to propagate Islam, to extend Islamic "ideology," to establish classes to that effect, and to establish groups for training speakers and teachers. They started to organize members into semi-secret ten-person groups. By November 1964, the leadership had decided to establish a military branch for targeting the regime's anti-Islamic figures. The following year they succeeded in killing Prime Minister Hasan Ali Mansur after the clerical committee issued a *fatwa* to that effect.[534] The *Vehme* assassinations executed in the early 1920s by the German *Freikorps* had found an echo.[535]

How to Organize Masses: The *Tudeh*

Iran had a confirmed tradition of urban and rural uprisings. In 1913, in the northern region of Ghilan which abuts the Caspian Sea, an anti-imperialist uprising with "radically Pan-Islamist" leanings had taken place against Russian and British encroachments, under the leadership of a religious figure, Mirza Kuchik Khan. The Muslim warriors were supported, funded and armed by the Germans and the Ottomans. Shortly after the collapse of the tsar's army in Iran, in 1917, "socialist ideas reached the Jengeli," contacts were made with Red movements in Azerbaijan and Persia. In June 1920, the Soviet commander of the Red Fleet in the Caspian, and member of the Central Asian Bureau of the Communist International, Admiral Raskolnikov, proclaimed an alliance with the Jengeli. The Soviet Socialist Republic of Ghilan was "the first Soviet satellite outside the Soviet Union."[536] Less than a year later, having chosen to turn Reza Shah into an ally, Moscow betrayed its Jengeli allies and established diplomatic relations with Tehran. In retaliation, Kuchik slaughtered the entire leadership of the Iranian Communist Party; he was then hunted down by the Iranians.

This first experience with Soviet reliability did not prevent the establishment, in September 1941, mostly by intellectuals, of an Iranian Communist Party. To avoid alienating the mullahs, the party's provisional program of February 1942, in typical "united front" manner, kept Marxist-tainted demands out. Stating its attitude toward religion, the party explained: "The *Tudeh* party has sincere faith in the true religion of Islam. Most of the members ... of our party are Muslims by background and believe in the religion of Muhammad. We shall never divert from the straight path of Islam." *Dar barih-i Eslam*, a party manifesto addressed to the clerics, averred: "Not only is the *Tudeh* party not against religion in general, but we feel a particular allegiance and deep respect toward Islam. We do not see any contradiction between the teachings of Islam and the principles that our party is advocating. We follow the same path and struggle for the same objectives. We hope that the *ulama* of Islam join us in this holy struggle and assure them of our loyalty to the true faith."[537] The Islamic technique of *taqiyeh*, dissimulating the truth to advance the cause and protect its partisans, was clearly not lost on the *Tudeh*.

In August 1946, as Soviet power rose and rose, three party members received cabinet positions in the government. The party was outlawed in 1949 but reemerged in 1951–1952 in the complex game played by multiple actors—the Shah, the clerical party, the bazaaris, the Soviet Union, the United States and Britain—over the issue of the nationalization of Iran's oil. *Tudeh* supported Dr. Mohammad Mosadeqh on and off, as suited its own goals, just as did the clerical party. Having built a remarkable apparatus to mobilize masses, the party was an essential player. It had established a large array of front organizations, each of which published periodicals openly propagating Marxist causes: youth, women, peasants, an association to fight illiteracy, a society for a

Free Iran, workers, journalists, a society against the imperialist oil companies, a society of the Partisans of Peace, high-school students, lawyers, teachers, engineers, civil servants.[538] The party was the first force ever in Iran to organize in this "European" manner, directly inspired by the way Socialists and especially Communists organized various layers of society. The party's ascent was not even dampened by Stalin's failed test-operation of setting up a satellite Soviet republic in a part of the Soviet wartime occupation zone of Iran closest to the USSR, Azerbaijan. When the puppet state collapsed, its leaders fled to the Soviet Union, where they were rounded up and either executed or shipped to Siberia. In the 1960s, the survivors returned to Iran. "Most remained true to their Communist ideal, although their faith in the Russians was spent. It was possible that their influence on the Communist movement in Iran is responsible for the emergence in the *Tudeh* party of a strong religious-national wing which in a curious way attempts to reconcile radical Islam and Marxism," researchers were able to report in 1979.[539] In that, the Iranians were rather successful—if not to the benefit of communism, certainly to that of radical Islam.

In July 1952, a few days before the resignation of Premier Mosadeqh, the Communist Party appealed to all anti-imperialist groups to join in a united front and "specifically requested [Ayatollah] Kashani to take the initiative toward this goal. When Kashani sent an appeal to the working and youth members of the *Tudeh* party, the Tehran press reported that an alliance had come into being between the *ulama* and the Iranian Communist Party." The day Mosadeqh effectively resigned, "Kashani sent a public letter to the pro-*Tudeh* organizations thanking them for their invaluable contribution to the national victory." The meanders of on-and-off alliances and enmities that mark the period are of lesser interest for this study—*Tudeh* now supported Mosadeqh, Kashani opposed him, but the Communists' influence and power grew by leaps and bounds. Three of its leaders again were members of the cabinet. By July, the *Tudeh* was the strongest and best organized political force in the country.[540] It was demanding official recognition for the Communist Party as such, the expulsion of American military advisers. When Stalin died, in March 1953, huge marches were organized along the breadth and length of the country. *Tudeh* was even recruiting prominent clerics, such as Sayyed Ali Akbar Burqai who campaigned for the Partisans of Peace. After the pro-Western counter-coup, *Tudeh* was banned, but maintained a prominent and efficient clandestine presence.

Even though Khomeini ranted against Marxism, materialism and the Little Soviet Satan, he allowed and encouraged his supporters to ally and cooperate with *Tudeh*. In turn, the latter sycophantically supported the Ayatollah. All the way into the 1979 Islamic Revolution and thereafter, this was true of Khomeini's trusted faithful who ran the mass-organizing: "The *Tudeh* ideologues, from whom the IRP [Islamic Revolutionary Party] cadre took many of their cues," were in a partial symbiosis with the Communists. [This persisted until the Imam decided to ban the party, arrest its members by the thousands, and exterminate its cadre. When that happened, in April 1983, the regime discovered several hundred *Tudeh* infiltrators in the military. The crackdown was probably motivated less by the party's influence in the intelligentsia, which lay supine under the Imam's spell or his killers' ways, but rather "the party's ideological impact on the clerics while they were novices in Iranian politics." In fact, "The militant clerics learned many of their political and journalistic tricks and tactics—first used during the anti-liberal, anti-nationalist smear campaign following the occupation of the American Embassy, their coining of political slogans and their models for political analysis from the *Tudeh* party."[541]

Ali Shariati's Theology of Liberation

The revolutionizing of radical Islam in Iran did not follow one line of communication only. We have already explored the cult of blood and redemptive violence that is a hallmark of Shariati's "Islamo-Marxism," the doctrine he called *tashayyo-e sorkh*, "Red Shiism."[542] We will now examine his doctrine and actions from the vantage point of their contribution to the transfer of Marxism and Bolshevism into radical Islam. Shariati is one of the most significant of the Gnostic *prophetae* of the contemporary age, whose influence on the Islamic Revolution was extraordinary, and extended far and wide into the entire spectrum of radical Islam, Shiite and Sunni alike.

The modern myth of revolution, as Eric Voegelin and Norman Cohn in particular have shown, is a modern form of the millenarian creed. Earthly redemption and the millennial kingdom, preached by all the totalitarian movements of the twentieth century, found especial resonance among religious masses whose creeds incorporated massive doses of apocalyptical and eschatological beliefs, such as the peculiar Mahdism of Shia Islam. The starting point of Mahdism, In Twelver Shia, the dominant sect of Shiism is the unbroken continuity of the Prophet's family's Imamate, through Fatima, Ali, Husayn and Hassan. It did not end with the disappearance of the Twelfth and last Imam.

Muhammad al-Mahdi ("the guided," b.868, d.?), who had been hidden since birth, appeared at the age of six to assert his claim to the Imamate, only again to disappear, this time down a well, to avoid the sad fate of his father and grandfather. For the next seventy years he maintained contact with his followers through a succession of four assistants, each known as *Bab* (Gate). On his deathbed in 941, the fourth *Bab*, as-Samarri, produced a letter from the Imam stating that there should be no successor to the latter and that henceforward the Mahdi would not be seen until he reappeared as champion of the faithful in the events leading to the Judgment Day. This long period, which has not come to an end yet, is known as the Greater Occultation. Some titles of the 12th Imam include: Master of the Age (*Sahib az Zaman*), Master of Command (*Sahib al Amr*), the one to arise (*al Qaim*), remnant of Allah (*Bagiyyat Allah*) and the awaited Imam (*Imam al Muntazar*).[543] This belief-structure was the perfect foundation on which to generate Gnostic-eschatological expectations, in short, Mahdism. In turn, the great renovator of Mahdism in the modern age—its prophet, the man who turned it into a political religion—Jamal al-Din al-Afghani, was a far-reaching influence on Shariati: "If Shariati's radical Islamism has deep roots and effects into Shia Islam, his political thought is inspired by the movement launched by Seyyed Jamaleddin Asabadi [al-Afghani]."[544]

Shariati's historiography is a hagiographic fairy tale made for the edification of the credulous. His supposed familiarity with Western intellectual currents is shallow and fractional, his sociology sophomoric and his scholarship embarrassingly feeble: he is an ideologue. Shortly before his premature death, he entrusted his (still unpublished) testament to Mohamad Reza Hakimi, a noted follower of Khomeini's, who in turn reported: "Of Shariati, let us first and foremost retain his potent and delicate gift as a communicator; with just a few words, simple slogans, he succeeded in radicalizing the mass of the people, which the clergy had been trying to do for a thousand years."[545] He cites one such slogan coined by Shariati at the time, *Shahid qalb-e tarikh ast*, "The martyr is the heart of history." The homology of Shariati's role and self-conception with that of Europe's medieval *prophetae* could not be more striking. He is, in Eric Voegelin's words, "the intellectual who knows the formula for salvation from the misfortunes of the world and can predict how world history will take its course in the future."[546]

The "Third International" merged with Russia, the "Third Rome; The "Third Reich" merged with the "third age" (Age of the Spirit) in the Gnostic parody of Christianity; likewise Shariati, like an alchemist, blended Islamic

Mahdism with Marx's Manichean millenarianism. Two Gnostic traditions intersected, recognized one another, and recombined their compatible strands. A suggestive simile to his undertaking was a group of Bolshevik leaders and intellectuals, today rather forgotten, but who individually and collectively played a major role in the Russian Revolution and the development of the Bolshevik Party. It is not uncommon—"Revolution devours its children"—for such groups to create an intellectual atmosphere conducive to the mobilization of revolution only to be discarded by the new masters once they are securely in power.

This Russian group called itself the "God Seekers;" its leaders were the internationally renowned pro-Bolshevik writer Maxim Gorki, the engineer and Bolshevik leader Alexksandr Bogdanov, and the future People's Commissar for Culture Anatolii Lunacharsky. These three had adopted Nietzsche's perspective of the "superman." In his hatred for "individualism," Gorki had dreamed of a Russian Superman who would lead the masses in a struggle for liberation. Lunacharsky and Gorki during the 1905 Revolution developed a Marxist surrogate religion of *Bogostroitel'stvo* (God-building). It extolled the heroic proletariat as savior of humanity, preached worship of collective humanity, and promised collective immortality to encourage people to risk death fighting for socialism, and to inspire heroism and self-sacrifice. It was in large part a response to Nietzsche, as was the obsession of the Russian radicals, from Chernychevsky onward, with creating a new culture and a New Man (*chelovek*) who would shed human nature and become more than the normal humans.[547] In the 1950s, Shariati was a member first of the "Movement for the Islamic Renewal," and then the *Nezhat-e Khoda-e Khoda-parastan-e Sosyalist*, the "Movement of the Socialist Worshippers of God."[548]

Shariati's children Ershan and Sarah Shariati, today both professors in France, report their father's fondness for his correspondent, the revolutionary Frantz Fanon, and his conception of "creating a new man." The raw material of the dream was to be "the oppressed masses." To convey that imitation of Marxian class struggle, Shariati borrowed Fanon's expression of "*les damnés de la Terre*," "the wretched of the earth," and translated it into Persian by reviving the Quranic term of *mostazafin*, "the disinherited,"—"a term that was to occupy a central position in the Islamic revolutionary rhetoric," since Shariati, even posthumously, was its leading sloganeer.[549]

Shariati also borrowed from the Quran and the stories of Muhammad's companions. In his fictionalized biography *Abuzar Qaffari the Socialist Worshipper of God*, he fished out this figure from relative obscurity to embody his theology of "liberation:" "I am the disciple of Abuzar, my doctrine, my Islam, my Shiism, my yearnings, my anger and my ideals are his. My purpose begins like his: in the name of God, God of the oppressed (*mostazafin*)."[550] Elsewhere, Shariati develops the fiction: "Abuzar, Companion of the Prophet, disciple of Ali.... He is a great revolutionary who fights against aristocracy, authoritarianism, capitalism [*sic*], misery and segregation. His word is higher than that of Proudhon."[551] And yet more: "A poor Bedouin, illiterate and rebellious to the idolatry of his time.... His material misery has endowed him with a keen sense of social justice; a man from the desert, remote from the depravation of the city, his illiteracy sheltered him from any reference other than Islam; his 'primitive' revolt against idolatry made him a proto-Monotheist, a *hanif*; his Islam is pure and coarse."[552] Abuzar, in other words, was a good savage, the degree zero of humanity: he was nothing, a man without attribute; therefore he was dispossessed and ready to become the apotheosis of super-humanity, the martyr. Of course, the Westernization, or modernization, of Iran, was a grievous attempt at further dispossessing the good savage of his authentic identity, culture and religion. Taking all the leaves from Fanon's book, Shariati hammered: "I hate modernism." He hated as well its effect on Iran, *qarbzadegi*, "plagued by the West," or in Al-i Ahmad's words, "Westoxication."

Prophet Muhammad himself was a revolutionary, but a Gnostic one who intended to establish God's perfect order on earth *hic et nunc*, just as Shariati: "The Prophet does not talk of a 'virtuous city,' of a 'divine city,' or of a 'promised land,' he implements it. It is not a theoretical construct but an objective one. The virtuous city of Islam is a real community (*Umma*). It is the city of the Prophet."[553] To him, the Quran was the blueprint for the perfect social life. Muhammad was "this revolutionary shepherd of the people."[554] Like his Bolshevik predecessors, and just as Dostoyevsky's "Possessed" equated God and the People, Shariati divinized the People: "Jihad in the way of God is jihad in the way of the People."[555] It was a "radically populist theory of revolution."[556] For this *propheta*, Marxism was a rival rather than an enemy. He himself was the great enlightener, endowed with a sacred mission, to redeem Iran from "cultural colonialism" and therefore redeem the Iranians to their true nature.

In a double movement, the Gnostic actualizes the Absolute by establishing Perfection in the finite and imperfect human world, and mobilizes the strivings of people for the same Absolute and Perfect. What is properly Gnostic in this double process is the claim that man can escape his condition, abolish his finite character—in other words, change his nature. This is the myth of revolution as embodiment of eschatological millenarianism. A utopia is essentially empty: it consists only of the desires projected into it by believers. So it had been for the Bolshevik Revolution of 1917, for the National-Socialist Revolution of 1933, for the Chinese Revolution of 1949, and so it was to be in 1979 for the Islamic Revolution of Iran.

Shariati's ideas contributed directly to the revolutionary outbreak through his influence on Iranian students and young intellectuals, especially the highly organized and motivated *Mojahedin-e Khalq*, who did some of the decisive fighting in the fateful days of February 1979. His ideas also had an important influence on the writings of the clerical pamphleteers and preachers, who were quick to take up the rhetoric of social justice and the cause of the disinherited. Furthermore, Shariati's writings won over a substantial part of the lay intelligentsia to Khomeini's side by leading them to believe the Islamic Revolution would be 'progressive.' Presumably a model to be followed was himself as a reformer, Shariati had written that Prophet Muhammad had preserved the form of traditional norms but had changed their contents in a revolutionary manner.[557]

This was the Nazi-Communist Muslim Brother Maaruf Dawalibi's "Marxist drink in a Muslim cup" all over again. The Islamic revolution was the Shiite millennium, the Imam-Mahdi reappearing in the shape of Ayatollah Khomeini.

Shariati's concept of the party as the instrument of revolution was a Leninist one: the party was the *locus* where belief (faith: *iman*) connects with revolutionary action (jihad). Shariati "succeeded to re-Islamicize a youth to which the religious leaders had lost access.... He transmogrified the Westernized youth into Islamic fighters. This psychological and behavioral transformation expressed itself as an increasing rejection of the Western model.... Shariati made himself the 'bridge' connecting the dynamic element of the [Islamist] middle class, the educated youth, and the people traditionally led by the clergy." This "triangle" carried out the revolution.[558]

Now, Shariati—the young Islamist disciple of semi-Marxists Herbert Marcuse, Jean-Paul Sartre and Frantz Fanon—was a darling of the radical Shiite clergy. "Very early on, the revolutionary clerics are in contact with him and throughout his life bestowed him with marks of respect and protection. The best-known *mujtahids* ... ayatollahs Taleqani, Tehrani, Beheshti, Mofatteh and especially Ayatollah Motahhari collaborated closely with him."[559] When clerical agents of the regime asked him to condemn Shariati, Ayatollah Khomeini pointedly refused.

Khomeini's point-man Mutahhari maintained a very close friendship and collaboration with Shariati. In 1965, Mutahhari (whose functions in the *Hetyat* included pronouncing on the killing of "enemies of Islam'") co-founded the *Huseiniyeh-ye Ershad* institute for research and education which later "played a major role in the religious movement of young activists before the Islamic Revolution." In November 1967, Mutahhari sent a letter to Shariati asking him to contribute to a book about the life of the Prophet the institute was going to publish, and soon afterward, he invited Shariati to come lecture there. "His lectures were livered with emotion, firing his audience with enthusiasm and were warmly welcomed by the young students, His teachings, too, had a major influence among the older men and women students. This essentially turned the Ershad Institute into the most attractive religious center in the country." In a letter Mutahhari wrote to the trustees, he depicted Shariati's lectures as "so popular during the four years [in question] that it exerted an influence on all groups of the country from the Grand Ayatollahs to the government officials."[560] Only Shariati's early death—probably at the hands of agents of SAVAK, the regime's secret police—prevented a continuation of his collaboration with Mutahhari: "In his late texts and lectures.... Shariati sought to modify his views and present an affirmative view of the *ulama* by mentioning their revolutionary and anti-imperialist role in contemporary Islam."[561] Shariati had journeyed to the West and brought back the worst he could find, which he then placed in the service of the Islamists' spirit of destruction.

Shariati's heirs were many, although in the end the legacy was channeled exclusively in the direction approved by the mullahs. Established at the beginning of the 1970s, the "Iranian People's Guerrilla," *Fadai-ye Khalq-e Iran*, which took its name from Navvab Safavi's old group, had started as a student group at Tehran University a half a dozen years before. Members became Marxists, read and discussed Che Guevara, Régis Dbray, the Brazilian theorist of urban guerrilla Carlos Marighela. Their theoretical pamphlets extolled guerrilla warfare, mass spontaneity, heroic activities; they added Castro, Mao and Giap to their repertoire. Another group, the *Guruh-e Furqan*, also established by Tehran University students, was the origin of the later *Mujahideen*. They read the Quran, Bazargan, Taleqani, but also literature on modern revolutions—Russia, China, Cuba, Algeria. A favorite was Algerian FLN ideologue Ammar Ouzegane's book *Le meilleur combat* (*The Highest Struggle*). Ouzegane, a former Communist, argued in his book that Islam was a revolutionary, socialistic creed and that the only way to fight imperialism was to resort to armed struggle and appeal to the religious sentiments of the masses. After years of study and debate, the *Mujahideen* assembled a team to provide its membership with their own theoretical handbook. They wrote a series of pamphlets, which included very primitive discussions of the theory of evolution, of Marx's theory of value, of "historical materialism," as well as a two-volume introduction to Quranic studies (*The Principle of Quranic Thinking*). Here they wrote that God is absolute evolution, not perfection; prayer is the connection between party members; the visible and invisible worlds are two hidden and overt stages of struggle and revolution; the afterworld is a socio-economic system of a higher world. They interpreted Quranic verses according to class struggle, and concluded that property was nothing more than a colonial phenomenon. This was very much in keeping with the pseudo-history that is always to be heard from the Gnostic revolutionaries from wherever they hark, and which Shariati, Maududi and Qutb in particular had refined to a great art.

The *Mujahideen* also issued two large booklets on the history of the prophets and on Imam Husayn. The interpretation was that of class struggle between rich and poor, ruled and rulers.[562] One of the *Mujahideen*'s leaders summed up their syncretic effort: "Our original aim was to synthesize the religious values of Islam with the scientific thought of Marxism … for we were convinced that true Islam was compatible with the theories of social evolution, historical determinism, and the class struggle.… [W]e say 'no' to Marxist philosophy, especially to atheism. But we say 'yes' to Marxist social thought, particularly to its analysis of feudalism, capitalism and imperialism."[563] The *Mujahideen* represented the inherent radicalism of Shiism, a form of socialism, a Muslim renaissance and reformation. They advocated an alliance with the Soviet Union. They were Shariati's "third way" to development.

The *Mujahideen* courted Ayatollah Khomeini. The story of their dealings sheds a fascinating light on the Islamic Revolution. The *Mujahideen* sent two members of their ideological team to Najaf in 1972 to ask Khomeini to give them his public support. With them they had letters of introduction from Ayatollahs Taleqani and Montazeri, old associate of Khomeini both, and from Ayatollah Mutahhari, who was in effect Khomeini's operational chief in Iran. The pair held twenty-four secret audiences with Khomeini, who urged them to de-Marxify themselves. He failed to grant his support, but he wrote letters to some of his followers in Iran urging them to support the families of *Mujahideen* who had been hurt by the Shah's repression. The *Mujahideen* and Khomeini were now in a united-front relationship. The *Mujahideen* had created an aura of organizational efficiency, of revolutionary fervor, of religious martyrdom around themselves. They made headways into the religious seminaries at Khunsar, Qom, Tehran; they debated with Taleqani, Shariati. One of their best-known slogans was *Bi nam-e Khuda va be Nam-e Khalq-e Qahraman-e Iran,* "In the name of God and in the name of the People of Iran." This infuriated the orthodox Gnostics, as it "gave God an associate"—the people—the very definition of the cardinal sin of polytheism in Islam.[564]

After some bloody internal conflicts, the *Mujahideen* published a "vehemently anti-Islamic manifesto" which discarded Islam in favor of Marxism-Leninism.[565] Khomeini's associate Mutahhari blasted the *Mujahideen* for their "new stratagem" and branded them "Batinists," an old insult denoting those who see allegorical and esoteric meanings in the Quran. The increasingly radicalized *Furqan* followed in the footsteps of the Medieval millenarians in developing a vision of an Islam without institutionalized leadership. They targeted and assassinated a number of the leading *ulama* and officials, starting in May 1979 with Murtaza Mutahhari himself.[566] Khomeini unleashed on them the full fire of his fury, calling them *munafiqun,* hypocrites—worse than unbelievers.

The falling out was inexorable. The chemical combination of Islam and Marxism is an unstable, and explosive one, but its syncretic-Manichean content is indisputable. Even when they slaughtered one another, they all promoted—Ayatollahs and lay *prophetae*—the same fundamental Gnostic gospel. Their views on who should preach it and be in power differed, as different mafia gangs compete for the loot but fight together against the authorities. The "Mobilization" (*Basije*), the regime's organization for the recruitment of the 12–14 year-old volunteers for death and martyrdom, was intellectually the joint offspring of both, of clerical and of lay revolutionaries.

Jihad and Revolution: Ayatollah Mutahhari

Mutahhari the cleric was no less of a Gnostic than his lay friend Shariati. Although human history externally consisted of wars and contradictions between the poor and the rich, or between the ruling and the ruled classes, internally these were wars between right and wrong, good and evil. Outwardly Mutahhari was a Marxian cleric, but inwardly he was a Gnostic Manichean one.[567] As he wrote in his discussion of martyrdom: "A martyr's motivation is different from that of ordinary people. His logic is the blind logic of a reformer, and the logic of a Gnostic lover.... A martyr's logic is unique. It is beyond the comprehension of ordinary people. This is why the word martyr is surrounded by a halo of sanctity."[568] But as a thinker, Mutahhari also was in a form of constant dialogue with Marxism, as if no clerical doctrine could be developed which did not, point by point, face and answer Marxism. In his biographer's words, "The importance of Mutahhari's works is based, first, on their comprehensiveness and complexity. While similar to Marxist totalism," [holism] they challenge it, since he "presents an alternative total Islamic system, Islamic world-view and social-political ideology...." How much he felt the urge to meet Marxism, rival but not enemy as Shariati had put it, emerges from his anguished interrogation regarding the attractiveness of Marxism for the young:

> Today, it is more or less established in the minds of youth that one must either be a theist—a peacemaker, complacent, calm, motionless, neutral—or a materialist—active, rebellious, opposed to colonialism, exploitation and despotism. Why has such an idea infiltrated the minds of young people?... They observe that it is just the supporters of materialism who lead uprisings, revolutions, battles and struggles, while theists are mostly static and neutral.... At present, the majority of heroic struggles against despotism [and exploitation] are guided by persons with more or less materialistic feelings. Undoubtedly, to a high extent, they have occupied the heroic trench.[569]

In order to reoccupy the heroic trench and recover the youth in it from Marxism, Islam had to Marxify itself. While it may be doubted whether Mutahhari and his fellow clerics would have seen the matter in this light, the wholesale adoption of Marxian categories to analyze the world and of Marxist-Leninist rhetoric to transform it, encapsulated in slogans a thousand times repeated, created an Islamo-Marxist hybrid—a monstrous laboratory experiment that was unleashed on the body of Iran and thence the rest of the world of Islam. The clerical agents of that innovation thought their immutable Islam immune to the loan-ideas, and probably saw themselves as both responding to urgent tactical requirements and cunningly borrowing effective devices from their rivals. The issues caused "a considerable division between the militant *ulama*." A delegation was sent to Najaf to ask Khomeini's ruling. "Although Khomeini took a cautious position and did not issue a statement, he privately supported Mutahhari."[570]

Mutahhari's project was to create an Islamic ideology, every bit as "holist" as Marxism. Just as Afghani before him, and Maududi, and Qutb, he sought an "ideologization" of Islam, to turn Islam into a political ideology similar to the secular religions of twentieth century totalitarianism, though couched in the Islamic cultural idiom.

> [The new Islamist ideology] meant the arrangement of readily available maxims constituting the sources of the Islamic tradition, the Quran and the sayings of the Prophet and the [Shiite] Imams, in accordance with a new pattern suggested by the Western total ideologies such as Communism and Fascism. A number of clerics took up the challenge of constructing the requisite Islamic total ideology. They were quick to learn the art of constructing an ideology from the lay intellectuals. They learned this art both from their opponents—most notably the ideologues of the *Tudeh* party—and their allies lay Islamist reformers such as [Mahdi] Bazargan and Shariati. Here, the importance of intense ideological debate between the *Tudeh* ideologues and the militant clerics in the Shah's prisons in the 1960s should be noted.[571]

In the economic and social planks of his total Islamic ideology, Mutahhari was a redistributionist Socialist, keen on limiting economic freedom and the market, willing to confiscate and nationalize wealth. The ambit of cases justifying state takeover was so huge and its terms so vague that it amounted to a case of confiscating everything except the bazaar and peasants' lands.[572] Mutahhari taught classes on Marxism, culled from the Farsi translations of third-hand and third-rate Western authors (rarely did he or most other clerics bother reading the original Western sources that they knew only from bowdlerized versions). But "because Marxism appeared to be the main alternative, Shia writers developed a dual attitude toward it: on the one hand, they tended to argue their own case through refutation of Marxism while, on the other, they tried to interpret Islamic laws and traditions as being no less revolutionary, just and so on, than Marxist ideals."[573]

Mutahhari's Marxian graft took to the Islamic stem. The project worked: "The major achievement of the clerical activists was to [offer] an ideology attractive to the intelligentsia and of maintaining their intellectual authority and leadership over the latter."[574] *Tudeh* and others had been the laboratory experiment, but the corporate interest reaping the fruit of their labor was the Islamic Revolution. The new jihad would be the result. Mutahhari's "three sacred concepts" of "faith, *hijrat* [migration] and jihad" were now applied to political struggles through their Marxist repatterning.[575] Materialism and monism were *tawhid*; the unity of God they meant fighting against oppressors, the *taghut*, idolaters; the Marxist proletariat was the Islamic *mostazafin*, the disinherited; the Shah was the anti-Christ, *ad-Dajjal* in the Muslim apocalyptic tradition; and Khomeini his messianic counter-image. All the facile dichotomies of a Gnostic worldview that erases differences and complexities were mobilized. Bevies of useful idiots from the Left, the intelligentsia and the good society enthusiastically joined the Islamic Revolution, typified perhaps by the first president of the Islamic Republic Abolhasan Bani-Sadr, one of the muddled ideologues of Islamo-Marxism. In the end, another slogan expressed the reality of the situation: "*Shah raft, Imam amad:*" "The Shah has gone, the Imam has come."

As the Islamic Revolution triumphed, it established a totalitarian apparatus of rule that came directly from the book of Hitler's, Lenin's, Stalin's and Mao's dictatorship. The militant clerics manned the Islamic Revolutionary Committees (*komiteh*—Farsi had to import the word), which meted out summary "justice" to the "enemies of God" and the "corruptors on earth," like once had the Cheka's flying 3-men tribunals and later the Gestapo's *Blockwart* system. The clerics created and manned the "Political-Ideological Bureaus" in the various branches of the Armed Forces—like the Red Army's *politruk* and the structure of political commissars. In 1979, they created an equivalent to the S.S., the Corps of the Guardians of the Islamic Revolution, *Sepah-e Pasdaran-e Enqelab-e Eslami*. In 1984, they established the Vigilante Patrols for Combating the Forbidden, *Gashta-ye Mobarazeh ba Moukarat*, a modern variation on the traditional moral police—the *mutawwa*, under the Central Bureau of the Revolutionary Committees. A Ministry of Intelligence—a KGB or S.S. *Sicherheitsdienst*, or better, the Nazi *Reichssicherheitshauptamt*, RSHA—was established in 1983, along with a Supreme Command of Islamic Propaganda that imitated the Soviet Central Committee's *agitprop* department. Islamic societies "were established in all organizations and enterprises of consequence to act as watchdogs for Islamic conformity"—precisely what Soviet party cells were designed to do. Islamic societies of ministries and government departments like the teachers, the military and factory workers have been particularly important. They have formed nationwide organizations, and there is a committee for the coordination of the Islamic societies of governmental departments and agencies. There is also a Council for the coordination of Islamic propaganda.[576]

But Khomeini went further. By 1980, he launched an "Islamic Cultural Revolution" aimed at re-Islamicizing society, reshaping the people and the state, de-secularizing the educational system, and fully establishing the Islamic

Republic as an ideological state. The cultural revolution, "an interesting extension of the modern myth of revolution due to Mao Zedong and the repercussions of the Chinese Revolution," was designed to eradicate all traces of Western cultural influence from high-schools and universities. "It was natural for [Khomeini and his clerical activists] to look at the latest model of revolution, with added features. Khomeini therefore ordered the creation of the Committee for Cultural Revolution to take charge of the Islamicization of the universities."[577]

The relationship between Islam and Marxism, between Islamists and Communists, Marxists and sundry ideologues, was never free of tensions, but ever an unstable coalition of Gnostics whose ideologies were convergent enough to permit cooperation and interchange, but divergent enough to cause strain and conflict. As long as they all fought uphill to oust the Shah, Khomeini cunningly kept silent or even encouraged the Leftist revolutionaries, and gave his clerics a wide mandate to work with them.

The Imam-Mahdi of the Revolution

In Iran's second presidential "election," in 1981, about five percent of the vote, or 400,000 ballots, were cast for the 12th Imam, the Mahdi. The myth was becoming flesh. In the event, the Mahdi did not become president, but he had a readily available substitute: over many years, with the fevered help from his host, Ayatollah Khomeini had painstakingly boosted himself to be the next best thing to the 12th Imam—a quasi-Mahdi.

Shiism owed its establishment in Iran to the supreme leader of an aberrant millenarian warrior order. The founder of the Safavid dynasty had claimed Mahdihood for himself in the sixteenth century. The intense personalization of the cosmic drama in Shiism, around the doomed figures of Ali, Husayn and Hasan, was a powerful, inherent booster to millenarian eschatology. The orthodox interpretation given over the ages by the *ulama* kept the millenarianism within bounds: the last Imam, the Mahdi, had gone into hiding, and would return at some unspecified time in the remote future; societies cannot exist in a permanent state of eschatological expectation, everlastingly suspended to a hypothetical. The millennium was a hope, not a daily matter. It was thus contained but not eradicated: the chiliastic belief lay now dormant, now fully reawakened. "As part of the general revival of religion in the late 1960s and

1970s, there was a marked increase in the popularity of *duaye nodbeh*, the supplication for the return of the Hidden Imam as the Mahdi, and special sessions were being arranged for its recital."[578] The etiology of millenarian upsurges has been presented: massive social dislocation and mental disorientation are preconditions and catalysts for its emergence as a mass phenomenon. Especially after the oil manna upset all norms and shook all rules as a result of the 1973 oil crisis, the Shah's Iran qualified as a society gripped by *anomie*. A fundamental dimension of the Islamic Revolution was the systematic exploitation, not least by Khomeini, of nostalgia for the old times, for the old stability.

The Egyptian Muslim Brotherhood had developed with a notion of supreme leadership—Hasan al-Banna was *al-Murshid*, the Guide. The charismatic Persian divine Musa al-Sadr, had organized the Lebanese Shiite community around a novel mix of social activism, belligerent identity politics and the fanning of millenarian expectations, and was called *Imam* by his followers. He was a harbinger of the future Khomeini as "leader of the Good in [the Lebanese Shiites'] Holy War against the forces of Evil."[579] Influenced by those examples, by 1970 Khomeini's militant followers were calling him *Imam*: "The acclamation of Khomeini as *Imam* by his followers was a startling event in Shiite history in Iran. Never since the majority of Iranians had become Shiite in the 16th century had they called a living person *Imam*. The term had hitherto only been used in reference to one of the twelve holy *imams* and its connotations in the minds of the Shiite believers as divinely-guided, infallible leaders undoubtedly worked to build up Khomeini's charisma."[580] It was now suggested that the Ayatollah was linked to the Hidden Imam of the Age, the Lords of Time.

"An unmistakably apocalyptic mood was observable during the religious month of Moharram 1399 (December 1978) among the masses of Tehran. Intense discussions were raging as to whether or not Khomeini was the Imam of the Age and the Lord of Time."[581] Khomeini's face was allegedly seen on the moon in provincial cities. Without claiming to be the returning Mahdi, Khomeini ingeniously exploited the messianic yearning by encouraging his acclamation as the *Imam*. He suggested that he was the forerunner of the Mahdi.

The slogan most frequently chanted by the "Followers of the Line of the *Imam*" was: "O God, O God, keep Khomeini until the Revolution of the Mahdi."[582] In September 1982, a clerical member of the Majlis, the parliament, predicted the imminent Advent of the Mahdi. A soldier wounded at the front during the war between Iran and Iraq reported that he had seen the Mahdi who had spoken to him thus: "Your prayer… has expedited my Advent by a few hundred years." The story was printed in *Sorush*, the intellectual journal of the Islamic militants in November 1982. The influential Ayatollah Saduqi of Yazd reported a miracle performed by Khomeini many years earlier: the Imam had created a spring in the middle of the desert under a scorching sun.

Khomeini's self-appointment as quasi-Mahdi was rooted in the revolutionary doctrine he had developed, that of the "government of the jurist," *velayat-e faqih*. In Islam, the law is *fiqh* and the jurist is the *faqih*. This covers a much wider ambit than is connoted by the English words, since, as Ignaz Goldziher had famously put it, "In Islam, theology is law and law is theology," a conception that derives seamlessly from the undivision of the religious and the political sphere. Khomeini now claimed absolute political power for the *faqih*, that is, himself. His theory overthrew centuries of accepted Shiite doctrine: during the Occultation of the 12th *Imam*—that is, until his Advent—the *ulama*'s mandate does not extend to the political sphere, and their mandate is a collective mandate, not one vested with any one individual. Khomeini rode roughshod over the traditions and the objections. From the 1963 riots onward, Khomeini and his followers stirred up the masses with the perspective of a political revolution; "to secure the leadership of this political revolution for themselves, they… revolutionized the Shiite political ethos."[583]

In January 1988, Khomeini asserted his God-given, absolute mandate to rule and govern as "the most important of the divine commandments [with] priority over all derivative divine commandments, even over prayer, fasting and pilgrimage to Mecca."[584] This was an extraordinary innovation in Islam, since the "derivative" commandments have always been considered the "Pillars of Islam." This clerical absolutism (hierocracy) exercised by one man, the quasi-Mahdi, became, as it were, Gospel truth in the Islamic Republic. Then-President Khamenei, now Supreme Guide himself—though lower in the scale of Mahdihood—asserted that the commandments of the ruling jurist, *vali-ye faqih*, "are like the commandments of God." He added: "It is the ruling jurist who creates the order of the Islamic Republic … and requires obedience to it. Opposing this order has become forbidden as one of the cardinal sins, and combating the opponents of this order has become a … religious duty."[585]

This extraordinary innovation had been enabled by, and was rooted in, the status of leadership in twentieth-century totalitarian states. In the Muslim world, Hasan al-Banna's role as *al-Murshid* had been one of the conveyors of this conception, but Antun Saada's Nazi-modeled Syrian Socialist National Party in Lebanon,[586] Ahmad Hasan in Egypt and others had shared and propagated it.

Al-Murshid was a notion with an old Sufi pedigree; it merged and blended with the *Duce* leading his *Stato totale*, with Hitler's *Führerprinzip*, with Stalin as the *Vozhd*. Ayatollah Khomeini in his incarnation as the *velayat-e faqih* was the very embodiment of Carl Schmitt's decisionist leader, as well as a repeat of the great Medieval *prophetae* of Europe, Thomas Müntzer, or the Anabaptist "king" of Münster. When in 1982 Khomeini ordered twenty-five Islamic organizations to merge into one "party of Allah," *Hezb-Allah*, it stood to reason, or unreason, that the slogan should be "Only one party, the party of Allah! Only one leader, Ruhollah!" It rhymes in Persian, with a similar ring to "*Ein Reich, Ein Volk, Ein Führer!*" and "Proletarians of all lands, *unite!*" Khomeini "represent[ed] Allah's will on earth," just as Hitler was the Will of the Race and Stalin the Will of History and The People.[587]

The results have been of the same order. The rampant jihad that has radiated from Tehran since 1979 has been one of the principal causes of destabilization and destruction in the region since; it has fanned the flames not only of Shiite jihad, but also of Sunni jihad. Indeed, Sunni-Shiite revolutionary and jihadi collaboration started the minute Khomeini returned to Tehran in 1979. Further, the Saudi-Wahhabi nexus was startled and frightened by the jihadi eruption across the Persian Gulf. The Kingdom's legitimacy as Custodian of the Holy Places was under relentless attack. The storming and seizure of the huge complex of the Great Mosque in Mecca, on November 20, 1979, the first day of the fifteenth century according to the Muslim calendar, shook the royal family to its foundations. The assailants had a Saudi core, but included in their ranks Egyptians, Kuwaitis, Sudanese, Iraqis, and Yemenis, among others. They had received military and tactical training in Libya and South Yemen from East German, Cuban, and Palestinian (members of the Popular Front for the Liberation of Palestine) instructors. They also included a contingent of apprentice terrorists trained in Iran.[588] The International Brigades of the new jihad were at work. As befits things modern, they had been born in a test-tube—the Palestine Liberation Organization—with a mad scientist operating the laboratory—the Soviet Union.

Coda: The PLO — Soviet Test-Tube and Incubator

Russia's inextinguishable thirst for conquest and territorial expansion propelled the tsar's armies into Chechnya in 1829. In self-defense the Sufi Brotherhoods, the Naqshbandiya-Muridiyya, declared a Holy War. After their first leaders Gazi Molla and Sheikh Mansur Ushirma were killed, a new leader emerged, Sheikh Shamil, whose role in the spread of Pan-Islamism has been examined earlier. Early Soviet literature "adopted a positive view of Shamil," as shown by textbooks of the time: "He was hailed as an able administrator, reformer, military leader and a patriot." This was in keeping with the original alliance between the Bolsheviks and the Pan-Islamists.[589] World War II saw a renewal of this favorable view, as Stalin contemplated ordering the Muslim religious leaders to declare a jihad against the Germans; in its aftermath, however, Shamil was the object of a virulent anti-Islamic campaign. His rehabilitation had to wait until after the Communist Party's 20th Congress in 1956. Soviet policy toward the Muslim world and the Middle East was undergoing a great new change. Shamil's symbolic value had to be activated.

The ultimate strategic failure of this renewed Soviet thrust in the world of Islam does not imply at all that it failed to have a powerful impact in that world, or that its effects were insignificant. A Soviet-centered analysis (as most approaches of the subject have been) will conclude that the strategy was a gigantic sinkhole for Soviet treasure and energy. An Islam-centered analysis will show a mighty penetration of Soviet ideas and practices, as has already been developed regarding the rise of Muslim national communism and the Bolshevik jihad.

Like the treatment of Shamil in Soviet literature, Soviet attitudes toward Islam followed the tactical meanders of Moscow's strategies. The World Peace Movement, founded in 1949 as the Soviets' premier front organization, scored resounding successes in the Middle East. Yet it did not preclude massive anti-Muslim persecutions within the USSR under the premiership of Nikita Khrushchev, whose policy was to eradicate all religions. Still, Khrushchev showed a notable ability to exploit developments in the Third World, the Muslim world inclusively. "The world was going our way," as the KGB stated.[590]

The Movement of the Non-Aligned convened its Bandung Conference in 1955. In spite of its bombastic name this group was strongly "anti-imperialist" and hence anti-American. It was also highly sensitive to the Soviets. With leaders such as the socialist Jawaharlal Nehru and the Communist Josip Broz, "Tito," philo-communism was a given—a point proven by the delirious welcome granted Chinese prime minister Zhou Enlai. With the Suez fiasco of 4

Accordingly, in the same year was established the Soviet Afro-Asian Solidarity Committee.

Moscow was developing its great proxy policy. Since the Warsaw Pact could not conquer Europe by conventional forces lest it set off a nuclear war that had been assessed to be virtually impossible to win, Soviet strategy would bypass and undermine the stalemate on the central front by weakening the periphery. It was a classic case of indirect strategy. As much as possible of the "Third World" would be the great proxy for Moscow's irregular warfare against the United States.

Delegations of Peace Partisans from the Arab world flocked to Cairo for the first Afro-Asian Solidarity conference. Soviet participation was significant, with the Soviet Union presenting itself as a "brotherly Muslim country."[591] In 1958, a first Muslim religious delegation led by the chief Mufti of Syria was in the USSR. "The desire of Soviet Muslims to volunteer to defend Arabism and Islam against Israeli imperialism" was stressed. The frequency of this kind of journey increased: the Chief Mufti of Egypt, the Grand Mufti of India, and others made the pilgrimage to the Third Rome. The same year, Nasser went twice to Moscow and began receiving a huge aid package, comparable over the next fifteen years only to what Cuba received. Soviet per capita nonmilitary aid to Egypt was fifteen times what India received, twenty times what China obtained, while the military aid was even larger. In 1964, Khrushchev journeyed to Alexandria: "The reception when he landed was quite indescribable. Many elements combined to make it a unique occasion. Nasser's prestige was at its height, and Khrushchev had become a legendary figure.... I saw there were tears in his eyes. Never anywhere had he been received as the Egyptian crowds had received him that day," reported Nasser's confidante Mohammed Heykal.[592]

"The Soviets presented themselves as the self-proclaimed protectors of colonized people and oppressed minorities."[593] As Khrushchev said, "The Soviet attitude is clear and precise: shackled with the chains of colonialism in Asia, Africa, Latin America or any other area of the globe. All peoples must be free! There is a close interconnection between the struggle of national liberation and the struggle for disarmament and peace. The struggle for general disarmament facilitates the struggle for national independence. The achievements of the National Liberation Movements, in their turn, promote peace and contribute to the struggle for disarmament."[594] Accordingly, the Kremlin toned down the anti-Muslim campaign at home, and began to create an Islamologic and Arabologic policy establishment. They of course discovered that "Islamic society ... may become a revolutionary anti-capitalist reformist movement."[595]

In brief, the wheel was being rediscovered, namely Stalin's and Sultan Galiev's original policy. The policy went through three channels: official—government, party, Communist youth, trade unions, universities, the Academy of Sciences, professional organizations such as the writers' union; KGB front organizations, such as the Partisans of Peace, bi-national friendship societies; and properly Islamic channels run through the Muslim Spiritual Directorates.[596] The latter was sending Soviet muftis as middlemen in delegations abroad; they were received by the religious authorities of the visited countries, and in turn they received the latters' contacts in the Soviet Union.[597]

The Central Committee's innocuously named International Department (I.D.) controlled the aforementioned Soviet Afro-Asian Solidarity Committee. The department was essentially the old Communist International (cosmetically dissolved in 1943 to please the Anglo-Americans), now directly integrated into the Central Committee. It was the leading voice in analyzing and formulating Soviet foreign policy. Run for decades by veteran *Komintern* functionary Boris Ponomarev, the I.D. also was the "orchestrating arms of the [Party] for the activities of the [military intelligence service] GRU, diplomats and related personnel abroad, and even KGB residencies abroad."[598]

In 1964, the party leadership, Politburo and I.D. decided to re-establish the "International Lenin School" (or Institute) that up to the purges of the late 1930s had operated as the top-level cadre school for international communism, but had been terminated by Stalin. The school's main focus was the Third World, the Muslim world in particular. Under the general supervision of Boris Ponomarev and his deputy Karen Brutents, the first head of the school was Fyodor Rizhenko, former head of the GIMO diplomatic school, the prestigious State Institute for International Affairs in Moscow. Rizhenko championed non-traditional methods of teaching for his special student body. The emphasis was on adapting the Marxist-Leninist creed to "local conditions," including religion and ideologies. As Rizhenko stated to the faculty: "Do not preach under the banner of Marxism-Leninism, use the Quran as a revolutionary book."[599] The school was training future secretary-generals and high-level leaders of Communist Parties, leaders of PFLP, PDFLP, the *Tudeh*, the Baath. The Patrice Lumumba University was a reprise of the old KUTVa; it trained lower level personnel and screened "candidates" for higher destinies and terror careers. It established a coherent phalanx of communist-terrorist cadre, trained in the crafts of "psychological warfare, subversive use of the media, as well as Marxist-Leninist ideology."[600] At the same time that the Politburo decided to establish the Lenin School, it also decided—as reported by Czech General Jan Sejna who defected to the West in 1968—drastically to increase Soviet investment in terrorist enterprises, by a tenfold factor.[601]

In that framework, the rise of the Castro regime was a boon for Soviet strategy. Cuba was to be a cover, a proxy and a re-dispatching center for the indirect strategy. It would be an essential coach, educator and mentor for subversive, terrorist and related activities in the Third World. The OSPAAL/Tricontinental established under the sponsorship of the Cuban *barbudos* gave a new luster to long-tarnished Soviet enterprises; it allowed for the recruitment of new layers inaccessible to direct Soviet entreaties. It provided an appropriately colored point of entry into the Third World as well as an elixir of revolutionary romanticism that Soviet bureaucrats had long been unable to grow. It is through Cuba and the Tricontinental that the test-tubes of modern Soviet terrorism—its cadre force, its methods—were cultivated. Top-fight Soviet agents such as Giangiacomo Feltrinelli, Henri Curiel, "Carlos" the Venezuelan, the Red Brigades of Italy, the Red Army Fraction of Germany, IRA and the Basque ETA rubbed shoulders under the aegis of the KGB, the East German *Stasi*, the Czech STB, Bulgarian intelligence, the Romanian *Securitate*. All of them in turn played a role in shaping, training and deploying Palestinian terrorism as well as Arab terror in general.

The Kremlin, for example, was extending its operations to the newly independent North Yemen, starting with a friendship pact with its pro-Nasser regime. At the Soviet Embassy in Saana, the job of the First Secretary "was to organize and direct guerrilla operations in Aden … control the embryonic liberation movement in Oman and Saudi Arabia and interface with the Front for the Liberation of South Yemen," wrote a Soviet defector.[602] But far-away Yemen was a sideshow, too primitive, too remote from the heartlands of Arabism and Islam. It may have been a useful training ground for future Soviet operations, but its usefulness rarely went beyond that of a strategic support station. Gradually, as Arab states disappointed their Soviet partners, notably after the Six

Days' War of 1967 and after Anwar al-Sadat expelled thousands of Soviet advisers from Egypt, Soviet policy de-emphasized state-to-state relations and increasingly turned to the indirect approach: the ascent of the PLO had begun.

The Palestinian national movement had a double pedigree line grafted onto its Islamic origins. The Grand Mufti of Jerusalem Amin al-Husayni, as we have seen, maintained a far-reaching cooperation with the Communists of Palestine from the late 1920s through the 1930s. He also gradually forged solid links of collaboration with the Axis powers, first by way of Rome and then by way of Berlin. His distant relative Yasser Arafat connected all sides, from his youthful membership in the Muslim Brotherhood in his native Cairo, to his lifelong partnership with the Soviet intelligence service, the KGB.

There is no point here in rewriting the history of the PLO and its longest-serving leader, which authoritative historians and journalists have already covered in detail.[603] What is presently of concern is the transfer to, and acquisition of, the Soviet art of terror by the Palestinian movement, and the role played in turn by this movement as a test-tube experiment for which methods worked and which did not—the lessons learned by its Soviet sponsors, by the movement itself, and by the Arab and Muslim world as well. For one of the keys to unlocking the mysteries and the complexities of modern jihad is the Palestinian cause célèbre.

The notion of "terrorism" as a series of more or less connected individual attacks carried out especially against civilians is an utter misnomer, a misleading label that warps and disguises the nature of the phenomenon beyond recognition. Terrorism is not the list of discrete bombings, gunning, knifings, hostage-takings and homicides perpetrated by small groups or networks of groups to protest this or that grievance or obtain redress. The Palestinian movement learned especially from its Soviet partners and sponsors what terror in the modern sense is. In the Soviet panoply of statecraft, terror was an instrument aimed at shaking, destabilizing, demoralizing, and cowing into submission an opponent one is not able or willing to attack frontally. The enemy's power will be eroded, rather than broken in one or several decisive battles, but in the end, or so the doctrine goes, the indirect approach will annihilate the enemy's will—the concept is Clausewitzian through and through.

This doctrine is a standard tenet of Marxist-Leninist doctrine: it is the "people's war," whose chief instrument is terror. Let us examine the Soviet conception of terror before advancing to people's war. Lenin rejected individual terrorism, such as was practiced by the *Narodniki* and the Socialist Revolutionaries

(S.R.) of Russia. But he repeatedly pointed out that rejecting terrorism out of principle was "philistine." To receive his license of approval, terrorism had to be part of an overall, concerted plan of action concocted by the party. As he wrote in *Left-Wing Communism*, "Of course, we rejected individual terror only on grounds of expediency, whereas people who were capable of condemning 'on principle' the terror of the French Revolution, or in general the terror employed by a victorious revolutionary party which is besieged by the bourgeoisie of the whole world, had always been ridiculed and laughed in scorn by revolutionaries."[604] In 1916, he emphasized: "We do not at all oppose political killing." So little did he, indeed, that the Bolsheviks in power launched a civil war and terror of proportions hitherto unknown in human history. The history of the Russian Civil War is one of countless atrocities perpetrated by both sides; but the very special contribution of the Bolsheviks was the systematic and deliberate mass murder of civilians not for what they did, or even for what they believed, but for what they were, from a "class standpoint." In civil wars throughout history, the opponent has been cruelly attacked on grounds of his belonging to the other camp, and on grounds of his religion: no innovation there. But the Bolshevik political police, the Cheka, launched a methodical campaign of extermination against the "bourgeois" class—men, women, old and young. The Cheka spent the day arresting the "guilty," and the night slaughtering them by the dozens and the hundreds, in the local or regional headquarters of the organization—a bullet in the neck, and mass graves in the forest.[605] Every leader and member of the party shared Lenin's concept. Trotsky even wrote a proudly vehement glorification of terror, *Terrorism and Communism*, which equated revolution with war, and terror with both. "The main object of revolution, as of war, is to break the will of the foe … if required, by terrorism."[606]

What distinguishes the totalitarian regimes of the twentieth century from their predecessors in despotism is that the terror they applied on their way to power did not abate as their grip on power consolidated; it worsened. Terror became a bureaucratically organized activity, sanctioned by parodies of laws and caricatures of tribunals. Mass graves were pushed eastward, to the archipelago of the Gulag. The terrorization of society paradoxically reached a climax after the 1934 Bolshevik Party congress that had named itself "The Victors' Congress." The show trials of the mid-1930s presented terror in iconic form. They incarnated terror's "crime and punishment' in the form of a bloodthirsty morality tale: anyone opposing even in the secret of his own mind the untrammeled rule of Stalin was a dead man. The terrible years of the great purges saw terror breaking into families and mowing people down by the hundreds of thousands. Society was truly terrorized.[607] Marx's analytical concept that "violence is the great midwife of history" had now turned to a prescriptive mandate. Just as the medieval millenarians had demanded "torrents of blood," the Goddess Revolution wanted its innumerable pounds of flesh. An Italian terrorist of the 1970s who was a linear descendent of Bolshevik terror wrote: "Violence is the auroral, immediate, vigorous affirmation of the necessity for Communism (…) A live animal, ferocious with his enemies, savage in its considerations of itself and its passion—that is how we like to foresee the constitution of a Communist dictatorship."[608] Terror as a permanent tool of statecraft: this is what the Soviets bequeathed their students. Rather than any particular tactics employed, this is the nature of "terrorism,"—the piecemeal if spectacular killing of civilians designated as the enemy of a given group.

An eerie similarity unites the Marxist-Leninist and the Islamic world-outlook. For the former, aggression is organic and specific to class society—by definition, the Soviet Union was peaceful, and capitalist societies were aggressors. Likewise, as we have seen in Maududi's and Qutb's writings in particular, Islam is axiomatically peaceful, since it represents the "Peace of Allah," the state of utter perfection on earth, whereas un-Islam is axiomatically troubling the peace by its very existence. The Orwellian inversion is permanent: any move taken in self-defense by the Other is *ipso facto* characterized as an attack on the One. Terror is therefore seen and proclaimed as an instrument in self-defense. He who represents either History and the Will of the People, or Allah's sovereignty "has no other choice," as the expression endlessly recurs in Islamist literature, but resort to terror. For one example in a thousand, the Palestinians judged in Athens for having fired into a crowd at the airport, addressed the United States in a courtroom speech: "We have decided to adopt your criminal methods and teach the first lesson to the people who are undertaking a campaign of extermination against us. We have discovered that in order to make you understand us and realize our right to live, we must begin to defend ourselves against all those who seek to exterminate us."[609]

The Cuban intelligence service (DGI) played an essential role in the grooming of the Palestinian movement. The January 1966 Tricontinental conference was held in Havana, with 513 delegates from 83 Third World groups, Communist countries, and "national liberation" movements. "The Palestinians, soon to become a second great magnetic pole for apprentice terrorists, began sending their own apprentices to Cuba in 1966. Cuban instructors have taught in the Middle East *fedayeen* camps since the early 1970s. The third pole closing the triangle was Soviet Russia itself, arming and training Palestinians on its own territory and turning out professional terrorists by the thousands."[610] This was no "spontaneous" terrorism, but rather state-conceived and state-organized and state-backed terrorism. The Soviet aim was "to do everything possible to exacerbate Arab alienation and anger with the West … and to embark on a vast expansion of subversion and terrorist operations."[611] British analyst Hugh Seton-Watson used another perspective to assess Soviet activities: the Soviets did not seriously expect that regimes similar to theirs would take root in the region, and did not aim at achieving that. "Rather they seemed to be aiming at the preservation and intensification of a state of chaos that could dangerously weaken their American enemy."[612] Defector Vladimir Zakharov confirmed: "The Soviet goal is to keep the conflict boiling on a low fire and to drag the Palestinians along. If everything was settled, how would the Soviets manipulate the Arabs?"[613]

Soviet interest in the Palestinians apparently started in earnest around the same time as their decision to change tack in their Middle Eastern policy. In other words, they went shopping for groups that would fit the particular bill they had in mind. It is likely, but not essential, that Arafat, with some of his Cairo acolytes, had taken part in the World Youth Conference held in Prague in 1956 that the intelligence services of the Soviet block used like a fishing pond for recruitment. The Palestine Liberation Organization had been established in 1964, at the behest of Nasser, at an Arab League Congress—and was meant by the Egyptian *rais* to be a weapon directed primarily against King Hussein of Jordan. By May 1966, the garrulous leader of the PLO, a former Saudi civil servant and Egyptian agent Ahmad Shuqairy, was meeting with Soviet prime minister Aleksei Kosygin. In January 1965, Arafat's *al-Fatah* had been set up by the Syrian intelligence service as a rival to Nasser's operation. Army intelligence deputy chief Ahmad Sweidani recruited would-be fedayeen in Palestinian camps in Lebanon. One of his agents was approached by a member of a group of eight, grandly entitled "Movement for the Liberation of Palestine," of which Arafat was one. On Sweidani's assignment, it carried out its first terrorist raid in January 1965.[614] Bulgaria, Czechoslovakia, and East Germany offered scholarships to members of the General Union of Palestinian Students, Arafat's fief.[615] The Soviet strategists singled out *al-Fatah* as a prime channel for their operations, and "Arafat appears to have been singled out as a focal point to effect that centralization."[616]

There were other groups. Every Arab country insisted on the honor of having its own Palestinian group. Splinter groups abounded, claiming their differences to be ideological (generally Marxist) ones, though in reality they were sectarian, tribal and geographical. George Habash and his Popular Front for the Liberation of Palestine went from being pro-Chinese to being pro-Soviet. He had been sought out by the Tricontinental in Beirut in 1967 and persuaded to go international.[617] Ahmad Jibril and his Palestine Liberation Front were fully KGB from the start. The PFLP was the most adept at absorbing Soviet ideology, or phraseology. It imitated Soviet rhetoric, calling Israel a "bridgehead for old and new imperialism" led by the United States, and it linked Zionism, racism and world imperialism.[618] Nayef Hawatmeh and his Democratic Popular Front for the Liberation of Palestine (PDFLP) "had the longest and the closest ties to the USSR of all the PLO factions."[619] The KGB's own Henri Curiel, a founder of the Egyptian Communist Party, was running an international support and logistics network for Latin American, Arab, European and Japanese terrorists out of Paris.[620]

For their own reasons, each and every Arab state was contributing to the PLO and the myriad splinter or pseudo-splinter groups that gravitated around it. The Saudi monarchy funded the PLO as a gesture of "Arab solidarity," and to prevent Nasser and the other contenders for "Arab leadership,"—the hackneyed but ever-new shibboleth of inter-Arab politics—from cornering the prestige that emanated from the Palestinian "market." The Gulf Emirates, led by the Kuwaitis, funded the PLO for the same reason, and also as an insurance policy to protect themselves: orienting Palestinian and pan-Arab sentiment against Israel was the safer way. Syria, Iraq, and in the end everybody, wanted a piece of the action all the more after 1956, 1967 and 1973 had shown challenging the Israelis militarily to be a guarantee of being badly mauled. The PLO was in effect a joint venture of Soviet and Arab shareholders: there seldom or never was a shareholders' face-to-face meeting; the executive was unreliable and unaudited; but everybody found their interest in its continued promotion.

After the Six Days' War some Soviet statements advocated an "Algerian" strategy against Israel. They suggested that there was a need for the Arabs to prepare for protracted guerrilla warfare and "a real people's war."[621] During the period known as the "Total Liberation Phase" (1969–1974), the PLO culturally and politically found its place in the ranks of other socialist anti-colonial liberation movements.[622] It called for a "people's war," inspired by guerillas in Algeria, China, Cuba, and Vietnam. The PLO's target in Israel, however, was not merely a government but the people themselves. Thus, since the PLO was at war with a society—not an army or simply the post-1967 occupation—every aspect and member of Israeli society was a legitimate target. The PLO's aim "is not to impose our will on the enemy," explained the PLO magazine *Filastin al-Thawra* in 1968, "*but to destroy him in order to take his place ... not to subjugate the enemy but to destroy him.*"[623]

The Palestinians sought to emulate the Algerian revolutionary experience and received expert advice in presenting their case. "Until they had consulted with the Algerians, the main Palestinian propaganda theme was 'throwing the Jews into the sea.' Under Algerian guidance, they introduced different terminology and themes"—such as "democratic, bi-national state" and other fictions.[624] The Palestinians' new mentors underlined that French public opinion and that of France's major allies had played a key role in the outcome of the war, as a result of the FLN's external propaganda. After the Six-Day War, M'hamed Yazid, minister of information in two Algerian wartime governments (1958–1962), imparted the following principles to Palestinian propagandists: "Wipe out the argument that Israel is a small state whose existence is threatened by the Arab states, or the reduction of the Palestinian problem to a question of refugees; instead, present the Palestinian struggle as a struggle for liberation like the others. Wipe out the impression ... that in the struggle between the Palestinians and the Zionists, the Zionist is the underdog. Now it is the Arab who is oppressed and victimized in his existence because he is not only facing the Zionists but also world imperialism."[625]

In 1970, China and Vietnam "reached out" to the PLO, inviting Yasser Arafat and Abu Iyad for a discrete visit. Zhou Enlai received them in China and granted them his country's full support.[626] In Vietnam, where Arafat and Iyad remained for two weeks, they were hosted by General Vo Nguyen Giap, the master of insurrectionary warfare of his generation. It is reported that Abu Iyad asked the Vietnamese why public opinion in the West considered the Palestinian armed struggle to be terrorism, while the Vietnamese struggle enjoyed praise and support. In response, the Vietnamese counseled the PLO to work for their goals in phases, which would conceal their real purpose, permit strategic deception, and give the appearance of moderation. They also coached the Palestinians on the manipulation of the American news media. Giap exhorted Arafat: "Fight by any method which can achieve victory.... If regular war can do it, use it. If you cannot win by classical methods, don't use them. Any method which achieves victory is a good one. We fight with military and political means and with international backing."[627] Abu Jihad, who later ran the PLO's military operations, had already visited China and North Vietnam, where he studied the strategy and tactics of guerilla war. He testified that these visits affected his military thinking for years to come to such an extent that he later preached the need for "a people's liberation war."[628] *Al-Fatah* translated the writings of Giap, Mao and Che Guevara into Arabic.[629]

The Soviets had unexpectedly found their panacea. Even though they were involved up to their eyeballs in funding, training, arming, supporting Palestinian terror; even though they provided it with permanent media, political and diplomatic cover, with sanctuary and every resource imaginable, Moscow could still deny its own "direct" involvement. The very chaos that the PLO was—this Brownian motion of fiercely competing rivals who literally raced for the honor of killing—favored Soviet designs, as it helped obfuscate the central strategy and role of the mastermind Arafat was meeting on a weekly basis with Soviet ambassador Aleksandr Soldatov, "generally regarded as a leading expert on urban guerrilla warfare," whose previous posting had been in Cuba.[630] The PLO was a major hub for Soviet operations, and under Soviet protection, was able to transfer Soviet methods and concepts to the entire region, bypassing borders and states that were often the prisoner of their declaratory pro-Palestinian stance (until the PLO crossed the line, and the Arab supporters slaughtered the Palestinians with gusto and in great numbers—the game of balance was fragile). The use of an endless string of soubriquets which all included the words "Palestine," "liberation," "democratic," or more colorful Arabic words, was but more sand in the eyes of the credulous beholders. For whoever wished to see with their eyes, there was of course no obfuscation or confusion; but the West's general attitude was to accept the Soviets' bold-faced lies: why compromise and endanger *détente* over a few casualties in the Middle East, or even in Europe?

A few days after the Shah's flight and Khomeini's return, in February 1979 Arafat arrived in Tehran. His retinue chanted: "Today Iran, tomorrow Palestine!" Arafat's association with Khomeini had begun in 1970 when the Ayatollah was an exile in Iraq.[631] A great many Iranian revolutionaries had trained in Palestinian camps in Lebanon, including Khomeini's own son.[632] The PLO had lent assistance to Musa al-Sadr's new paramilitary force, which later turned into Hezbollah's military wing. They had exchanged personnel. In November 1979, shortly after the takeover of the U.S. Embassy in Tehran, Arafat had ordered all *Fatah* cadres to help the Iranian Revolution—with terror operations in particular. The PLO had lent many of its Lebanese assets to Iran, the most effective one being Imad Mugniyah of the PLO's elite Force 17. Mugniyah was an important *Fatah* intelligence figure in his own right, and later headed Hezbollah's terror apparatus.[633] It was *Fatah* and Iranian intelligence that planned and organized the 1983 destruction of the U.S. Embassy in Beirut and the October bombing of the Marine Corps barracks. Arafat had not been mendacious when he had declared on his arrival in Tehran in 1979: "The path we have chosen is identical; we are moving forward on the same path; we are fighting the same struggle, the same revolution; our nation is one, we have always lived in the same trenches for the same goal and the same slogan, Our slogan is: we are all Muslims; we are all Islamic revolutionaries, all fighting for the establishment of one body of Islamic believers. We will continue our struggle against Zionism and move towards Palestine alongside the Iranian revolutionaries."[634] When Khomeini set up a three-man committee to create the Iranian terror network under the leadership of Hodjatoleslam Fazlallah Malahati, several PLO-trained advisers served in a senior capacity in the venture.[635]

The PLO was the great educator of Middle Eastern jihad, the principal transmitter of the Soviet art of terror. The lessons learned were of primordial importance for the jihadis, and were duly assimilated and replicated in years and decades to come. Arafat and his companions taught that violence was glamorous; that maximalism, an all-or-nothing policy, paid off because it frightened Western leaders; that "blood and iron" was the only way; and that "armed struggle restores a lost personal and national identity. An identity taken by force… can only be restored by force."[636]

Arafat applied Guevara's concept of the revolutionary *foco* to all the places he succeeded to dominate for a time, whence hords of terrorists then went to plague other countries, whether in Europe or the Middle East.

Arafat relentlessly explored and pushed the limits of lawlessness, as in the case of the "Black September" movement which he created, as yet one more terror group "which I do not control"—the group was made up entirely of *Fatah* intelligence personnel, using *Fatah*'s facilities and funds![637] He showed that armed gangs were above any law, order and authority, any tradition and norm: the Cause was "sacred" and therefore surpassed any conceivable human and divine conception. Few crimes were not committed in the name of the Cause under his authority. "The PLO was free of all checks and accountability, secular or religious. There were neither written nor custom-established laws to which the rulers had to refer."[638] The absence of any territorial parameters allowed the PLO to set up [quasi-military] facilities in many countries and endowed it with a larger potential for the unacceptable without the possibility of any retribution from the society of nations."[639]

Arafat showed the power of egregious threats. In the summer of 1995, he stated to his Israeli interlocutor: "I know there are two ways to reach a Palestinian state, through the negotiating table and through a war of independence. We can accept a lot of casualties, 30,000 martyrs. Can you accept 500 Israeli soldiers killed?"[640]

Arafat showed how timorous the most famed Western leaders were, and how they could be made to pay ransom. European governments freed imprisoned killers as their planes were being hijacked and their nationals kidnapped and slaughtered. European airlines—Air France, Lufthansa and others—submitted to being racketed by the PLO so that their planes would not get into trouble. The British Foreign Office, the Austrian chancellor, socialist Bruno Kreisky, the Socialist International leader Willy Brandt, the U.S. Department of State and every French president fell over themselves to make nice to the PLO and pretend that they believed Arafat's solemn assurances that he condemned terrorism. Henry Kissinger wrote in 1973: "The PLO had potential for causing trouble all over the Arab world; we wanted it to be on its best behavior during the early stages of our approaches to Egypt and while we were seeking Saudi support."[641] Recently declassified archives have shown that the U.S. Government had direct and incontrovertible evidence of Arafat's personal orchestration of terror against the United States but chose to ignore it for diplomatic reasons.[642]

Arafat also unwittingly taught another lesson which the jihadis assimilated: he was—his people were—the prisoners of their own web of delusion. They had conjured up a maze of fiction which they mistook for reality, and then willed themselves to act according to this self-deception. When Arafat clashed with reality and lost—as he always did, in Jordan, in Lebanon, in Tunis, in Ramallah—he invented new fictions that further alienated him and his faithful from reality by explaining away their failures. But it was also the case that "despite actual failure, he achieved symbolic success by persuading his followers that it had been a victory."[643]

In brief, Arafat demonstrated that a high risk, high reward strategy paid off. He operationally established a new price/earning ratio (PER) for terror: For the PLO, the expense required to win the kind of victories it craved was minimal; for its enemies, the expense to be incurred to hunt the PLO down was huge, the benefits always tenuous in the short term that Western politics, especially, indulged in.

The PLO was the first school and its chief the headmaster of international jihad. The rewards for this unending series of crimes were international accolade, Arafat's pistol-wearing appearance at the United Nations' General Assembly of 1974, and, twenty years later, the Oslo Agreements with a Nobel Peace Prize thrown in. In 1966, in his message to the first conference of the Tricontinental, Che Guevara had said: "We must above all keep our hatred alive and fan it to paroxysm. Hate as a factor of struggle, intransigent hate of the enemy, hate that can push a human being beyond his natural limits and make him a cold, violent, selective and effective killing machine."[644]

Osama bin Laden's aide Abu Ubeid al-Qurashi reported that the model for the September 11, 2001, operation had been the PLO's Munich massacre of the Israeli Olympics athletes. "Munich," he averred, "was the perfect media victory."[645]

PART III
MODERN JIHAD AS TERROR

Futuwwah, Not Netwar

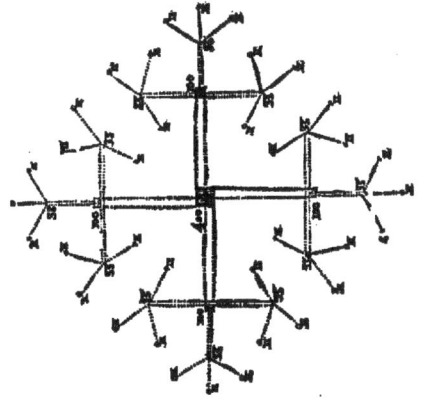

Much has been written since 2001 about al-Qaeda and international Islamic terrorism. The jihadis' use of the Internet and the apparent decentralization of their operations have led to an analysis of modern jihad and jihadi warfare as "networks." The diagram above was published in 1660 in *La Description d'Ukraine* by Guillaume Le Vasseur de Beauplan. It illustrated the way in which 400 mounted Tatar warriors deployed in the Eurasian steppe.[646] This was "a Tatar strategy for hiding a troop of horsemen in the steppe.... Four hundred men would divide into successively smaller squads and then meet at a prearranged rendezvous. The trails of the smaller groups would soon disappear from the steppe grass leaving no trace for enemy scouts to follow."[647]

Allegorically, the diagram suggests that we may seek some of the organizational and sociological "secrets" of today's jihadis in the historical structures of the societies that generated them, rather than in the silicon instruments they use. It shows a remarkable ability to scatter forces and grant them great initiative and flexibility, based on what modern military lingo calls "commander's intent," or, in the classical, nineteenth century German conception, *Auftragstaktik*: the ability of the lower echelons of the officer corps to fathom the strategic sense of the plan they are part of, and take their local decisions within that general framework. Sir Basil Liddell Hart had already pointed out that remarkable characteristic of the Mongol war machine.[648] "To a unique degree, [the Mongol armies] had attained ... 'intellectual discipline.'... The supreme command was in the hands of the Emperor; but once the plan was decided upon, the subordinate generals executed the actual operations without interference and with but the rarest communication with the supreme command...." The 10,000-strong *touman* was capable of acting as an independent force. Enormous flexibility was allowed in the execution. Further, "all Mongol campaigns... [were] prepared for by the employment of an extensive spy system, combining propaganda among the enemy peoples with a wonderful service of information.... The Mongols were the pioneers of [the] attack on the rear."

If the hypothesis presented in the first part of this study regarding the "Nomadic way of war" is correct, the same principles apply here, with minor variations. All tribally organized societies past the primitive stages of human existence generate similar modes of thought, organization and action. Much of al-Qaida is organized along familial, clan and tribal lines.[649] The analyst should look into the traditional modes of organization of paramilitary action in the Arab and Muslim world. For the default modes of organization inscribed in a culture's genetic code are the first to be implemented, since everybody knows how to practice them, and they require little training or education. After all, this is the way "things are done here."

From the times of Classical Islam, in much of the *umma*—Syria, the "Jazirah" (Arab Iraq), Persian Iraq, Khurasan—various bodies of townsmen were organized on a more or less permanent militia basis. Sometimes these were sectarian groups. Sometimes they represented the lower-class elements in the towns but were more or less tied to the established authorities. They formed centers of power to be reckoned with, if they could be effectively mobilized.[650] "Many townsmen came to be organized in socially conscious bodies called most frequently, in Arabic, the *futuwwah*, or men's clubs, ceremonially devoted to the manly virtues. The word *futuwwah*, literally 'young manhood,' expresses manly ideals of comradely loyalty and magnanimity (the term was taken from the Bedouin tradition but was given a special meaning when used to render urban notions...)."

At first, *futuwwah* was mainly applied to upper-class organizations, but gradually it evolved downward. A parallel may be drawn with the boisterous, rowdy "circus factions" of the Byzantine Empire—lower-class sportive men's clubs that doubled as rent-a-crowd riff-raff for politico-theological factions of the Byzantine power games. Likewise the *futuwwah* which had "militia potentialities; they affected peculiarities of dress and were sometimes even referred to likewise as 'the young men.'... Some of the men's clubs were dedicated entirely to sports, others more to mutual aid. Occasionally the members lived, or at least ate, in a common clubhouse. They were formed among several different social strata; "probably some were essentially youth gangs, bands of adolescents and young men asserting their personal independence, while (at least later) some were general tradesmen's associations." It may seem almost impossible to deal with such groups under one heading, but... there must have been an unbroken spectrum of such organizations, from one extreme form to another; and certain sorts of ideals and expectations were acknowledged by most of them," and their common role was their ability to function as the matrix for urban militias.

A common feature to all *futuwwah* was an unconditional loyalty of the members to one another, and some sort of private ritual: the initiate received investiture. "In each town there were likely to be several independent *futuwwah* clubs, each of which kept jealously separate from the others, claiming alone to represent true *futuwwah*. Each such club, then, was closely organized into smaller units, within which the ceremonial life chiefly took place, and it was expected that each *futuwwah* man should be unquestioningly obedient to the head of his particular unit." The clubs "so strongly stressed the ties of mutual loyalty among the club members that other social ties might be disregarded; some clubs even insisted on their members cutting the ties to family, and admitted only bachelors; this would be especially true of those that could be called youth gangs. At the same time, they prided themselves on their ethical standards, particularly their hospitality; those whose members were substantial tradesmen might be first to offer hospitality to strangers in town." One may infer that the *futuwwah* clubs were a highly important network and networking organization—more of which later.

"The *futuwwah* naturally tended to supplement an interest in sports with a degree of military discipline; and such discipline was normally directed at least potentially against the established powers.... *Futuwwah* members readily took to bearing arms, allegedly to defend at need their *futuwwah* brethren. At times *futuwwah* clubs carried out military expeditions on behalf of their ideals—while at other times they carried out riots which frightened wealthier elements in a town. When riots did occur, some made a point of plundering only the houses of the rich.… Even their opponents credited them with a strict code of honor in such matters. Some clubs undertook 'protection rackets.'… Sometimes even the criminal and beggar elements of a town seem to have assimilated their organizations to the *futuwwah*; indeed, such elements were likely to be more tightly organized than were more established groups.… [*Futuwwah* clubs] always were potentially at odds with the established order controlled by the notables."

Marginal, *futuwwah* could be influential. Rebellious, they were connected to powers. Underground, they could be called on. Bridges existed. "Many of the [trade and craftsmen's] guilds seem to have been organized as *futuwwah* clubs—and they maintained an appropriately independent spirit." Further, "The *futuwwah* guilds gained spiritual stability to support such a role through a close association with Sufism. Even in the High Caliphal Period, many Sufis had adopted some of the *futuwwah* language for expressing loyalty and magnanimity.… Some writers interpreted the *futuwwah* as a sort of lesser Sufi way for those unable to achieve the full mystical way." The *futuwwah* had become, Hodgson concludes, at least in some places, "essentially the Sufi dimension of guild organization."

The association between *futuwwah* and Sufism is crucial, as Sufism developed as the dimension of popular devotion in Islam that was unfulfilled by the formalism of the *ulama*'s dry and legalistic version of Islam. Sufism—which took time to be accepted in the mainstream of Sunni orthodoxy—developed as an underground, or at least parallel form of religious organization, and always retained this character. From its early beginnings, ca. the middle of the tenth century, Sufis organized themselves in the form of many "schools," or rather, Sufi masters, the *pîrs*, acquired disciples and organized orders (or brotherhoods), the *tariqas*, from a word that means "ways." The *tariqas* "were loosely organized bodies of *pîrs* and *murids* [followers, disciples] following well-defined and even hierarchically-controlled 'ways' of mystical discipline, each with its rituals, its chiefs, and (of course) its endowments. These were founded on the relationship between master and disciple."[651]

Further, "the *tariqa* orders were many of them international and at least at first there was a certain subordination of *pîrs* and *khaniqahs* [Sufi house] at a distance to the headquarters of the head of the order—usually at the founder's tomb. In this way, the several *tariqas* formed a flexibly interlocking network of authorities, which paid no attention to the political frontiers of the moment and was readily expandable into new areas." Sufism and Sufi orders thus were a flexible, international network, sustaining popular devotion and high mysticism, but also representing an alternative social outlook.

Futuwwah, guilds and Sufi order are facets of similar phenomena—secret societies. A secret society, with esoteric codes, was endowed with "its own institutions, mores, hierarchies and secret values, its beliefs, its more or less strange non- or infra-Islamic local rituals.... [T]his esoteric proclivity inherent in every self-enclosed grouping... [was] fostered by contacts with the leading political secret societies: Batinites, Qarmats, who more or less leaned toward a terrorism that was all at once anti-Sunni in religious affairs, anti-Caliphal in political affairs, and opposed to big landowners in social-economic terms. "[T]he world of craftsmen and trades was ...closely related to the criminal underworld," but, being rooted in above-ground commerce and production, it gradually purified the thieves' honor code—"honor and brotherhood, succor to the weak and luckless"—and "exalted it into esoteric and initiatic yearnings."[652]

Field studies would urgently be required today to ascertain whether any such form of organizations have been or are connected to jihadi terror groups. After all, there is extensive evidence of the association of bandits, outlaws, and clandestine guilds of brigands and thugs with modern revolutionary movements. Stalin recruited Russian organized crime to work with the Bolsheviks.[653] Mao Zedong was intimately connected to various Triad gangs.[654] Marxist historian Eric Hobsbawm even devoted a book to the glorification of the coalescence of outcasts, outlaws and revolutionaries in the form of what he called "social bandits."[655] Many reports have been filed regarding the dealings between al-Qaeda, Hezbollah and other Islamists on the one hand, and drug, diamond and smuggling gangs on the other.[656] In periods of great social dislocation and of ensuing *anomie,* the lower depths rise up to the surface, and tie up with elements in society they would not have known or associated with under normal circumstances—just as the *futuwwah* used to do. Criminal individuals and organizations that have already broken with the standard norms of social behavior and violated the usual respect for the law, the property and the life of others can easily slide into the personality and the behavior of the "political" criminal and terrorist. The borderline between revolutionary terrorist and criminal killer is so gray that it has been crossed back and forth many a time by both sides during the twentieth century's totalitarian and terror wars.

A How-To of Modern Jihad: Algeria

"[A] section of our opinion… thinks obscurely that the Arabs have acquired the right somehow to slit throats and to mutilate."

ALBERT CAMUS

"We must above all keep our hatred alive and fan it to paroxysm. Hate as a factor of struggle, intransigent hate of the enemy, hate that can push a human being beyond his natural limits and make him a cold, violent, selective and effective killing machine."

ERNESTO "CHE" GUEVARA

The Soviets had strongly advised the Palestinian movement to emulate the "Algerian model." By forcing the French out of Algeria, the Algerian insurrection had been a signal success. It had become the poster boy, as it were, of the anti-imperialist, anti-colonialist struggle of the "oppressed and exploited people"—the living embodiment, in other words, of Leninist ambitions; the Baku Congress come to life. After the victory of the Viet Minh against the French Army in 1954, the Algerian war was the next great nexus of the Third World revolt against "capitalism." Support for the Algerian cause was the main headline at the 1955 Bandung Conference of the Non-Aligned Movement. Propaganda poured out of Nasser's Cairo, notably on the waves of "Voice of the Arabs" radio, and along with the multitudinous organs of pan-Arabism, incessantly drummed up the glories of the Algerian FLN.

The victory of the Vietnamese Communists—who consistently posed as nationalists—had been for Arabs and for Muslims a great and heartening example of the "small oppressed people" throwing off the yoke of a "great Western power." It was as much myth as reality—the cover and sanctuary accorded the Viet Minh by Russia and China had been crucial to their victory—but it gave Muslim revolutionaries great confidence that the world and history were going their way. Although the Vietnam War was inspiring, however, it was emotionally remote: culturally and intuitively, Arabs and Muslims had little in common with Ho Chi-Minh's cohorts. They were able to learn from them to some extent, but conditions and traditions in Asia were far-off. The war waged by fellow-Arabs and fellow-Muslims in Algeria was much closer to their hearts; it was easier to understand and easier to imitate. During his first trip to postwar Algeria, Arafat's oldest companion Abu Iyad confirmed that the Algerian "revolution," for the Palestinian movement, "symbolized the success we dreamed of."[657]

The Algerian War was presented internationally as a national liberation movement. Moscow broadcast it as such and foreign correspondents were writing it; but to Algerians, it was a jihad. The FLN's initial proclamation of November 1954: "To the Algerian People" announced the "launch [of] the true revolutionary struggle" and made it clear that it was "freeing itself from any possible compromise." It stated its goal as "national independence through …the restoration of the Algerian state, sovereign, democratic and social, within the framework of the principles of Islam." It also proposed external objectives, "internationalization of the Algerian conflict," and the "pursuit of North African unity in its national Arab-Islamic context." The message was clear: Christians and Jews would be *dhimmis* in the projected new Algeria, and the Berbers, a large proportion of the population, would be second-class persons.[658] The name of FLN's principal newspaper, to make the point explicit, was *al-Moudjahid*.

Arab and Islamic, the insurgency did not hide its colors—at home. "When the Algerian revolution calls itself Arab, it concerns a reaction—of a cultural-linguistic nature … —against the influence of the French, or more generally, Western culture. When the Algerians accentuate their Arab civilization and ethnic origins, it is an attempt to give a content … to a nationalism which is still too new to be able to set itself up as autonomous in any other way than by opposing the cultural presence of France.… When it calls itself Muslim … 'Islamism,' then consists in showing that a certain feeling of equity, of solidarity, of social justice, is common to the teaching of the Prophet and to Socialist conviction; at a more subtle level it is maintained that the revolution is nothing more than the modern way of realizing the aims of religion."[659]

Since the FLN leadership was more pragmatic than ideological, a mix of Islam and Marxism, or rather of Leninist techniques, was characteristic.[660] "Essentially inward-turned the FLN leaders as a whole do not impress one as having been well-read on revolutionary practice and theory; if they had absorbed the techniques of the Viet Minh, it was through the direct experiences some had had as members of the ill-fated French forces in Indochina."[661] The "Nine Historical," the group of leaders that launched the insurrection, "deeply admired Ho Chi Minh."[662] They were shortly to be Mao's guests of honor in Beijing, and "placed ostentatiously ... to the right of Mao" for the October 1 Revolution Day parade.[663] Tito's Yugoslavia gave "staunch support both in arms and on international platforms."[664] And, as soon as Fidel Castro came to power, "the Cubans were counted among the warmest friends of the Algerians."[665] The leading theoretical voices in the FLN were the former Communist Ammar Ouzegane, who was especially close to Ahmed Ben Bella, and Frantz Fanon, the Gnostic inspiration for Ali Shariati.

As might be expected, there was a significant Nazi contribution to the FLN. A number of FLN cadres were former Nazis, like Mohammed Said, leader of the *wilaya 3* (one of the six regions into which the FLN had divided its operations), who had joined the Muslim SS Legion formed by the Mufti of Jerusalem, Haj Amin al-Husayni, during World War II. "In 1943, he was parachuted into Tunisia as an *Abwehr* [German military intelligence]." Always coiffed with a Wehrmacht steel helmet, he made no secret about his wartime commitment: "I believed that Hitler would destroy French tyranny and free the world."[666]

The FLN carried out its jihad by way of three principal means: the first was the systematic slaughter of Algerian Muslims to show everybody, French and Muslims, who was boss; the second was atrocious terror against the French *pied noirs* (native to Algeria); the third was to court support from the international Communist movement, the Non-Aligned and all Westerners who for whatever reasons found it convenient or expedient to support the future winners against the French.

The first act of the Algerian War occurred nearly ten years before its effective outbreak, in 1945 In the city of Setif, on V.E.-Day, graffiti on the walls loudly proclaimed: "Muslims, awaken!" "It's the Muslim flag that will float over North Africa!" "*Français*, you will be massacred by the Muslims!" A report on those days' events states: "As violence erupted, small groups of killers, the scent of blood in their nostrils, now fanned out by taxi, bicycle or even on horseback into the surrounding countryside, spreading the word that a general jihad ... had broken out.... For five dreadful days the madness of demonstrators run amok, killing, rape and pillage, continued.... The accepted casualty reports made grisly reading: 103 Europeans murdered and another hundred wounded, a number of women brutally raped.... Many of the corpses were appallingly mutilated: women with their breasts slashed off, men with their severed sexual organs stuffed into their mouths...."[667]

When the insurrection started for real, on All Saints' Day 1954, its first action was highly symbolic: a bus was stopped in the middle of the countryside. FLN fighters ordered the passengers to disembark, and killed two civilians, a left-leaning French schoolteacher and a Muslim notability. The symbol could not have been clearer.

"At first, the [FLN] terrorism was aimed mainly at the Muslims, in order to dissuade them from cooperating with the French authorities or to enroll them by force, and to make them respect, out of fear, the orders given to the population."[668] It was a permanent, deliberate, systematic modus operandi through the eight years of "a savage war of peace." The doctrine was very similar to that developed in Latin America by Brazilian Communist leader Carlos Marighela: "It is necessary to turn political crisis into armed conflict by performing violent actions that will force those in power to transform the political situation of the country into a military situation. That will alienate the masses, who, from then on, will revolt against the army and the police and blame them for this state of things." Marighela's strategy demanded blind terrorism to polarize and exacerbate the situation, which would eradicate the "soft center." In effect, he wanted to create violent persecution against those in whose name he was supposed to fight.[669] Marighela was the accomplished Communist Gnostic: he knew better than them what was good for them, and how to get there, in the name of the Doctrine that he (not them) knew to be True. The same went for the FLN. As we shall now see, they needed to terrorize the Algerian masses into becoming subservient to their "saviors."

By the winter of 1954–1955, "Fear was everywhere. The bodies of loyal Muslims would be discovered, often appallingly mutilated or having been subjected to slow deaths." For instance, "the village policeman was found with his throat slit and eyes gouged out, a scrap of paper signed 'FLN' pinned to his skin."[670] By 1955, "[t]error had taken hold" in the whole country, wrote the French governor General Jacques Soustelle. French counter-measures diverted the FLN from hardened or risky targets. "Brutal murders of Muslim 'friends of France,' from caids [judges] to humble village constable, multiplied, totaling 88 in April [1955] alone, with a similar number hideously mutilated—as terrible warning to the rest." The FLN ordered all to stop smoking or drinking. The penalty for a first offense was the cutting off of lips or nose; for the second one, the slitting of the throat."[671] The massive use of the weapon of terror and savagery propelled the FLN to world-wide fame, resulting in the new organization being invited to the Bandung conference. The conference condemned colonialism in particular and in general, and then unanimously adopted an Egyptian motion proclaiming Algeria's right to independence. There the FLN leaders met Ho Chi Minh, ever ready to supply his own recipes, among which mass murder and terror featured prominently. Five months later, the "Algerian Question" was formally inscribed on the agenda of the United Nations General Assembly. Terror paid. Soustelle, an old left-winger, pointed out that the FLN "never sought to attach the rural populations to their cause by promising them a better life, a happier and freer future; no, it was through terror that they submitted them to their tyranny."[672] The initiation ritual for new recruits was the killing of a designated Muslim 'traitor' or French petty official. "In their actual techniques of liquidation FLN operatives consciously endeavored to achieve the gruesome. A loyal *garde-champêtre* [rural constable] would be found tied to a stake, his throat cut...." Marching orders were: "Kill the *caids*.... Take their children and kill them. Kill all those who pay taxes and those who collect them. Burn the houses of Muslim NCOs away on active service.... Liquidate all personalities who want to play the role of *interlocuteur valable*.... Kill any person attempting to deflect the militants."[673] Over the first two and a half years of the war, the FLN killed six Muslims for every one Frenchman. It was not even only pro-French "collaborators" whose death was ordained. In the summer of 1955, the cruel *wilaya* head Ait Amouda, a.k.a. Amirouche, had his forces encircle a *maquis* run by the Algerian National Movement (MNA) in East Kabylia; all 500 guerrillas were slaughtered. In a village near Bougie, (today's Annaba), Amirouche ordered the liquidation of 1,000 or more "dissident" Muslims. Any Muslim beneficiary of land grants in the framework of the French-initiated land reform was ordered to be killed.

At the 1956 "Soummam" leadership summit of the FLN, which adopted a strongly Marxist oriented platform, "indiscriminate terrorism was espoused."[674] On May 31, 1956, the French authorities announced that the *mechta* (village) of Melouza had been the theater of a frightful massacre: "Three nights earlier, the FLN had rounded up every male above the age of 15 from the surrounding area, herded them into houses and into the mosque, and slaughtered them with rifles, pick-axes and knives: a total of 301 in all.... Sickened by the massacre, world opinion ... for a brief time animadverted against the FLN."[675]

The precision is important: anaesthetized by the Holy Cow of "anti-colonialism," press correspondents who covered the war soon reverted to their apologies of the Noble Savage in His struggle against Evil incarnate, and the unspeakable massacre soon faded into oblivion, while every atrocity committed by the French Army—and those were not few—found its place in the automatic pigeonhole that fit the overall narrative. No less a figure than Albert Camus, a leftwing *pied-noir* with a passionate love for Algeria, exploded in saddened anger against "a section of our opinion [which] thinks obscurely that the Arabs have acquired the right somehow to slit throats and to mutilate."[676] Prominent parts of the cult in support of the right to slit throats were Jean-Paul Sartre, who made it into a theory in his 1961 introduction to Frantz Fanon's *Les damnés de la terre*[677] and Simone de Beauvoir, who compared the French Army to the Nazis. Their confederate Francis Jeanson, who organized a logistical support network for the FLN, explained that Stalin's crimes were "made almost unavoidable by the hostility of the entire world." This attitude was not unique to wayward French intellectuals. Prominent British Labour Party left-wing leader Barbara Castle explained on the "Algeria Day" decreed on the Soviet model that "terrorism was the result of repression, not its cause."[678] The Algerian War was indeed a model for much of what was to come.

Arab corpses mattered only if killed by the French. By 1957, the FLN had begun a vicious war in mainland France—against fellow Muslims who opposed the FLN, or were merely neutral, but especially against the MNA. By 1960 this campaign had already claimed several thousand lives, "[T]he killings reached a crescendo as the FLN stepped up its campaign to achieve total ascendancy. Barely a day went by without a corpse fished out of the Seine or found hanging in the Bois de Boulogne …a blanket of terror successfully imposed by the FLN."[679] The climax was reached right after "independence" had been achieved, when anywhere between 30,000 and 150,000 *harkis*, Muslim auxiliaries of the French, and their families, were exterminated by the victorious FLN. In total, it is estimated that if the French killed 141,000 FLN male combatants, the FLN killed 172,000 to 232,000 male Muslims.[680]

The war against Algerian Muslims waged by the FLN was completed by a war of terror carried out against French civilians; Muslims were the softest of targets, only followed by French civilians. After the Battle of Algiers and General Challe's highly successful military campaign, the FLN was liquidated as a military force. Its organized military forces huddled in Tunisia, the prime sanctuary enjoyed throughout the war by the FLN, and stopped trying to cross the mined and electrified "Ligne Morice" erected by the French. In the dying years of the war, terror was as essential to the FLN strategy as it had been in its early years.

Wilaya 2 commanders decided "to launch a total war on all French civilians, regardless of sex and age." Justifying it, the *wilaya* commander Youssef Zighout declared: "To colonialism's policy of collective repression, we must reply with collective reprisals against the Europeans, military and civilian, who are all united behind the crimes committed against our people. For them, no pity, no quarter!"[681] The hapless small town of Philippeville was chosen to highlight this commitment. In August 1955, the FLN mobilized: "The largest possible number of Algerians, even hastily armed with only sticks, pitchforks, axes, sickles and knives, was to be involved." It was a typical mafia tactic: make the people accomplices to the crime, make them burn their bridges. Here is what happened: "Muslims of both sexes swarmed into the streets in a state of frenzied, fanatical euphoria. Grenades were thrown indiscriminately into cafés, passing European motorists dragged from their vehicles and slashed to death with knives or even razors. Altogether, some 26 localities came under sudden attack. The peak of horror was reached at Ain-Abid, 24 miles east of Constantine, and at el-Alia … close to Phlippeville. The attackers [at el-Alia] went from house to house, mercilessly slaughtering all the occupants regardless of sex or age, and egged on by Muslim women with their *you-you* chanting.… In some of the attacked towns, the muezzins even broadcast from their minarets exhortations to slit the throats of women and nurses in the cause of the 'Holy War.'" When the French Army arrived on the scenes, "an appalling sight greeted them. In houses literally awash with blood, European mothers were found with their throats slit and their bellies slashed open.… Children had suffered the same fate, and infants in arms had had their brains slashed out against the wall."[682]

At Ain Abid, an entire *pied-noir* family called Mello perished atrociously: "a 73-year-old grandmother, and an 11-year-old daughter, the farmer killed in his bed, with his arms and legs hacked off. The mother had been disemboweled, her five-days-old baby slashed to death and replaced in her opened womb. There were similar scenes of such revolting savagery in attacks elsewhere that day, and what heightened the horror … was the carefully premeditated planning which clearly lay behind them."[683] Bodies strewed the streets.

French reprisals were atrocious, and the number of Muslims who perished perhaps ten times higher. The FLN had "succeeded:" they ardently desired that a river of blood separate the two communities. It did. The same awful scenario was replayed in the terrible defeat suffered by the FLN with the Battle of Algiers in 1957, which the French won, if at a terrible price. There, the FLN called a general strike, and the French Army broke it. But the 1,400 operatives of the terror network were laying bombs in cafés, dancing bars, at the General Post Office of Algiers. "The casualties of the innocent were … almost equally divided between Muslims and Europeans." Only, in the mind of the jihadis waging total war, "there are no innocents," as the Palestinian Marxist George Habash later said. The bombing campaign "struck equally at ordinary, working-class Muslims and at Europeans."[684] Mass arrests, mass torture: the French military harvested all the actionable intelligence they needed, and nabbed or killed virtually the entire FLN organization, including its leadership. Algiers would be relatively peaceful for several years.

De Gaulle's absolute commitment to liquidate the French presence in Algeria, and to liquidate the war, so as to reshuffle the country's entire foreign policy, tore the guts out of the French military victory. De Gaulle wanted France to be the leader of the Non-Aligned while being covered by the American nuclear umbrella. To be loved by the Third World, the Arab world in particular, which he was going to spend much of his foreign policy efforts attempting, he needed to leave the Algerian theater. Starting negotiations with the FLN demoralized the pro-French forces among the Algerians, who knew they had no mercy to expect from a victorious FLN, infuriated the *pied-noir* community who saw no future under an FLN government, and maddened the officer corps. It led to full parleys, and in 1962, to independence. *"La valise ou le cercueil:"* "Your choice is to pack your bags or get a coffin" was the FLN's promise to the *pieds-noirs*. Here is a typical, all-too-familiar FLN killing in 1961: "they killed a shop inspector in his car, a man who had never done anything to anyone. They sliced open his skull, took out his brains, and carefully placed them on the ground—like a milestone on the roadside."[685]

The great Kabyle writer and friend of Albert Camus Mouloud Feraoun wrote in distraught tones: "There is French in me, there is Kabyle in me. But I have a horror of those who kill.... Vive la France, such as I have always loved! Vive l'Algérie, such as I hope for! Shame on the criminals! Shame on the cheaters! When Algeria lives and raises her head again… it will remember France and all it owes to France." Alas, Feraoun was machine-gunned by those Frenchmen who had become as beastly as their enemy, the OAS. Hopes for the kind of enlightened brotherhood he had in mind had been murdered along with all the civilians. The FLN's view was voiced by Frantz Fanon: "Come now, comrades, the European game has finally ended; we must find something different. We today can do everything, so long as we are not obsessed by the desire to catch up with Europe. Europe now lives at such a mad, reckless pace that she has shaken off all guidance and all reason."[686] This Gnostic *everything is possible, everything is permitted* was indeed the break with what Europe had to offer on its best side, but also an embrace of Europe's worst.

First under the lunatic socialist despotism of Ahmed Ben Bella and then under the implacable military dictatorship of Houari Boumediene, the triumphant new class looted Algeria to the bone. The victorious *mujahdin* of yesterday confiscated power and riches. The new Algeria was ruled under a pale of silent terror where people disappeared and did not come back. It was gradually, but forcibly Arabized—at the expense of the few remaining Europeans, and mostly at the expense of the Berbers of Kabylia—it was Islamicized. The non-Arab, non-Muslim population was increasingly treated as *dhimmis*.

After three decades of misrule that squandered the nations' oil and natural gas wealth, and forced a large part of the population to emigrate–mostly to France!—the youth rose in revolt under the leadership of the only available alternative, the very Islamists that the regime had encouraged to destroy the influence of Western culture. The callous Algerian military leadership was ready to repeat its wartime exploits in order to keep power. In the atrocious civil war of the 1990s, perhaps 150,000 were slaughtered, either by the military or by the Islamists—it was often very difficult to know who the culprits were. The very methods used by the FLN were now repeated either by its heirs or by its challengers, this time without an extraneous third party: villages were exterminated, busses stopped and passengers gunned down or killed by slitting their throats, entire families were murdered during "house visits," babies were slaughtered, thousand of young women were raped, etc. The GIA (*Groupe Islamique Armé*) and the "Salafist Group for Preaching and Combat" had assimilated the lesson taught by the FLN: he who wants to rule must terrorize and despise human life as an incidental instrumentality in his quest for power. The FLN won the Algerian War at the price of "freeing" the country from its most educated and skilled element, of purging a large part of the population, of creating a permanent dictatorship, of making it incapable of sustaining its population, and, perhaps worst of all, of durably imprinting terror as the favored means of political action in the souls of surviving Algerians. This nightmare that haunted the nation without apparent end was the curse of the Algerian War. The means used by the FLN in the accomplishment of their goal predetermined the face of the future Algeria: it was to be an endless repeat of the same nightmare.

This is the model of which Arafat and his friends "dreamt." The Tricontinental, the entire international Left, the Soviet propaganda apparatus, never stopped singing the praise of the Algerian revolutionaries. The Iranian clerics and the lay intellectuals, the entire Palestinian movement, empathized with them and studied their actions. Many of the Soviet-allied networks that supported the rise of Palestinian terror coalesced during the Algerian War (1954–1962). After the victory of the Algerian insurgents, Algiers became a place of pilgrimage for revolutionary kooks, charlatans, academics, Messiahs and killers, Black Panther Eldridge Cleaver and Cuban hero Che Guevara, Nazi international leader François Genoud, old hands from the *Komintern*. By the end of October 1963, some 686 Cuban combatants, equipped with Soviet tanks and artillery, had arrived in Oran to secure the newly established leftist regime of President Ahmed Ben Bella.[687] With Ben Bella's approval, in 1964 Castro entrusted Guevara and some 250 Cuban military advisers to set up a logistics base outside Algiers.

"Strike Terror in the Heart of the Enemy"

"The word 'jihad' conjures up the vision of a marching band of religious fanatics with savage beards and fiery eyes brandishing drawn swords and attacking the infidels wherever they meet them and pressing them with the edge of the sword...."

ABUL ALA MAUDUDI

General Zia ul-Haq took power in Pakistan in 1977 in a coup d'Etat, after a tenure as chief of Army staff, the highest ranking officer in that country's military. A devout Deobandi, Zia maintained a close relationship with Saudi Arabia and the Wahhabi, such that in the terse formulation of compatriot Shahid Mahmud, "If it had been possible, Zia would have imported all the sands of Saudi Arabia to make Pakistan resemble it."[688] Abul Ala Maududi was a political partner, an adviser, a guru.

In 1979, the newly minted dictator wrote a foreword to a book, *The Quranic Concept of War*, published by his subordinate Brigadier S.K. Malik at the latter's behest. Zia's foreword was short and to the point: "I … commend Brigadier Malik's book … to both soldier and civilian alike. *Jihad fil sabil Allah* is not the exclusive domain of the professional soldier, nor is it restricted to he application of military force alone."[689] Former justice minister of Pakistan Allah Bukhsh K. Brohi wrote the preface to the book. "The most glorious word in the vocabulary of Islam is jihad," he intoned.[690] The former advocate-general of Pakistan gave a more than extensive definition of the *casus belli* that must provoke jihad: "When a believer sees that someone is trying to obstruct another believer from traveling on the road that leads to God, [the] spirit of jihad requires that such a man who is imposing obstacles should be prevented from doing so and the obstacles placed by him should also be removed."[691] The definition was exactly that given by Maududi and Sayyid Qutb: just about anything and anyone was liable to fall within the purview of the *casus jihadi*. This is the definition used by Osama bin Laden and the other jihadis: the very existence of the Other and the lowliness of Islam's stature in the world are the causes of jihad. Brohi continued: "Defiance of God's authority by one who is His slave exposes that slave to the risk of being held guilty of treason and such a one, in the perspective of Islamic law, is indeed to be treated as a sort of that cancerous growth on [the] organism of humanity…. It thus becomes necessary to remove the cancerous malformation even if it be by surgical means (if it would not respond to the other treatment), in order to save the rest of humanity."[692] As a result, our Islamic jurist concluded, "The believers have no option, but in sheer self-defense, to wage a war against those who are threatening aggression." To make sure that the point was not missed, he added, "[The Muslims'] role on earth is to communicate the same message of God and his practice (*Sunnah*) which they have inherited from their Prophet and if there be anyone who stifles their efforts and obstructs them from communicating the Message it will be viewed as constituting membership in *darul Harb* and liable to be dealt with as such."[693]

This is a warrant for mass murder. Brigadier Malik supplied the theory, the Quranic concept of war. The ISI and the Army of Pakistan, creators of the Taliban, the power behind the Kashmir jihad, patrons of Mollah Omar and protectors of Osama bin Laden, absorbed it. The book, *The Quranic Concept of War*, was highly commended in the Pakistani military. "Zia's Islamic theory of war written by S.K. Malik has been compulsory course for indoctrination of its army and the ISI [Inter-Service Intelligence, the all-powerful military intelligence service which largely runs the country]," wrote Air Marshal Malik, vice-chief of staff (no relation).

The brigadier, after a long scholastical retreading of quotations from the Quran and *hadith* on the subject, lists the cases in which jihad will be invoked, and must be. They are so extensive as to constitute an unlimited mandate, provided forms are respected. "Punitive, retaliatory and preventive purposes" as well as "unbearable and provocative manner" on the part of the enemy are *casus belli*, while Muslims should "enter into armed hostilities in sympathy with their brethren living in another state," but of course "but only after scrutinizing each case or its own merit and not as a matter of general rule."[694] Quranic rules "revolutionized warfare" and "conferred upon the Muslim armies a complete and total protection and immunity against all the psychological and moral attacks that the enemy could bring to bear upon them.... [They] became immortal and invisible."[695]

So, what is jihad? "Jihad is total strategy," the brigadier answers. It is

> the near-equivalent of total or grand strategy.... Jihad entails the comprehensive direction and application of "force." Jihad is a continuous and never-ending struggle waged on all fronts including political, economic, social, psychological, domestic, moral and spiritual to attain the object of policy. It aims at attaining the overall mission assigned to the Islamic state, and military strategy is one of the means available to it to do so. It is waged at individual as well as collective level; and at internal as well as external front.[696]

Having defined the function of jihad, Malik then defined the aim of jihad:

> The Quranic military strategy thus enjoins us to prepare ourselves for war to the utmost in order to strike terror into the hearts of the enemies, known or hidden, while guarding ourselves from being terror-stricken by the enemy. In this strategy, guarding ourselves against terror is the "Base," preparation for war to the utmost is the "Cause:" while the striking terror into the hearts against the enemies is the "Effect." The whole philosophy revolves there.... In war, our main object is the opponent's heart or soul, our main weapon of offense against this object is the strength of our own souls, and to launch such an attack, we have to keep terror away from our own hearts.[697]

The phrase "strike terror (into the hearts of) the enemies of Allah and your enemies" is a well-known verse from the Quran (8:60). Malik then waxes Sun Zi-like: "So spirited, zealous, complete and thorough should our preparation for war [be] that we should enter the 'war of muscles' having already won the 'war of will.' Only a strategy that aims at striking terror into the hearts of the enemies for the preparation stages can produce direct results."[698] War is peace, and peace is war, he insists. Peacetime preparation for jihad is "vastly more important than the active war."

> [Preparation] must be to the utmost, both in quality and in quantity. It must be a continuous and never-ending process. Preparation should be at the plane of total strategy, that is, jihad and not the military instrument alone.... The lesser the physical resources the greater must be the stress and reliance on the spiritual dimensions of war. Terror struck into the hearts of the enemies is not only a means, it is the end in itself. Once a condition of terror into the opponents' heart is obtained, hardly anything is left to be achieved. It is the point at [which] the means and the end meet and merge. Terror is a means of imposing decision upon the enemy, it is the decision we wish to impose upon him.[699]

Brigadier Malik concludes, in pure Gnostic fashion, with a strong dose of Leninist voluntarism, or Nietzschean *Wille zur Macht*:

> Terror cannot be struck into the hearts of an enemy by merely cutting its lines of communication or depriving it of its route of withdrawal. It is basically related to the strength or weakness of the human soul. It can be instilled only if the opponent's Faith is destroyed. Psychological dislocation is temporary; spiritual dislocation is permanent. Psychological dislocation can be produced by a physical act but this does not hold good of the spiritual dislocation. To instill terror into the heart of the enemy, it is essential … to dislocate his faith. An invincible faith is immune to terror. A weak faith offers inroads to terror.[700]

The mind of jihad has spoken.

CONCLUSION

Modern jihad erupted in full force with the Islamic Revolution in Iran in 1979 in both the Shiite and the Sunni world. It was a reflection, a result and a concentrate of all the main political pathologies of the twentieth century, led by the parade of motley totalitarian ideologies, but transformed by its absorption into the Islamic cultural matrix.

What a striking historical paradox this was: the world of Islam was falling behind the fast-paced progress made by the modern world and those areas of the world that had taken up the challenges of modernity. It was falling behind not only because it did not invent modernity or did not espouse it, but because it actively rejected it. On the other hand, it avidly absorbed the dark shadow of modernity, its evil side—the totalitarian ideologies that sprung up as the corruption of modernity, Bolshevism, fascism, Nazism, post-modernism.

Some parts of the world of Islam accepted at least components of modernity—Turkey in the first place, and others to lesser degrees. These all occurred in "hybrid" civilizational areas outside the Arab core of Islam where those in power accepted to borrow other, more constructive creations of the West. Those who did not went shopping in Europe for nihilism, the destructive hatred and the self-destructive passions that neo-Gnosticism had loosed on the continent.

The European totalitarian ideologies themselves were an echo from older times, a secularized form of pseudo-religion. They were largely the violent spasms that responded to the torments and dislocations of modernity, and were rooted in the medieval, millenarian, apocalyptical, eschatological insurgencies that wreaked havoc in Europe from the eleventh through the early sixteenth century. Just as the medieval sectarians had lived in a "second reality" of their own making, their messianic successors in modern Europe made class or race or state the divinized ordering point of their delusional world. Both the medieval and the modern sectarians shed torrents of blood to bring about their version of perfection on earth.

Likewise, modern jihad, which massively drew on the modern sectarians, has its roots in traditional jihad, and has stirred the tidal messianic hopes of disoriented masses, their dislocated lives, their incensed ruminations, and is twice promising them the Gnostic Paradise, in Allah's kingdom erected on earth, and in Paradise as martyrs. Modern jihad is the modern form of Mahdism. It is Islamic in its cultural idiom, its form and content. There is no firewall between Mahdism and mainstream Islam, since it is all "in the Book," in the Quran, in the vast *hadith* literature, in the *fiqh*, the jurisprudence derived from both, in the folktales and collective memory of Muslim peoples.

Grafted onto a tribal social structure—in the sociology of society, in the structure of the religion, in the minds of its members—a toxic combination of jihad and totalitarianism appeared on the market, conveyed by numerous and complex contacts and cooperation between the European retailers and the Islamic purchasers. It was expressed in and symbolized by the jihadis' worship of violence, their predilection for blood and their cult of death: "We love death more than you love life." This was a society going terminal and descending into a nihilistic frenzy of destruction.

This is the mind of jihad. This is the enemy we are facing in the great war declared on us on September 11, 2001. This is his way of war.

ENDNOTES

1 Andrew G. Bostom, ed., *The Legacy of Jihad: Islamic Holy War and the Fate of Non-Muslims* (Amherst, NY: Prometheus Books, 2005), p. 28.

2 On *taqiyeh*, see Ignaz Goldziher, *Introduction to Islamic Theology and Law* (Princeton, NJ: Princeton University Press, 1981) pp. 180-81.

3 This kind of dishonest "scholarship" has been thoroughly debunked by, *inter alia*, David Cook as well as Andrew Bostom, *loc.cit*. Linguistic legerdemains based on the fact that *jihad* originally means "exertion" are disingenuous at best—as if one claimed that the English words "war" does not mean violent struggle because its Germanic root *werra* means "confusion."

4 On *bida*, unlawful innovation, see *i.a.* Ignaz Goldziher, *op.cit* , esp. pp. 232–245.

5 Laurent Murawiec, *The Mind of Jihad* (Washington, DC: Hudson Institute, 2005), esp. part 3, "The Gnostic Mahdi," pp. 119–168.

6 This irony is identical with that that marked the rebellion of other cultures against modernity. In their book *Occidentalism; The West in the Eyes of its Enemies* (New York: Penguin Press, 2004), Ian Buruma and Avishai Margalit have nicely outlined how massively Japanese, Russian (and Soviet), Chinese and other radical nationalists who upheld the purity, unicity and superiority of their culture's purported "soul," against the materialist, inorganic, inauthentic West: it all came from Fichte and his romantic successors. The thought of course would be anathema to the Islamists, whose extreme ignorance alone protects them from such a shocking acknowledgment.

7 "Jihad made in Western academia" contributed as well, from its post-Marxist, post-modern groves, as we will indicate *passim*.

8 A conception well developed by Dr. Shmuel Bar.

9 Note that the "plasticity" referred to above allowed an egregious violation of the principle of contradiction: while the hijackers were praised as "the magnificent 19," it was stated that Muslims could not possibly have planned and executed the hits. Additionally, since the only way a Muslim may be declared and considered a non-Muslim is *takfir*, and no authority of any sort in the world of Islam had declared any of the terrorists *takfir*, they were indeed Muslims. The credibility of the argument would depend on the declaration having been made that they were apostates.

10 Laurent Murawiec, "Empire? Quel Empire?" in *Le Débat* 133 (janvier-fevrier 2005), Paris.

11 Habakkuk, 1:6–9. King James Version (New York: New American Library, 1974), p. 731.

12 *Ibid.*, p. 183.

13 René Grousset, *L'Empire des steppes: Attila, Genghis Khan, Tamerlan*, (Paris: Payot, 1965), p. 12.

14 The Gobi desert is an example of the landlocked desert. It is "a cheerless solitude of sand, rock or gravel that extends 1,200 miles.... Vegetation is confined to scrub and grassy reeds; the climate is

extreme; icy sandstorms blow furiously in winter and spring. Rain falls but seldom… The Takla-Makan is a smaller Gobi, so swept is summer by choking dust storms that travel across it is tolerable only in winter. The Dasht-I Kavir, or Persian Desert, 800 miles wide, consists less of sand than of water swamps, but [is] dotted with oases…." John Keegan, *A History of Warfare* (New York: Vintage Books, 1994), p. 174.

15 Halford J. Mackinder, *Democratic Ideals and Realities: A Study in the Politics of Reconstruction* (London: Henry Holt & Co., 1919), Reprint (Washington, DC: National Defense University, 1996), pp. 55–56.

16 *Ibid.*, pp. 57, 60.

17 Erik Hildinger, *Warriors of the Steppe: A Military History of Central Asia, 500 B.C. to 1700 A.D.* (New York: Da Capo, 1997), p. 6.

18 Erik Hildinger, *op.cit.*, pp. 5–6.

19 *Ibid*. My emphasis, LM.

20 Miklós Jankovich, *They Rode into Europe: The Fruitful Exchange in the Arts of Horsemanship between East and West* (New York: Charles Scribner's Sons, 1971), p. 23. [*Pferde, Reiter, Völkerstürme*] (Munich: BLV Verlagsges, 1968).

21 Paul Kahn, ed., *The Secret History of the Mongols: The Origin of Chingis Khan* (San Francisco: North Point Press, 1984), esp. 27ff.

22 Robert L. O'Connell, *Of Arms and Men: A History of War, Weapons and Aggression* (Oxford: Oxford University Press, 1989), pp. 98–99.

23 Erik Hildinger, *op.cit.*, pp. 6–8.

24 René Grousset, *op.cit.*, p. 14.

25 Miklós Jankovich, *op.cit.*, p. 66.

26 René Grousset, *op.cit.*, p. 12.

27 *Ibid.*, p. 13.

28 Robert L. O'Connell, p. 100.

29 The distinction between Us and Them is an anthropological constant, which is by no means unique to nomads. Nevertheless, it does not necessarily lead to a license to exterminate wholesale. The Greeks considered the *barbaroi* as lesser, inasmuch as they did not speak Greek; the Chinese equally consider the *yemanren*, the barbarian, as inferior on account of his not participating in the world of Chinese culture: in neither case did the status of barbarian make the latter liable to be slaughtered at will. Settled peoples do not have the same mores as nomads.

30 John Keegan, *op.cit.*, p. 161.

31 René Grousset, *op.cit.*, p. 58.

32 Miklós Jankovich, *op.cit.*, p. 27.

33 B.H. Liddell Hart, *Great Captains Unveiled* (New York: Da Capo, 1996), p. 5.

34 Colin McEvedy and Richard Jones, *Atlas of World Population History* (London: Penguin Books, 1978–1980), pp. 164, 168, 145.

35 Patricia Crone, "The Early Islamic World," *in* Kurt Raablauf & Nathan Rosenstein, *War and Society in the Ancient and Medieval Worlds, Asia, the Mediterranean, Europe and Meso-America* (Cambridge, MA.: Harvard University Press, 1999), pp. 309–332 (314).

36 Stanislav Andreski, *Military Organization and Society* (Berkeley, CA: University of California Press, 1971), p. 33.

37 Halford J. Mackinder, *op.cit.*, p. 70.

38 Erik Hildinger, *op.cit.*, p. 30.

39 See also Gérard Chaliand: "The decisive weapon on the nomadic horseman, since it enables him to harass without risking a frontal fight. The latter only occurs once the opponent has been weakened, unhinged ou thrown into disarray by the assault given by heavy cavalry armed with spears as the Scythians, the Huns' double-edged rapier, the Arabs' saber [curved sword]." *Les Empires nomades: de la Mongolie au Danube, Vè siècle av. J.-C-XVIè siècle* (Paris: Perrin, 1995), p. 54.

40 Herodotus, *Histories*, IV.

41 Erik Hildiger, *op.cit.*, p. 38.

42 Plutarch, *Lives*, "Crassus," VII.

43 Erik Hildiger, *op.cit.*, pp. 46–47.

44 Miklós Jankovich, *op.cit.*, p. 52.

45 Erik Hildiger, *op.cit.*, p. 63.

46 Ammianus Marcellinus, in *The Medieval World: 300–1000,* edited by Norman F. Cantor (New York: Macmillan, 1963), pp. 68–69.

47 "The Huns' conquests were not due to superiority of numbers, but to the mobility of small bands of horse-archers who could concentrate rapidly at any given point, quickly disperse and reconcentrate at another… a cyclonic strategy was developed; operations took the form of whirlwind advances and retirements. Whole districts were laid waste and entire populations annihilated, not only in order to establish a heat of terror which would evaporate opposition, but also to leave the rear clear of all hostile manpower and so to facilitate withdrawals. The tactics adopted may be defined as… fury, surprise, elusiveness, cunning and mobility… 'Try twice, turn back the third time' is as much a Hunnish as a Turkoman proverb, and as Amédée Thierry points out: 'The nomads, unlike ourselves, do not consider flight a dishonor. Considering booty of more worth than glory, they fight only when they are certain of success. When they find their enemy in force, they evade him to return when the occasion is more opportune.'" J.F.C. Fuller, *op.cit.*, p. 288.

48 Erik Hildiger, *op.cit.*, p. 77.

49 Marco Polo, *The Travels of Marco Polo the Venetian* (New York: AMS Press, 1968), p. 136.

50 Gérard Chaliand, *op.cit.*, pp. 131–33.

51 René Grousset, *op.cit.*, pp. 284–285.

52 *Ibid.*, p. 128.

53 Erik Hildiger, *op.cit.*, p. 13.

54 Robert L. O'Connell, *op.cit.*, p. 100.

55 René Grousset, *op.cit.*, p. 114.

56 *Ibid.*, p. 97.

57 *Ibid.*, p. 291.

58 *Ibid.*, pp. 291–309, *passim*.

59 *Ibid.*

60 *Ibid.*, p. 429.

61 *Ibid.*, p. 507.

62 *Ibid.*, pp. 507–510.

63 "Whole districts were laid waste and entire populations annihilated, not only in order to establish a heat of terror which would evaporate opposition, but also to leave the rear clear of all hostile manpower and so to facilitate withdrawals." J.F.C. Fuller, *op.cit.*, 288.

64 "Timur of Samarkand… operated on a very large scale indeed, conquered powerful states and sacked great cities…. His operations were… little more than gigantic raids. It was this very propensity for raiding that made the steppe people very difficult to deal with" Erik Hildiger, *op.cit.*, p. 12.

65 Elmer C. May, Gerald P. Stadler, John F. Votaw, *Ancient & Medieval Warfare: The History of the Strategies, Tactics and Leadership of Classical Warfare*, edited by Thomas E. Griess, The West Point Military History Series (Wayne, NJ: Arley Publishing Group, 1984) p. 109.

66 "[T]heir ships were better designed than Greek or Roman vessels, overcoming water resistance to a degree not equaled until modern times…. Speed and seaworthiness were built into them at the sacrifice of size, for the largest of the raiding vessels held fewer than 200 men. Yet such small craft proved fit either to cross the Atlantic or to penetrate far up the rivers into the interior of Europe." Lynn Montross: *War through the Ages*, revised and enlarged 3rd ed. (New York: Harper & Row, 1960), p. 98. And: "Contrary to legend, the Vikings were seldom interested in fighting for the sake of fighting. They felt it no disgrace to take to flight with their plunder; but once hemmed in by an aroused countryside, they never refused a battle against any odds. Man for man, they proved more than a match for the soldiery of Europe. Surprise and velocity served them well as moral weapons. Leaving their warships under guard after reaching the limit of a river's navigability, they spread out in fleet bands to sack every village and abbey in the district. Before the peasantry could arm against them, the plunderers were on their way to sea…. The expeditions grew progressively more bold, until by 850 the raiders were strong enough to sack London and push far up the Meuse and the Loire. Permanent bases were established at the river mouths as the manhood of Scandinavia took up the profitable new career…. Europe had no adequate defenses for several decades." *Ibid*, 99.

67 Erik Hildiger, *op.cit.*, 110.

68 J.F.C. Fuller, *op.cit.*, p. 286.

69 Erik Hildiger, *op.cit.*, p. 122.

70 Ellis H. Minns, Proceedings of the British Academy, 1942, pp. 51–52, quoted by J.F.C. Fuller, *A Military History of the Western World*, Vol. 1, *From the Earliest Times to the Battle of Lepanto* (New York: Da Capo, 1987), p. 287.

71 Fuller is quoting E.A. Thompson, *A History of Attila and the Huns* (London: 1948), pp. 208–209.

72 Erik Hildiger, *op.cit.*, p. 11.

73 Erik Hildiger, *op.cit.*, p. 111.

74 *Ibid.*, p. 119.

75 *Ibid.* My emphasis, LM.

76 Ibn Khaldun, *The Muqaddimah: An Introduction to History*, translated by Franz Rosenthal, edited and abridged by N.J. Dawood (Princeton, NJ: Princeton University Press, 1989), p. 93.

77 Henri Pirenne, *Mahomet et Charlemagne*, Presses (Paris : Universitaires de France, 1970), p. 109.

78 René Grousset, *op.cit.*, pp. 277–278.

79 *Ibid.*, p. 249.

80 Joseph Henninger, "La société bédouine ancienne," *in* Francesco Gabrieli, *L'antica società beduina, Studi raccoti da Francesco GabrieliI, Rome, Centro di studi semitici, Instituto di studi orientali*, (1959), p. 83. Also see Ibn Khaldun, *op.cit.*, I, p. 6.

81 Hans Delbrück, *History of the Art of War, Vol III, Medieval Warfare* (Lincoln, Nebraska, and London: University of Nebraska Press, 1990), p. 204.

82 Hans Delbrück, *op.cit.*, p. 203.

83 *Ibid.*

84 John Keegan, *op.cit.*, p. 192.

85 Laurent Murawiec, *Princes of Darkness: The Saudi Assault on the West* (Lanham, MD, and Oxford: Rowman and Littlefield, 2005).

86 Quoted by Robert Lacey, *The Kingdom: Arabia and the House of Saud* (New York: Avon, 1981), p. 230.

87 Jean-Paul Charnay, "Monde arabe," *in* André Corvisier, ed., *Dictionnaire d'art et d'histoire militaire* (Paris: Presses universitaires de France, 1988), pp. 30–36.

88 Ibn Khaldoun, *Le Livre des exemples, Muqaddima* (Paris : Bibliothèque de la Pléiade, Gallimard, 2002). The quotes are drawn, *passim*, from Book II, chapters 2, 5, 8, 9, 15, 24, 25, 26 and 27.

89 Edmund Bosworth, *Armies of the Prophet*, pp. 201–212.

90 Reuben Levy, *The Social Structure of Islam* (London and New York: Routledge, 1957), p. 407.

91 Jean-Paul Charnay, *loc.cit.*.

92 John Keegan, *op.cit.*, p. 22.

93 Reuben Levy, *op.cit.*, 428.

94 Gérard Chaliand, *op.cit.*, 87.

95 Reuben Levy, *op.cit.*, p. 436.

96 Patricia Crone, *loc.cit.*, p. 321.

97 David Nicolle, *Armies of the Muslim Conquest* (Oxford: Osprey, #255, 1993), p. 10.

98 Reuben Levy, *op.cit.*, pp. 408–409 and Hans Delbrück, *op.cit.*, pp. 205–206.

99 Reuben Levy, *op.cit.*, p. 428.

100 Hans Delbrück, *op.cit.*, pp. 206–207.

101 Edmund Bosworth, op.cit., p. 202.

102 David Nicolle, *op.cit.*, p. 8.

103 Lynn Montrose, *op.cit.*, p. 121.

104 *Ibid.*, p. 123.

105 My emphasis, LM.

106 Patricia Crone, *Pre-Industrial Societies: Anatomy of the Pre-Modern World* (Oxford: One World, 1989), p. 35.

107 As Patricia Crone argues, *loc.cit.*, p. 312.

108 C.W.C. Oman, *The Art of War in the Middle Ages: A.D 378–1515*, revised and edited by John H. Beeler (Ithaca, NY: Cornell University Press, 1963), p. 37.

109 Reuben Levy, *op.cit.*, p. 412.

110 David Nicolle, *op.cit.*, p. 14.

111 *Ibid.*, p. 204.

112 Hans Delbrück, *op.cit.*, p. 204. The *hadith* is quoted from Wellhausen, "Die religiös-politischen Oppositionsparteien im alten Islam," Abhandlungen der königlichen Gesellschaft der Wissenschaft zu Göttingen, Phil. Hist. Kl., new series, 5, 2.10.

113 Quoted *ibid.*, p. 122.

114 Henri Pirenne, *op.cit.*, pp. 107–108.

115 *Ibid.*

116 John Keegan, *op.cit.*, pp. 195–96.

117 Alfred Morabia, *Le jihad dans l'Islam médiéval: le combat sacré des origines au XIIè siècle* (Paris : Albin Michel, 1993), p. 93.

118 Patricia Crone, *loc. cit.*, p. 311.

119 *Ibid.*, p. 312.

120 Quoted *in* Edmund Bosworth, *op.cit.*, p. 203.

121 Patricia Crone, *loc. cit.*, p. 313.

122 David Cook, *op.cit.*, p. 44.

123 See entry "*ribat*," H.A.R. Gibb & J.H. Kramers, *Shorter Encyclopedia of Islam* (Leiden: E.J. Brill, 1953), pp. 473–475.

124 David Cook, *op.cit.*, p. 45.

125 Gérard Chaliand, *op.cit.*, p. 149.

126 Alfred Morabia, *op.cit.*, p. 60.

127 Quoted in Andrew Bostom, *The Legacy of Jihad: Islamic Holy War and the Fate of Non-Muslims* (Amherst, NY: Prometheus Books, 2005), p. 61.

128 Edmund Bosworth, *op.cit.*, p. 201.

129 *Ibid*. See also Jean-Paul Charnay, *loc.cit.*

130 *Hadith* quoted by Alfred Morabia, *op.cit.*, p. 164.

131 There is evidence to show that the idea for the Christian Crusaders' chivalric-religious orders with their warring monks, Templars, Hospitallers, etc., were originally imitated from the murabitun, which the Western European knights and the Church encountered on the extreme limes of the umma, Muslim-occupied Spain—just as the Christian concept of crusade was probably inspired by the example of jihad. See Hans Prutz, *Die Geistlichen Ritterorden: Ihre Stellung zur kirchlichen, politischen, gesellschaftlichen und wirtschaftlichen Entwicklung des Mittelalters* (Berlin: Haube & Spener, 1908).

132 Patricia Crone, *op.cit.*, p. 314.

133 Hans Delbrück, *op.cit.*, p. 207.

134 John Keegan, *op.cit.*, p. 207.

135 Patricia Crone, *op.cit.*, p. 317.

136 Of course, there remained minorities of men who were neither slaves nor marchland nomads, who were willing to leave all to fight the holy war. Those men were generally the ardent pious. An example was a group in Kufa, a part of the army there that banded together and was called "The Readers" because of their constant reading of the Quran. Hans Delbrück, *op.cit.*, p. 211.

137 Reuben Levy, *op.cit.*, 454. Also see Edmund Bosworth, *op.cit.*, p. 202.

138 John Keegan, *op.cit.*, p. 193.

139 Edmund Bosworth, *op.cit.*, p. 201.

140 Patricia Crone, *Pre-Industrial Societies*, p. 1.

141 Alfred Morabia, *op.cit.*, p. 224.

142 Jacques Ellul, *Les Chrétientés d'Orient entre Jihad et Dhimmitude, VIIè-XXè siècle*, 1991, quoted by Bat Ye'Or, *The Decline of Eastern Christendom under Islam* (Cranbury NJ: Fairleigh Dickinson University Press, 1998), pp. 18–19.

143 Alfred Morabia, *op.cit.*, p. 91.

144 The expression of "Muslim lands" so often used in the political discourse of Islam is extremely significant: it is rooted in the notion that any area that once, ever so briefly or tenuously, was ruled by Muslims, has thereby *ad aeternam* acquired a substantial quality, has been organically transformed into a 'Muslim land,' no matter what its prior or subsequent history may have been or what its inhabitants desire. Thus Spain may be claimed as well as Provence, Sicily as well as Sardinia, India as well as Israel.

145 Alfred Morabia, *op. cit.,* p. 198.

146 Bassam Tibi, "War and Peace in Islam," in Terry Nardin, *The Ethics of War and Peace: Relations and Security Perspectives* (Princeton, NJ: Princeton University Press, 1996), pp. 128–145.

147 Alfred Morabia, *op.cit.*, p. 172.

148 *Hadith* quoted by Alfred Morabia, *op.cit.*, p. 160.

149 Victor Davis Hanson, *Carnage and Culture* (New York: Anchor Books, 2002), p. 147.

150 *Ibid.*, pp. 121–122.

151 W.R.W. G*ardner, "Jihad,"* in *Moslem World, 2 (1912)*, pp. 347–357, in Andre Bostom, *op.cit.*, p. 299. On the concept of abrogation in the Quran: "None of Our Revelations do We abrogate or cause to be forgotten, but We substitute something better or similar: knowest thou not that Allah hath power over all things" (Q., 2:106).

152 Quoted by David Cook, *op.cit.*, p. 23. Also Alfred Morabia, *op.cit.*, pp. 150, 373.

153 Jean-Paul Charnay: *La Charia et l'Occident*, Paris, 2001, Editions de l'Herne.

154 Bernard Lewis, *The Political Language of Islam* (Chicago: University of Chicago Press, 1988), p. 28.

155 Majid Khadduri, "The Law of War: the Jihad" in: *War and Peace in the Law of Islam, Bk. 2: The Law of War: the Jihad* (Baltimore: Johns Hopkins University Press, 1955), pp. 49–73.

156 Quoted by Alfred Morabia, *op.cit.*, 163, from *Concordantia*, I, p. 388.

157 Majid Khadduri, *loc.cit.*

158 Quoted by Alfred Morabia, *op.cit.*, p. 168; from *Concordantia*, VI, p. 249.

159 Quoted by David Cook, *op.cit.*, p. 23, from one of the six canonical collections of *hadith*, the *Sunan* of Abu Daud.

160 Quoted by Alfred Morabia, *op.cit.*, p. 160, from *Concordance*, I, 389 A.D.

161 Quoted by Alfred Morabia, *op.cit.*, p. 199.

162 Joseph Schacht, *An Introduction to Islamic Law* (Oxford: Clarendon Press, 1964), p. 130.

163 *The History of al-Tabari*, vol. 12 (Albany, NY: State University of New York Press, 1992), p. 167, quoted in Andrew Bostom, *op.cit.*, p. 26.

164 *The Mind of Jihad, I* (Washington, DC: Hudson Institute, 2005), part 4: "Manichean Tribalism."

165 Quran, 10:25.

166 Antoine Fattal, *Le statut légal des non-musulmans en pays d'Islam*, 71, quoted in Andrew Bostom, *op.cit.*, p. 96.

167 Rudolf Peters, "Jihad: An Introduction," in *Jihad in Classical and Modern Islam* (Princeton, NJ: Markus Wiener, 1966), pp. 1-8, quoted in Andrew Bostom, *op.cit.*, p. 98.

168 William Marçais, "Pérenne Islam: principes de connaissance et d'action," in *L'Afrique et l'Asie*, 39, 1957, quoted in Alfred Morabia, *op.cit.*, p. 75.

169 Bassam Tibi, *loc.cit.*, p. 328.

170 Alfred Morabia, *op.cit.*, p. 97.

171 *Ibid.*, p. 122.

172 Bassam Tibi, *loc.cit.*, p. 328.

173 Roger Arnaldez, *The Holy War According to Ibn Hazm of Cordova*, in Andrew Bostom, *op.cit.*, 268.

174 Shaykh ul-Islam Taqi-ud-Deen Ahmad ibn Taymiyyah, *The Religious and Moral Doctrine of Jihad*, http://www.sullivan-county.com/z/tay.htm.

175 Quoted by Alfred Morabia, *op.cit.*, p. 160.

176 Alfred Morabia, *op.cit.*, pp. 172–174.

177 David Cook, *op.cit.*, p. 13.

178 David Cook, *op.cit.*, p. 47.

179 David Cook, *op.cit.*, p. 39.

180 David Cook, *op.cit.*, p. 13.

181 http://inshallahshaheed.wordpress.com/mashari-al-ashwaq-ila-masari-al-ushaaq/

182 David Cook, *op.cit.*, p. 56.

183 Notions bandied about of jihad meaning 'exertion' and of a spiritual 'major jihad' being more important than a 'minor jihad' with military overtones, are disingenuous at best and more often outright apologetic lies. The later conception of a greater jihad, which relies on one lone *hadith*, was developed—no earlier than the ninth century—as "false advertisement," as Prof. David Cook has emphatically put it, to endow devotional matters with the cachet of the prestigious military jihad. To sum up the matter, the purported 'greater' jihad is a personal matter of personal exertion, whereas jihad in general, the so-called 'minor' jihad, is war *fil sabil Allah*, in the way and for the sake of Allah. Reforming Muslims of the late nineteenth century, who desired to amend Islam and modernize it, especially in India, leveraged the former to make their Islam a more peaceful one; apologetic scholars in the West and in the Muslim world are merely being disingenuous in their claims.

184 David Cook, *op.cit.*, p. 26.

185 This list is drawn from Bostom's compilation of texts to that effect by those authors, *op.cit.*, pp. 141–250.

186 Arthur Jeffery, "The Political Importance of Islam," 388 (1942), quoted by Andrew Bostom, *op.cit.*, p. 95.

187 Clément Huart, "Le droit de la guerre," pp. 332–333, quoted by Andrew Bostom, *op.cit.*, p. 94.

188 Henri Lammens, *Islam: Beliefs and Institutions* (London, Frank Cass & Co. 1929), quoted by Andrew Bostom, *op.cit.*, p. 95.

189 Alfred Morabia, *loc.cit.*, p. 200. The author also specifies that in practice, after the great conquests, many Muslim rulers waged mostly defensive wars. His specification falls under the rubric of the balance-of-forces-dictated defensiveness.

190 Quoted by K.S. Lal, "Muslims Invade India," in *The Legacy of Muslim Rule in India* (New Delhi: Aditya Prakashan, 1992), pp. 80–114.

191 Eric Hildiger, *op.cit.*,

192 Laurent Murawiec, *Princes of Darkness: The Saudi Assault on the West*, *op.cit.*, esp. ch. 13, pp. 145–159.

193 David Cook, *op.cit.*, pp. 74–81.

194 *Ibid.*, pp. 86–90.

195 David Cook, *op.cit.*, p. 93.

196 L. Murawiec, *The Mind of Jihad,* I.

197 On this issue, see, *inter alia*, Gustav E. von Grunebaum, *Classical Islam: A History, 600*A.D.*–1258*A.D., (Chicago, IL: Aldine Publications Co., 1970), p. 94; H.A.R. Gibb, *Mohammedanism* (Oxford: Oxford University Press, 1970), p. 76; Christoph Luxenberg, *Die Syro-Aramäische Lesart des Koran, Ein Beitrag zur Entschlüssselung der Koransprache*, (Berlin: Das Arabische Buch, 2000), *passim;* Tillman Nagel, *Geschichte der islamischen Theologie. Von Mohammed bis zur Gegenwart,* (Munich: C.H.Beck, 1994).

198 G.E. von Grunebaum, *Modern Islam: The Search for Cultural Identity*, (Berkeley: University of California Press, 1972), pp. 180, 186. 209.

199 Quoted by L. Bercher, *Revue des etudes islamiques*, IX (1935) 75–86, quoted in G.E. v. Grunebaum, *Modern Islam, op.cit.*, p. 228.

200 Quoted by Martin Kramer, "Political Islam," The Washington Papers, #73, vol. VIII, CSIS/Georgetown, (Beverly Hills/London: Sage Publications,1980), p. 20.

201 K.H. Ansari, "Pan-Islam and the Making of Early Indian Socialism," *Modern Asian Studies*, vol. 20 (1986): pp. 509–537.

202 Martin Kramer, *Islam Assembled: The Advent of the Muslim Congresses* (New York: Columbia University Press, 1986), p. 3.

203 Bernard Lewis, "The Middle East Crisis in Perspective," in *Islam in History: Ideas, People, and Events in the Middle East*, New Edition, Revised and Expanded, (Chicago & La Salle, IL: Open Court, 1993), pp. 405–420; Bernard Lewis, *What Went Wrong: The Clash Between Islam and Modernity in the Middle East,* (New York: Perennial, 2003).

204 This caused a phenomenon not strictly identical to, but comparable to the release of newly urbanized masses of peasants and workers from their traditional allegiances and identifications (village, family, church) in nineteenth-century Europe [Mosca, Michels].

205 Jacob M. Landau, *The Politics of Pan-Islam: Ideology and Organization* (Oxford: Clarendon Press, 1990), p. 48.

206 Kemal H. Karpat, *The Politicization of Islam: Restructuring Identity, State, Faith and Community in the late Ottoman Empire*, (Oxford: Oxford University Press, 2001), p. 48.

207 Jacob M. Landau, *op.cit.*, p. 5.

208 Jamal al-Din al-Afghani, in an 1884 article in his Paris-based journal *al-Urwa al-Wuthqa*, quoted by Jacob Landau, *op.cit*, p. 16.

209 Martin Kramer, *Islam Assembled, op.cit,* p. 1.

210 In a limited but useful sense, we may compare the relationship of the imagined community of Islam to the extant Muslim polities, with the relationship between the *Reichsidee* and Germany as a *Kulturnation*, and the actual German-speaking polities of centuries past.

211 Albert Hourani, *op.cit.*, p. 107.

212 Jacob Landau, *op.cit.*, p. 11.

213 Albert Hourani, *Arabic Thought in the Liberal Age 1798–1939*, (Oxford & New York: Oxford University Press, 1970), p. 106.

214 Martin Kramer, *op.cit.*, p. 4.

215 Kemal Karpat, *op.cit.*, pp. 162, 176.

216 From a report by Lord (Henry) Layard, quoted by Joan Haslip, *The Sultan: The Life of Abdülhamid II*, (London: Cassell, 1958), p. 124.

217 Quoted by Martin Kramer, "Political Islam," *loc.cit.*, p. 12.

218 Jacob Landau, *op.cit.*, p. 41.

219 Arminius Vambéry, quoted by Landau, *ibid.*, p. 64.

220 *Ibid.*, pp. 65–66.

221 Kemal Karpat, *op.cit.*, p. 136.

222 Jacob Landau, *op.cit*, pp. 51–52.

223 Kemal Karpat, *op.cit.*, p. 35.

224 The paradox has often occurred: it shook Hohenzollern Prussia faced with extinction at the hands of Napoleon, the Bourbons of Spain, as well as the British ruler who empowered the Colonists to fight the French and Indian Wars.

225 Kemal Karpat, *op.cit.*, pp. 124–125.

226 Jacob Landau, *op.cit.*, p. 9.

227 Ignaz Goldziher, *Introduction to Islamic Theology and Law,* pp. 161–162.

228 See L. Murawiec, *The Mind of Jihad*, *op.cit.*, p.29f, 163–165.

229 Jacob Landau, *op.cit.*, p. 14.

230 Jacob Landau, *op.cit.*, p. 19., and Nikki R. Keddie, *Sayyid Jamal al-Din al-Afghani: A Political Biography* (Berkeley, San Francisco, London: University of California Press, 1972), pp. 133–138.

231 Kemal Karpat, *op.cit.*, p. 188.

232 So wrote the eminent Turkish intellectual Celal Nuri (1877–1939) in his 1913 book, *The Past, Present and Future of Islam: Views About World Civilization and Its Political and Social Doctrines*, Jacob Landau, *op.cit.*, p. 83.

233 Jacob Landau, *op.cit.*, p. 88.

234 Jacob Landau, *op.cit.*, pp. 86–93.

235 Jacob Landau, *op.cit.*, p. 135.

236 Jacob Landau, *op.cit.*, p. 137.

237 On the entrance of the Ottoman Empire in the war, Efraim Karsh and Inari Karsh, *Empires of the Sand: The Struggle for Mastery in the Middle East, 1789–1923*, (Cambridge, MA: Harvard University Press, 2001). On the CUP, Bernard Lewis, *The Emergence of Modern Turkey*, (Oxford: Oxford University Press, 1975).

238 Bernard Lewis, *The Emergence of Modern Turkey*, *op.cit.*, p. 82.

239 Wolfgang G. Schwanitz, "The German Middle East Policy, 1871–1945," *in* Wolfgang G. Schwanitz & Bernard Lewis (Eds.), *Germany and the Middle East*, Princeton Papers, vol. X–XI, (Princeton, NJ: Marcus Wiener Publishers, 2001), pp. 1–23.

240 Thomas L. Hughes, "The German Mission to Afghanistan, 1915–1916," *ibidem*, pp. 25–63.

241 Wolfgang G. Schwanitz, "Djihad 'made in Germany'," *op.cit.*, p. 24.

242 Fritz Fischer, *Griff nach der Weltmacht: Die Kriegspolitik des kaiserlichen Deutschland 1914–1918*, Düsseldorf, Droste Verlag, 1961–1967, Nachdruck 2004, p. 11.

243 Hans-Ulrich Seidt, *Berlin Kabul Moskau: Oskar von Niedermayer und Deutschlands Geopolitik*, (Munich: Universitas Verlag, 2002), p. 56.

244 Fritz Fischer, *Griff nach der Weltmacht, op.cit.*, p. 110.

245 As a belated response to Russia's declaration of war on November 2 and the two Western allies' own declaration of war on November 5.

246 Full text, translation and presentation by Geoffrey Lewis, "The Ottoman Proclamation of Jihad in 1914," *The Islamic Quarterly*, XIX, 3 and 4 (July–December 1975), London, pp. 157–163.

247 *Ibid.*, pp. 157–158.

248 *Ibid.*, pp. 160–162.

249 Walter Nicolai, *Geheime Mächte, Internationale Spionage und ihre Bekämpfung im Weltkrieg und Heute*, Berlin, 1923 [*The German Secret Service, by W. Nicolai. Translated, with an additional* chapter, by George Renwick, London, S. Paul, 1924]. p. 94. It comes as no surprise that the Turkish Republic asked Walter Nicolai in 1926 to set up a national intelligence service. Nicolai in the meantime had become a fervent advocate of a German alliance with Soviet Russia.

250 Tilman Lüdke, *Jihad Made in Germany: Ottoman and German Propaganda and Intelligence Operations in the First World War* (Münster: LIT, 2005), pp. 75–82.

251 Martin Kramer, *Islam Assembled, op.cit.*, p. 55.

252 Wolfgang G. Schwanitz, "Djihad 'Made in Germany:' Der Streit um den Heiligen Krieg 1914–1915," *Sozialgeschichte,* Leiden, 18 (2003), pp. 2, 7–34.

253 Bernard Lewis, *The Emergence of Modern Turkey, op.cit.*, p. 225.

254 By German historian Wolfgang G Schwanitz.

255 Wolfgang G. Schwanitz, *Germany and the Middle East, op.cit.*, p. 7.

256 Fritz Fischer, *op.cit.*, p. 113.

257 Max von Oppenheim, "*Denkschrift betreffend die Revolutionierung des islamischen Gebiete unserer Feinde*," pp. 2–3. Politisches Archiv des Auswärtigen Amtes, Berlin, P Arch AA R 20938. My gratitude goes to Dr. Wolfgang Schwanitz who kindly communicated this text to me, as well as many other crucial elements of this story.

258 *Ibid.*, pp. 7–14.

259 *Ibid.*, pp. 20–30.

260 *Ibid.*, p. 54.

261 *Ibid.*, p. 58.

262 *Ibid.*, p. 60.

263 *Ibid.*, p. 71.

264 See David Fromkin, "The Importance of T. E. Lawrence," *The New Criterion*, Vol. 10, No. 1, September 1991.

265 Max von Oppenheim, *op.cit.*, pp. 81–82.

266 *Ibid.*, pp. 90–92.

267 *Ibid.*, pp. 126–127.

268 Fritz Fischer, *op.cit.*, p. 116.

269 Wolfgang G. Schwanitz, *The German Middle East Policy*, *op.cit.*, p. 9.

270 Jacob Landau, *op.cit.*, pp. 102–103.

271 *Ibid.*

272 Jacob Landau, *op.cit.*, pp. 104–105.

273 This was implicitly or explicitly the sense of the geopolitics of Friedrich Rätzel, (*Erdenmacht und Völkerschicksal*, Kröners Taschenausgabe, Stuttgart, 1941), and Karl Haushofer, *Der Kontinentalblock. Mitteleuropa – Eurasien – Japan*), Zentralverlag der NSDAP, München, 1941) the two intellectual leaders of the German school of geopolitics.

274 Thomas Hughes, « *The German Mission…* » *op.cit.*, p. 32.

275 Hans-Ulrich Seidt, *.op.cit.*, p. 49.

276 Thomas Hughes, *op.cit.*, p. 39.

277 Hans-Ulrich Seidt, *op.cit.*, p. 77.

278 *Ibid.*, pp. 84–87.

279 Thomas Hughes, *op.cit.*, p. 38.

280 M.N. Roy, *Memoirs*, New Delhi, Ajanta Publications, 1964 (reprint 1984), p. 286.

281 *Ibid.*, p. 40.

282 Hans-Ulrich Seidt, *op.cit.*, p. 85.

283 Jacob Landau, *op.cit.*, p. 184.

284 Jacob Landau, *op.cit.*, p. 198.

285 Thomas Hughes, *op.cit.*, p. 31.

286 Jacob Landau, *op.cit.*, p. 205.

287 *Ibid.*, p. 214.

288 M.N. Roy, *Memoirs*, *op.cit.*, p. 455.

289 The following is mostly drawn from an article by K.H. Ansari, "Pan-Islam and the Making of Early Indian Muslim Socialists," *op.cit.*

290 M.N. Roy, *Memoirs, op.cit.*, p. 3.

291 Jacob Landau, *op.cit.*, p. 176.

292 K.H. Ansari, *op.cit.*, p. 514.

293 *Ibid.*, p. 518.

294 I am grateful to Professor Bernard Lewis for having suggested this very notion.

295 James H. Billington, *The Icon and the Axe: An Interpretive History of Russian Culture* (New York: Vintage Books, 1970), esp. pp. 456–519; Mikhail Heller and Aleksandr M. Nekrich, *Utopia in Power: The History of the Soviet Union from 1917 to the Present*, (New York: Summit Books, 1982); Tomas G. Masaryk, *The Spirit of Russia*, (London: Allen & Unwin, 1961).

296 See Alain Besançon, *Les origines intellectuelles du Léninisme*, Paris, Calmann-Lévy, 1977; René Fülöp-Miller, *Geist und Gesicht des Bolschewismus*, (Vienna, Althea, 1929).

297 See Ian Buruma, Avishai Margalit, *Occidentalism*.

298 A phrase coined by Jacob Burckhardt in a letter of 24 July 1889 to Friedrich von Preen: p. 203 in Jacob Burckhardt, *Briefe*, ed. Max Burckhardt, vol. 9 (Basel/Stuttgart, 1980).

299 Also see Stefan Possony, *Lenin: The Compulsive Revolutionary*, Dmitri Volkogonov, *Lenin: Life and Legacy*, (London: HarperCollins, 1994); Richard Pipes, *The Russian Revolution*, (New York: Vintage Books, 1991), esp. pp. 361–392.

300 Winfried B. Scharlau, Zbyn k A. Zeman, *Freibeuter der Revolution: Parvus-Helphand, Eine politische Biographieî*, (Cologne: Verlag Wissenschaft und Politik, 1964), p. 137.

301 *Ibid.*, p. 248.

302 *Ibid.*, p. 266.

303 Hans-Ulrich Seidt, "When Continents Awake, Island Empires Fall! Germany and the Destabilization of the West 1919–1922" in Wolfgang G. Schwanitz (Ed.), *The German Middle East Policy*, pp. 65–83. Also see E.H. Carr.

304 On Seeckt, his personality, career, views and power, John Wheeler-Bennett, *The Nemesis of Power: The German Army in Politics, 1918–1945*, (London: Mamillan Press, 1960) esp. pp. 84–120.

305 Hans-Ulrich Seidt, *Berlin, Kabul, Moscow*, *op.cit.*, p. 135.

306 Hans-Ulrich Seidt, "When Continents Awake…," *op.cit.*, p. 65.

307 Hans-Ulrich Seidt, *Berlin, Kabul, Moscow*, *op.cit.*, p. 119.

308 Quoted *ibidem*, p. 131.

309 Quoted *ibidem*, p. 133.

310 *Ibidem*, p. 140.

311 M.N. Roy, *Memoirs, op.cit.*, p. 411.

312 Hans-Ulrich Seidt, "When Continents Awake…," *op.cit.*, p. 72.

313 Hans-Ulrich Seidt, *Berlin, Kabul, Moscow*, *op.cit.*, p. 146.

314 Martin Kramer, *Islam Assembled…, op.cit.*, p. 70–71.

315 M.N. Roy, *Memoirs, op.cit.*, p. 398.

316 M.N. Roy, *Memoirs, op.cit.*, p. 398.

317 K.H. Ansari, *op.cit.*, p. 527.

318 Sibnarayan Ray (Ed.), *Selected Works of M.N. Roy*, vol. 1, Delhi, Oxford University Press, 1987, p. 37.

319 http://www.globalwebpost.com/farooqm/study_res/default.html, Dr. Farooq's Study Resources Page.

320 Banglapedia, http://banglapedia.search.com.bd/HT/R_0243.htm

321 Rear Admiral Paul von Hintze, formerly Ambassador to Mexico had made a secret deal with the former Mexican dictator general Huerta: in return for weapons, the latter had agreed, to cut off oil supplies to Great Britain in the event of war with Germany; later the Admiral became the Kaiser's last Foreign Minister and the negotiator of the 'supplementary treaty' of Brest-Litovsk of August 27, 1918 between Soviet Russia and Germany.

322 M.N. Roy, *Memoirs, op.cit.*, p. 14.

323 *Ibid.*, 66–81.

324 On National Bolshevism, see *i.a.*, Jean-Pierre Faye, *Langages totalitaires : La raison critique de l'économie narrative*, Paris, Hermann, 1972.

325 M.N. Roy, *Memoirs, op.cit.*, p. 295.

326 See *Selected Works of M.N. Roy*, vol. 1, *op.cit.*, pp. 171–178.

327 M.N. Roy, *Memoirs, op.cit.*, p. 390.

328 *Selected Works of M.N. Roy*, vol. 1, *op.cit.*, pp. 165–169.

329 *Ibid.*

330 *Ibid.*, p. 326.

331 *Congress of the People of the East, Baku, September 1920*. Stenographic Report, translated and annotated by Brian Pearce, (London: New Park Publications,1977), pp. 4, 1, 2.

332 *Ibid.*, pp. 25–37.

333 *Ibid.*, p. 192.

334 Provision must also be made for the influence of the Fabian Socialist doctrines which were immensely influential amongst less radical and more upper class elements of the colonial world. There was however a coherence between the radical (Bolshevik) and the moderate (Fabian) socialism: the theory of 'imperialism' originated with the British Liberal Hobson and was then adopted by Fabian and Bolsheviks alike, before being retreaded for the colonials. See Laurent Murawiec, "*Impérialisme?*," *Le Débat*, Paris, Winter 2004.

335 *Ibid*, pp. 38–52.

336 *Ibid.*, pp. 61–63.

337 *Ibid.*, pp. 75–76.

338 *Ibid.*, pp. 76–79.

339 *Ibid.*, pp. 113–114.

340 *Ibid.*, 16 p. 1.

341 *Ibid.*, pp. 167–173.

342 Hans-Ulrich Seidt, *Berlin, Kabul, Moscow, op.cit.*, p. 140.

343 Hans-Ulrich Seidt, *Berlin, Kabul, Moscow, op.cit.*, p. 142.

344 Hans-Ulrich Seidt, *Berlin, Kabul, Moscow, op.cit.*, p. 144.

345 Hans-Ulrich Seidt, *Berlin, Kabul, Moscow, op.cit.*, p. 143.

346 Hans-Ulrich Seidt, *Berlin, Kabul, Moscow, op.cit.*, pp. 146–155.

347 M.N. Roy, *Memoirs, op.cit.*, p. 417.

348 *Ibid.*, p. 420.

349 *Ibid.*, p. 419–421.

350 K.H. Ansari, *op.cit.*, p. 518.

351 *Ibid.*, p. 519.

352 M.N. Roy, *Memoirs, op.cit.*, p. 468.

353 K.H. Ansari, *op.cit.*, p. 515.

354 Pursuing his own track, Hasan succeeded in convincing the Ottoman governor of Hijaz Ghalib Pasha to issue a letter to all Muslims all over the world proclaiming jihad on behalf of Caliph against the enemies of Islam. "[A]ttack the tyrannical Christian government" wherever they suffer under its "bondage." *Ibid.*, pp. 515–517.

355 Martin Kramer, *Islam Assembled, op.cit.,* p. 59.

356 K.H. Ansari, *op.cit.*, p. 525.

357 *Ibid.*, p. 530.

358 M.N. Roy, *Memoirs, op.cit.*, p. 464.

359 M.N. Roy, *Memoirs, op.cit.*, pp. 436–437.

360 M.N. Roy, *Memoirs, op.cit.*, p. 439.

361 M.N. Roy, *Memoirs, op.cit.*, p. 447.

362 M.N. Roy, *Memoirs, op.cit.*, p. 326.

363 M.N. Roy, *Memoirs, op.cit.*, p. 526.

364 M.N. Roy, *Memoirs, op.cit.*, p. 537.

365 M.N. Roy, *Memoirs, op.cit.*, p. 538. My emphasis, LM.

366 Alexander A. Benningsen & S. Enders Wimbush, *Muslim National Communism: A Revolutionary Strategy for the Colonial World*, (Chicago: University of Illinois Press, 1979), p. 110.

367 *Ibid.*, pp. 29 and 143.

368 Gerhard von Mende, *Der nationale Kampf der Russlandtürken. Ein Beitrag zur nationalen Frage in der Sowjetunion*, Weidmannsche Buchhandlung, Berlin, 1956, p. 139.

369 Quoted *ibidem*, p. 147.

370 Quoted by Alexander A. Benningsen & S. Enders Wimbush, *Muslim, op.cit.*, p. 75, from *Mwetody Revoliutsionnoi: Kommunicheskoi propagandy na Vostoke,* Zhizn Naytsionalnostei, 8(14) 1922.

371 S. Dimanshtein, *Revoliutisiia I Natsionalny Vopros*, Moscow, 1930, 3:288, quoted by Alexander A. Benningsen & S. Enders Wimbush, *op. cit.*, p. 22.

372 Jacob Landau, pp. 161–162.

373 Gerhard von Mende, *op.cit.*, p. 181.

374 Alexander A. Benningsen & S. Enders Wimbush, *op.cit.*, p. 22.

375 Alexander A. Benningsen & S. Enders Wimbush, *op.cit.*, pp. 27, 29.

376 *Ibid.*, p. 29.

377 *Ibid.*, p. 36.

378 *Ibid.*, p. 29.

379 *Ibid.,* from Hanafi Muazzar's unpublished 1922 book *Din ve Millet Meseleri [Religious andNational Problems]* as quoted in A. Arsharuni and Kh. Gabidullin, *Ocherki Panizlamizma I Panturkisma v Rossii*, Moscow, 1931.

380 Interview in *Bombay Chronicle,* Aug. 1, 1925, quoted in A. Battal-Toymas*, Musalla Jarullah Bigi,* Istanbul, 1958, p. 23.

381 Alexander A. Benningsen & S. Enders Wimbush, *op.cit.*, p. 27.

382 Gerhard v. Mende, *op.cit.*, 156, quoting from A. Arsharuni.

383 Mir-Said Sultan Galiev, in *Zhizn Natsionalnostei*, 42 (50), 1919, quoted by Alexander A. Benningsen, *op.cit.*, p. 134.

384 *Ibid.*, p. 207.

385 Gerhard v. Mende, *op.cit.*, n.3, p. 147.

386 *Ibid.*, pp. 66, 85, 87.

387 Gerhard v. Mende, *op.cit.*, p. 156.

388 Mir-Said Sultan Galiev, Speech at the Regional Congress of the Kazan Organization of the Russian Communit Party (Bolshevik), March 1918, quoted by Arsharuni, *op.cit.*, 78. From Alexander A. Benningsen, *op.cit.*, p. 42.

389 *Ibid.,* p. 43.

390 *Ibid.*, 46. From Z.I. Gimranov, 9th Conference of the Tatar Obkom, 1923, published in *Stenograficheskii otchot 9oi obstnoi konferentsii Tatarskoi organisatsii, RKP(b),* Kazan, 1924, p. 130.

391 Quoted by Tobolev in *Kontrrivoliutsiyon soltangaliëvchekele karshy,* Kazan, 1929, p. 39, *in* Alexander A. Benningsen & S. Enders Wimbush, *op.cit.*, p. 47.

392 *Ibid.*, p. 52.

393 Quoted by Alexander A. Benningsen & S. Enders Wimbush, *op.cit.*, *ibid.*, from L. Rabinstein, *V borbe za Leninskuiu Natsionalnuiu politiku,* Kazan, 1930, pp. 37–9.

394 *Ibid.*, 54. From Tobolec, *op.cit.*, p. 14.

395 Alexander A. Benningsen & S. Enders Wimbush, *op.cit.*, p. 58.

396 Alexander A. Benningsen & S. Enders Wimbush, *op.cit.*, p. 108–109.

397 "The Methods of Antireligious Propaganda among the Muslims," *Zhizn Natsionalnostei* 29(127) & 30(128), 1921, quoted in Alexander A. Benningsen & S. Enders Wimbush, *op.cit.*, pp. 145–147.

398 *Ibid.*, pp. 147 and 157.

399 Quoted by B. Nikitine, "Le problème musulman selon les chefs de l'émigration russe" in "Le Bolchévisme et l'Islam," II. Hors de Russie, *Revue du Monde Musulman,* décembre 1922 (p. 52), pp. 55–82, from V. Chernov, *Revoliutsionnaya Rossiya*, 3, Feb. 1921,

400 Jules Monnerot, *Sociologie du Communisme*, Paris, Gallimard, 3ème édition, 1949, esp. chapter 1, « L' « Islam » du XXè siècle, » pp. 20–22.

401 A comparison may be made with Lucian Pye's analysis of the various *guanxi* networks of influence inside the Chinese Communist Party. It is the *guanxi* that elects and ideological marker to differentiate itself from other contenders for power, rather than ideological differences that determine the formatio of a *guanxi* network. See Lucian Pye, *The Spirit of Chinese Politics*, (Cambridge, MA: Harvard University Press, 1992).

402 Walter Z. Laqueur, *Communism and Nationalism in the Middle East*, (New York: Praeger, 1956), p. 11.

403 *Ibid.*, pp. 259.

404 *Ibid.*, p. 6.

405 *Ibid.*, p. 17.

406 *Al Akhbar*, Aug. 15, 1952, quoted by Walter Z. Laqueur, *ibid.*, p. 239.

407 Walter Z. Laqueur, *ibid.*, p. 236.

408 This entire sub-section will follow Walter Laqueur's narrative.

409 Walter Laqueur, *ibid.*, p. 78.

410 *Ibid.*

411 *Ibid.*, p. 236.

412 *Ibid.*, p. 242.

413 *Ibid.*, p. 250.

414 *Ibid.*, p. 256.

415 *Ibid.*, p. 137.

416 *Ibid.*, p. 167.

417 Fouad Ajami, *The Dream-Palace of the Arabs: A Generation's Odyssey*, (New York: Pantheon Books, 1998), and *The Arab Predicament: Arab Political Thought and Practice Since 1967*, (Cambridge: Cambridge University Press, 1981).

418 Bernard Lewis, *The Emergence of Modern Turkey*, *op.cit.*, 227.

419 Elie Kedourie, *Politics in the Middle East*, (Oxford: Oxford University Press, 1992), esp. 277*ff*, 295*ff*.

420 Albert Hourani, *Arabic Thought in the Liberal Age,* esp. ch. xi, "Arab Nationalism," esp. pp. 310–323.

421 Wolfgang G. Schwanitz, "The German Middle East Policy…," *op.cit.*, p. 10.

422 Quoted by Bernard Lewis, *Semites and Anti-Semites: An Inquiry into Conflict and Prejudice,* (New York: W.W. Norton & Co., 1987), p. 140.

423 Quoted *in* Martin Kramer, *Islam Assembled, op.cit.*, p. 158.

424 Wolfgang G. Schwanitz, "The German Middle East Policy" *op.cit.*, p. 12.

425 Bernard Lewis, *Semites, op.cit,* 142.

426 Lukasz Hirszowicz, *The Third Reich and the Arab East,* (London: Routledge & K. Paul; Toronto: Toronto University Press, 1966), p. 30.

427 On this subject, see Laurent Murawiec, *The Mind of Jihad, I, op.cit., passim.*

428 Bernard Lewis, *Semites, op. cit.,* 149.

429 Bernard Lewis, *Semites, op.cit.,* 144.

430 Bernard Lewis, *Semites, op.cit.,* 148.

431 Olivier Carré & Gérard Michaud [Michel Seurat] (présenté par), *Les Frères musulmans 1928-1982,* Paris, Julliard, 1983, p. 22.

432 Bernard Lewis, *Semites, op.cit.,* 149.

433 "Study of German Intelligence Activities in the Near East and related areas prior to and during World War II," pp. 34 and 41. Secret. Declassified 27 September 1976, declass.#NND943072. National Archives, RG263 records of the CIA, "Formerly security classified Special Studies relating to foreign intelligence agencies." Box 2.

434 "Study of German Intelligence Activities in the Near East," *op.cit.*, p. 29.

435 "Study of German Intelligence Activities in the Near East," *op.cit.*, p. 106.

436 Laurent Murawiec, *The Mind of Jihad, op.cit.*, p. 42.

437 "Study of German Intelligence Activities in the Near East…" *op.cit.*, p. 161.

438 Much of this information from E. Lévi-Provençal, "L'Emir Shakib Arslan," Cahiers de l'Orient contemporain, 4è année (IX–X), 1er-2è trimestre 1947, pp. 5–19.

439 "Study of German Intelligence Activities in the Near East," *op.cit.*, pp. 6 and 154.

440 Martin Kramer, *Islam Assembled, op.cit.*, 149.

441 "Study of German Intelligence Activities in the Near East," *op.cit.*, pp. 148–149.

442 Bernard Lewis, *Semites, op.cit.*, 142.

443 "Study of German Intelligence Activities in the Near East," *op.cit.*, pp. 9 and 148.

444 "Study of German Intelligence Activities in the Near East," *op.cit.*, p. 4.

445 Pol. Archiv, AA, Nachlass Werner Otto von Hentig, vol. 84, Memo Max von Oppenheim, 25.07.40, 7 pp., quoted *in* Wolfgang G. Schwanitz, *op.cit.*, 18.

446 Bernard Lewis, *Semites,* op. cit., 147.

447 Jillian Becker, *The PLO: The Rise and Fall of the Palestine Liberation Organization,* (New York: St. Martin's Press, 1984), *op.cit.*, 19.

448 Martin Kramer, *Islam Assembled*, *op.cit.*, pp. 124–134.

449 Martin Kramer, *Islam Assembled*, *op.cit.*, p. 155.

450 Bernard Lewis, *Semites*, *op.cit.*, 150.

451 General der Flieger Hellmuth Felmy, "Part One" in "German Exploitation of Arab Nationalist Movements in World War II," Historical Direction Headquarters U.S. Army Europe, Foreign Military Studies Branch, MS#P207, National Archives, p.2.

452 Wolfgang G. Schwanitz, "The German Middle East Policy," *op.cit.*, p. 15.

453 Bernard Lewis, *Semites*, *op.cit.*, p. 158.

454 Bernard Lewis, *Semites*, *op.cit.*, pp. 150–151.

455 Daniel Carpi, "The Mufti of Jerusalem, Amin al-Husayni and His Diplomatic Activity during World War II, (October 1941-July 1943)" in *Studies in Zionism*, no. 7 (Spring 1983), quoted by Bernard Lewis, Bernard Lewis, *Semites*, *op.cit.*, p. 151.

456 Bernard Lewis, *Semites*, *op.cit.*, p. 152.

457 "Study of German Intelligence Activities in the Near East," *op.cit.*, p. 6.

458 Wolfgang G. Schwanitz, "The Jinnee and the Magic Bottle: Fritz Grobba and the German Middle East Policy, 1900–1945," pp. 86–117, in Wolfgang G. Schwanitz, Wolfgang G. Schwanitz & Bernard Lewis (Eds.), *Germany and the Middle East*, Princeton Papers, vols. X–XI, (Princeton, NJ: Marcus Wiener Publishers, 2001).

459 Martin Kramer, *Islam Assembled*, *op.cit.*, p. 158.

460 Karlheinz Roth, "Berlin—Ankara—Baghdad: Franz von Papen and German Near East Policy During the Second World War," in Wolfgang G. Schwanitz, Wolfgang G. Schwanitz & Bernard Lewis (Eds.), *Germany and the Middle East*, (pp. 181–214), pp. 203–204.

461 Bernard Lewis, *Semites*, *op.cit.*, p. 156.

462 Bernard Lewis, *Semites*, *op.cit.*, p. 155.

463 *The Testament of Adolf Hitler,* in *The Hitler-Bormann Documents,* February-April 1945, p. 71, quoted by Martin Kramer, *Islam Assembled*, *op.cit.*, 163.

464 Wolfgang G. Schwanitz, "The Jinnee and the Magic Bottle: Fritz Grobba and the German Middle East Policy, 1900–1945," *op.cit.*, p. 100.

465 Jillian Becker, *The PLO*, *op.cit.*, pp. 29–31.

466 "Study of German Intelligence Activities in the Near East," *op.cit.*, pp. 2*ff.*

467 *Ibid.*, pp. 4–6.

468 Bernard Lewis, *Semites*, *op.cit.*, p. 160.

469 *Ibid.*, 102.

470 Claire Sterling, *The Terror Network: The Secret War of International Terrorism* (New York: Holt, Rinehart Winston, 1981), p.113.

471 *Ibid.*, p. 116.

472 Bernard Lewis, *Semites, op.cit.*, p. 149.

473 *Deutsche Nationalzeitung,* May 1, 1964. Quoted in Bernard Lewis, *Semites…, op.cit.*, p. 162.

474 Eric Voegelin, *Autobiographical Reflections*, (Columbia, MO: University of Missouri Press, 2006), 46–47.

475 Quoted in Martin Kramer, "Political Islam," *The Washington Papers*, #73, vol.VIII, 1980, from Ayatollah Ruhollah Khomeini, *al-Hukuma al-Islamiyya (The Islamic State)*, p. 134.

476 Another *hadith* reports Muhammad as having said: "Verily, at the end of every century, Almighty Allah will send such a person to the *Umma*, who will revive the religion for them." Yet another one says: "Allah has indeed raised a *mujaddid* at the beginning of every century" or "Allah will raise a *mujaddid*."

477 Bernard Lewis, Islamic Concepts of Revolution," in P.J.Vatikiotis (Ed.), *Revolution in the Middle East and Other Case Studies*, (Totowa, NJ: Rowman & Littlefield, 1972), pp. 30–40.

478 In particular, *Federalist Papers*, p. 10.

479 Tocqueville, *La démocratie en Amérique, Œuvres, II,* Paris, Ed. de la Pléiade, Gallimard, 1992, and *L'Ancien régime & la Révolution, Œuvres, III, ibid.*

480 See Gertrud Himmelfarb, *The Roads to Modernity: The British, French, and American Enlightenments* (New York, Knopf, 2004).

481 Bernard Lewis, *The Political Language of Islam*, pp. 95–96.

482 Ayatollah Khomeini, "An Islamic State – Point of View," in *Concept of the Islamic State*, London, Islamic Council of Europe, 1979, p. 7.

483 Martin Kramer, "Political Islam," *op.cit.*

484 Mr. Ramin Parham brought this point to my attention.

485 Sayyid Abul Ala Maududi, *Jihad fi sabilillah (Jihad in Islam)*, Translated by Prof. Khushid Ahmad, Ed. By Huda Khattab, UKIM Dawah Center, n.d.

486 This and following quotes from Ahmad S. Moussalli, *Radical Islamic Fundamentalism:The Ideological and Political Discourse of Sayyid Qutb*, (Beirut: American University of Beirut, 1992), pp. 200–203.

487 Sayyid Qutb, *Maalim fi al-Tariq*, pp. 69–71.

488 See especially Albert Hourani, *Arab Thought in the Liberal Age*, Elie Kedourie, *Democracy and Arab Political Culture*.

489 Maxime Rodinson, *Marxism and the Muslim World*, trans. by Michael Pallis, (London: Zed Press, 1979), pp. 41–42.

490 Marcel Gaboriau, "Le néo-fondamentalisme au Pakistan: Maududi et la Jamiaat Islami," pp. 33–76, in Olivier Carré & Paul Dumont, *Radicalismes islamiques, vol 2, Maroc, Pakistan, Inde,Yougoslavie, Mali,* (Paris: L'Harmattan, 1986).

491 Marcel Gaboriau, "Le néo-fondamentalisme au Pakistan," *loc.cit.*, pp. 38 and 40.

492 Quoted by Seyyed Vali Reza Nasr, *Maududi and the Making of Islamic Revivalism* (Oxford: Oxford University Press, 1996), p. 31.

493 Marcel Gaboriau, "Le néo-fondamentalisme au Pakistan," *loc.cit.*, p. 46.

494 Abul Ala Maududi, *Musalman awr mawjutah siyas*, Lahore, Kashmakash, 1940, 3:31, quoted in Seyyed Vali Reza Nasr, *Maududi, op.cit.*, p. 55.

495 Marcel Gaboriau, "Le néo-fondamentalisme au Pakistan," *loc.cit.*, p. 44.

496 Sayed Abul Ala Maududi, *Jihad in Islam*, Lahore, Islamic Publications, 1998–2001, p. 19.

497 Seyyed Vali Reza Nasr, *Maududi, op.cit.*, p. 130.

498 Marcel Gaboriau, "Le néo-fondamentalisme au Pakistan," *loc.cit.*, p. 70.

499 Marcel Gaboriau, "Le néo-fondamentalisme au Pakistan," *loc.cit.*, p. 58.

500 Abul Ala Maududi, *A Short History of the Revivalist Movement in Islam*, Lahore, 1963, p. 35, quoted in Seyyed Vali Reza Nasr, *Maududi, op.cit.*, p. 136.

501 Marcel Gaboriau, "Le néo-fondamentalisme au Pakistan," *loc.cit.*, p. 70.

502 Abul Ala Maududi, *Mizajshinasi rasul*, Lahore, Tafhimat, 1965, 1:102, quoted in Seyyed Vali Reza Nasr, *Maududi, op.cit.*, p. 137.

503 Abul Ala Maududi, *Toward Understanding Islam*, 14th ed., 176, quoted in Marcel Gaboriau, "Le néo-fondamentalisme au Pakistan," *loc.cit.*, p. 43.

504 Abul Ala Maududi, *Moral Foundations of the Islamic Government*, quoted in Marcel Gaboriau, "Le néo-fondamentalisme au Pakistan," *loc.cit.*, p. 51.

505 Quoted *in* Seyyed Vali Reza Nasr, *Maududi, op.cit.*, p. 77.

506 Marcel Gaboriau, "Le néo-fondamentalisme au Pakistan," *loc.cit.*, pp. 51–58.

507 Abul Ala Maududi, *Al-Jihad fil Islam*, quoted in Marcel Gaboriau, "Le néo-fondamentalisme au Pakistan," *loc.cit.*, p. 59.

508 Quoted *in* Seyyed Vali Reza Nasr, *Maududi, op.cit.*, pp. 71 & 76.

509 Abul Ala Maududi, *Jihad in Islam*, Lahore, Islamic Publications, 1998–2001, p. 8.

510 Abul Ala Maududi, *Jihad in Islam, op.cit.*, pp. 9–10.

511 Abul Ala Maududi, *Jihad in Islam, op.cit.*, pp. 13, 14, 17.

512 On 'logocracy,' see Jean-Paul Charnay, *La charia et l'Occident*, Paris, Ed. de l'Herne, 2001.

513 Abul Ala Maududi, *Jihad in Islam, op.cit.*, p. 21.

514 Abul Ala Maududi, *Jihad in Islam, op.cit.*, pp. 21–2.

515 Abul Ala Maududi, *Jihad in Islam, op.cit.*, pp. 22–24.

516 Seyyed Vali Reza Nasr, *Maududi…, op.cit.*, p. 70.

517 Georges Sorel, *op.cit.*, pp. 122–123.

518 Seyyed Vali Reza Nasr, *Maududi, op.cit.*, p. 19.

519 G.E. von Grunebaum, *Modern Islam*, *op.cit.*, p. 224.

520 Said Amir Arjomand, *The Turban for the Crown: The Islamic Revolution in Iran*, (Oxford: Oxford University Press, 1988), p. 105.

521 Said Amir Arjomand, *The Turban for the Crown*, *op.cit.*, p. 97.

522 Said Amir Arjomand, *The Turban for the Crown*, *op.cit.*, p. 94.

523 Olivier Carré, "Introduction," in Olivier Carré & Paul Dumont, *Radicalismes islamiques, vol. 1, Iran, Liban, Turquie*, (Paris: l'Harmattan, 1985), p. 8.

524 Amir Taheri, *Holy Terror: The Inside Story of Islamic Terrorism,* (London: Sphere Books, 1987), p. 42.

525 Mahmood T. Davari, *The Political Thought of Ayatollah Murtaza Mutahhari: An Iranian Theoretician of the Islamic State*, (London & New York: Routledge Curzon, 2003), p. 20.

526 Mahmood T. Davari, *The Political Thought of Ayatollah Murtaza Mutahhari*, *op.cit.*, p. 21.

527 Yann Richard, "L'organisation des *fedaiyan-e Eslam, mouvement intégriste musulman en Iran (1945–1956)*, 23-82, in Olivier Carré & Paul Dumont, *Radicalismes islamiques, op.cit.*, pp. 24–28.

528 Yann Richard, "L'organisation des *fedaiyan-e Eslam,*" *op.cit.*, pp. 35, 40, 51.

529 Mahmood T. Davari, *The Political Thought of Ayatollah Murtaza Mutahhari, op.cit.*, pp. 22.

530 Yann Richard, "L'organisation des *fedaiyan-e Eslam,*" *op.cit.*, pp. 54–63.

531 Amir Taheri, *op.cit.*, p. 81.

532 See Farhad Khorokhavar, *Les nouveaux martyrs d'Allah*, (Paris: Flammarion, 2002), *passim*.

533 Yann Richard, "L'organisation des *fedaiyan-e Eslam,*" *op.cit.*, p. 81.

534 Mahmood T. Davari, *The Political Thought of Ayatollah Murtaza Mutahhari, op.cit.*, 39 and Said Amir Arjomand, *The Turban for the Crown, op.cit.*, p. 95.

535 Robert G.L. Waite, *Vanguard of Nazism: The Free Corps Movement in Postwar Germany 1918–1923*, (New York: W.W. Norton, 1969).

536 Alexander A. Benningsen & S. Enders Wimbush, *Muslim National Communism, op.cit.*, pp. 79–80.

537 Said Amir Arjomand, *The Turban for the Crown, op.cit.*, pp. 24–25.

538 Said Amir Arjomand, *The Turban for the Crown, op.cit.*, pp. 25.

539 Alexander A. Benningsen & S. Enders Wimbush, *Muslim National Communism, op.cit.*, pp. 111–112.

540 Mahmood T. Davari, *The Political Thought of Ayatollah Murtaza Mutahhari, op.cit.*, pp. 26–27.

541 Said Amir Arjomand, *The Turban for the Crown, op.cit.*, pp. 157–159.

542 Laurent Murawiec, *The Mind of Jihad, op.cit.*, esp. pp. 47–57, 130–137, and 215–223.

543 Encyclopedia of the Orient, http://lexicorient.com/e.o/12thimam.htm

544 Nouchine Yavari-d'Hellencourt, "Le radicalisme chiite de Ali Shariati," (pp. 84–118) *in* Olivier Carré & Paul Dumont, *Radicalismes islamiques, vol. 1, Iran, Liban, Turquie*, Paris, l'Harmattan, p. 113.

545 Nouchine Yavari-d'Hellencourt, "Le radicalisme chiite de Ali Shariati," *loc.cit.*, p. 117.

546 Eric Voegelin, *Science, Politics & Gnosticism*, (Washington, DC: Regnery, 1977), p. 67.

547 Luciano Floridi, "Nietzsche: Impact on Russian Thought" (London: Routledge, Chapman & Hall, 1988). http://lists.paleopsych.org/pipermail/paleopsych/2006-August/005656.html

548 Nouchine Yavari-d'Hellencourt, "Le radicalisme chiite de Ali Shariati," *loc.cit.*, p. 111.

549 Said Amir Arjomand, *The Turban for the Crown*, *op.cit.*, p. 94.

550 Ali Shariati, *Che bayaad kard?*, Tehran, Complete Works, 20, 1982, p. 249, quoted in Nouchine Yavari-d'Hellencourt, "Le radicalisme chiite de Ali Shariati," *loc.cit.*, p. 86.

551 Ali Shariati, *Baz-gasht*, Tehran, Hoseiniye Ershad, Complete Works, 4, 1978, p. 308.

552 Quoted by Nouchine Yavari-d'Hellencourt, "Le radicalisme chiite de Ali Shariati," *loc.cit.*, p. 87.

553 Ali Shariati, *Che bayad kard?*, *op cit.*, 417, quoted in Nouchine Yavari-d'Hellencourt, "Le radicalisme chiite de Ali Shariati," *loc.cit.*, p. 90.

554 Ali Shariati, *Jehat-giri-e tabaqati-e eslam*, Tehran, Complete Works, 10, 1980, quoted in Nouchine Yavari-d'Hellencourt, "Le radicalisme chiite de Ali Shariati," *loc.cit.*, p. 96.

555 *Ibid.*, p. 89.

556 Said Amir Arjomand, *The Turban for the Crown*, *op.cit.*, p. 93.

557 Said Amir Arjomand, *The Turban for the Crown*, *op.cit.*, p. 94.

558 Nouchine Yavari-d'Hellencourt, "Le radicalisme chiite de Ali Shariati," *loc.cit.*, p. 110.

559 *Ibid.*, p. 101.

560 Mahmood T. Davari, *The Political Thought of Ayatollah Murtaza Mutahhari*, *op.cit.*, p. 42–44.

561 Mahmood T. Davari, *The Political Thought of Ayatollah Murtaza Mutahhari*, *op.cit.*, p. 63.

562 The foregoing is a paraphrase of Davaris' report on the matter, *op.cit.*, pp. 75ff.

563 Quoted by E. Abrahamian, *Radical Islam: the Iranian* Mojahedin, London, Tauris, 1988, p. 92.

564 Mahmood T. Davari, *The Political Thought of Ayatollah Murtaza Mutahhari*, *op.cit.*, p. 79.

565 Mahmood T. Davari, *The Political Thought of Ayatollah Murtaza Mutahhari*, *op.cit.*, pp. 76–77.

566 Mahmood T. Davari, *The Political Thought of Ayatollah Murtaza Mutahhari*, *op.cit.*, pp. 81–82.

567 Mahmood T. Davari, *The Political Thought of Ayatollah Murtaza Mutahhari*, *op.cit.*, p. 48.

568 Morteza Motah-hari [Murtaza Mutahhari], *The Martyr*, (Houston TX: Free Islamic Libraries, 1980), p. 14.

569 Mahmood T. Davari, *The Political Thought of Ayatollah Murtaza Mutahhari*, *op.cit.*, pp. 64–65.

570 *Ibid.*, p. 63.

571 Said Amir Arjomand, *The Turban for the Crown*, *op.cit.*, p. 97.

572 Mahmood T. Davari, *The Political Thought of Ayatollah Murtaza Mutahhari*, *op.cit.*, pp. 103–106.

573 Mahmood T. Davari, *The Political Thought of Ayatollah Murtaza Mutahhari*, *op.cit.*, pp. 87.

574 Said Amir Arjomand, *The Turban for the Crown*, *op.cit.*, p. 97.

575 Morteza Motah-hari [Murtaza Mutahhari], *The Martyr*, *op.cit.*, p. 8.

576 Said Amir Arjomand, *The Turban for the Crown*, *op.cit.*, pp. 163, 165, 170.

577 *Ibid.*, pp. 142–143.

578 *Ibid.*, p. 101.

579 See Amir Taheri, *Holy Terror, op.cit.*, pp. 65–73.

580 Said Amir Arjomand, *The Turban for the Crown, op.cit.*, p. 101.

581 *Ibid.*

582 *Ibid.*, p. 152.

583 *Ibid.*, p. 181.

584 *Ibid.*, p. 182.

585 *Jomhuri-ye Eslami*, January 1988, in Said Amir Arjomand, *The Turban for the Crown, op.cit.*, p. 183.

586 Jillian Becker, p. 114.

587 Amir Taheri, *Holy Terror…, op.cit.*, p. 80.

588 Laurent Murawiec, *Princes of Darkness: The Saudi Assault on the West*, esp. Ch. 2.

589 Kemal H. Karpat, *op.cit.*, pp. 38–39.

590 Christopher Andrew and Vassili Mitrokhin, *The World Was Going Our Way: The KGB and the Battle for the Third World* (New York: Basic Books, 2005), esp. pp. 139–261.

591 Alexandre Benningsen, Paul B. Henze, George K. Tanham, S. Enders Wimbush, *Soviet Strategy and Islam* (New York: Saint Martin's Press, 1989), p. 32.

592 Mohammed Heykal, *The Sphinx and the Commissar: The Rise and Fall of Soviet Influence in the Middle East* (New York: Harper & Row, 1978), pp. 134–135.

593 Roberta Goren, *The Soviet Union and Terrorism*, (London: Allen & Unwin, 1984), p. 76.

594 *Soviet News*, July 11, 1962, quoted in Roberta Goren, *op.cit.*, p. 86.

595 Quoted in Alexandre Benningsen, Paul B. Henze, et al., *op.cit.*, p. 37.

596 Quoted in Alexandre Benningsen, Paul B. Henze, et al., *op.cit.*, p. 38.

597 Quoted in Alexandre Benningsen, Paul B. Henze, et al., *op.cit.*, pp. 41–48.

598 Roberta Goren, *op.cit.*, pp. 102–103.

599 Personal report to the author from a participant.

600 'Annual of Power and Conflict,' 1973–1974, London, Institute for the Study of Conflict.

601 U.S. Congress, Judiciary Committee, U.S. Senate Hearings on Terroristic Activity, Part 4, 94th Congress, 14 May 1975; and Jan Sejna, *We Will Bury You*, London, Sidgwick & Jackson, 1982, and Claire Sterling, *The Terror Network: The Secret War of International Terrorism*, p. 14.

602 Quoted in Alexandre Benningsen, Paul B. Henze, et al., *op.cit.*, 105. See also John B. Kelly, *Arabia, The Gulf and the West*, (New York: Basic Books, 1980), esp. Ch. 1, "The Abandonment of Aden," pp. 1–45.

603 See inter alia, Christopher Dobson, Roberta Goren, Jillian Becker, Ephraim Karsh, Barry and Judy Colp Rubin, and Ion Pacepa.

604 Quoted by Roberta Goren, *op.cit.*, p. 22.

605 The most graphic depiction of Cheka terror in the civil war is in an autobiographical novella written by the Bolshevik chief of the Cheka in the large city of Omsk during the Civil War: *Zazubrin, Shchepka*, published in French translation as *Le tchékiste*, (Paris: Chr. Bourgois, 1990); see also Richard Pipes (Ed.), *The Unknown Lenin: From the Secret Archives*, (New Haven: Yale University Press, 1996).

606 Leo Trotsky, *Terrorism and Communism*, (Ann Arbor, MI: AA Paperback, 1961), p. 58.

607 Robert Conquest, *The Great Terror: Stalin's Purge of the Thirties*, (New York: Macmillan, 1973).

608 Quoted by Roberta Goren, *op.cit.*, pp. 212–213.

609 Quoted by Christopher Dobson, *op.cit.*, pp. 152–153.

610 Claire Sterling, *op.cit.*, p. 15.

611 Alexandre Benningsen, Paul B. Henze, et al., *op.cit.*, p. 89.

612 *Ibid.*, p. 91.

613 Vladimir Zakharov, *High Treason*, (New York: Ballantine, 1981), p. 251, quoted in Alexandre Benningsen, Paul B. Henze, et al., *op.cit.*, p. 91.

614 Jillian Becker, *op.cit.*, pp. 41, 43.

615 Roberta Goren, *op.cit.*, pp. 106-7.

616 *Ibid.*, p. 108.

617 Claire Sterling, *op.cit.*, p. 39.

618 Roberta Goren, *op.cit.*, p. 109.

619 *Ibid.*, p. 119.

620 Claire Sterling, *op.cit.*, pp. 54*ff.*

621 MER, v.3, 1963, 3, quoted by Roberta Goren, *op.cit.*, pp. 107.

622 Hussam Mohammad, "PLO Strategy: From Total Liberation to Coexistence;" http:/pij.org/site/vhome.htm?g=a&aid=4282.

623 Barry Rubin, *Revolution until Victory? The Politics and History of the PLO* (Cambridge, MA: Harvard University Press, 1994), p. 24. My emphasis, LM.

624 Joel S. Fishman, "Ten years since Oslo: the PLO's "people's war" strategy and Israel's inadequate response," Jerusalem Viewpoints, No. 503, 1–15 September 2003, Jerusalem Center for Public Affairs, http://www.jcpa.org/jl/vp503.htm

625 Raphael Danziger, "Algeria and the Palestinian Organizations," in *The Palestinians and the Middle East Conflict*, Gabriel Ben-Dor, ed., (Tel Aviv: Turtledove, 1979), pp. 364-365, quoted by Joel S. Fishman, *ibid*.

626 Abu Iyad [Salah Khalaf] with Eric Rouleau, *My Home, My Land*, trans. Linda Butler Koseoglu, (New York: Times Books, 1978), pp. 65–67. Quoted by Joel S. Fishman, *ibid*.

627 Joel S. Fishman, *op.cit.*

628 See entry of Khalil al-Wazir in Guy Bechor, ed., *The PLO Lexicon*, (Tel Aviv: Ministry of Defense,

1991), p. 90. See also "Biography of Khalil al-Wazir (Abu Jihad)," *Encyclopedia of the Palestinians,* Philip Mattar, ed. (New York: Facts on File, 2000). Quoted by Joel S. Fishman, *ibid.*

629 Y. Harkabi, "Al Fatah's Doctrine," in Walter Laqueur and Barry Rubin, eds., *The Israel-Arab Reader: A Documentary History of the Middle East Conflict,* (New York: Penguin Books, 1991), p. 395.

630 Roberta Goren, *op.cit.*, pp.140–141.

631 Roberta Goren, *op.cit.*, p. 132, n. 154.

632 Barry Rubin & Judith Colp Rubin, *op.cit.*, p. 84.

633 Barry Rubin & Judith Colp Rubin, *op.cit.*, p. 97.

634 BBC/ME, February 21, 1979; quoted *in* Martin Kramer, "Political Islam," *op.cit.*, p. 14.

635 Amir Taheri, *op.cit.*, pp. 88-89.

636 Quoted by Barry Rubin & Judith Colp Rubin, *op.cit.*, pp. 27, 28.

637 Barry Rubin & Judith Colp Rubin, *op.cit.*, p.61.

638 Jillian Becker, *op.cit.*, p. 141.

639 Roberta Goren, *op.cit.*, p. 181.

640 Quoted by Barry Rubin & Judith Colp Rubin, *op.cit.*, p.157.

641 Henry Kissinger, *Years of Upheaval,* (New York: Simon and Schuster,1982), pp. 626–627.

642 See for example: Caroline Glick, "The Longest-Running Big Lie," *Jerusalem Post,* Jan. 1, 2007.

643 Quoted by Barry Rubin & Judith Colp Rubin, *op.cit.*, p. 41.

644 Che Guevara, Message to the Tricontinental Conference, cited in the *Brigate Rosse*'s *Contro Informazione,* July 1978, quoted by Claire Sterling, *op.cit.*, p. 8.

645 Al-Ansar, February 27, 2002, translated by MEMRI, #353, March 12, 2002.

646 Guillaume Le Vasseur de Beauplan, *La Description d'Ukraine,* (Ottawa: Presses de l'Université d'Ottawa, 1990), pp. 116–117.

647 Eric Hildiger, *op.cit.*, 118.

648 B.H. Liddell Hart, "Jengis Khan and Sabutai," *Great Captains Unveiled, op.cit.*, pp. 7*ff.*

649 See Laurie Mylroie's documentation of the role of Khaled Sheikh Muhammad's extended family in the 1993 and 2001 World Trade Center attacks: *Study of Revenge: Saddam Hussein's Unfinished War Against America* (Washington, DC: AEI Press, 2000).

650 This discussion of the *futuwwah* is largely drawn from Marshall G.S. Hodgson, *The Venture of Islam*, vol. 2, *The Expansion of Islam in the Middle Periods,* (Chicago: University of Chicago Press, 1974), pp. 128*ff.*

651 Marshall G.S. Hodgson, *op.cit.*, pp. 214, 220*f.*

652 Jean-Paul Charnay, *Principes de stratégie arabe*, Paris, L'Herne, 1984, 8.

653 E.E. Smith, Edward Ellis Smith, *The Young Stalin; the Early Years of an Elusive Revolutionary,* (New York: Farrar, Straus and Giroux, 1967).

654 Jean-Louis Margolin, in Stéphane Courtois, Nicolas Werth, Jean-Louis Panné, *Le livre noir du communisme – Crimes, terreur et repression*, (Paris: Robert Laffont, 1998).

655 Eric Hobsbawm, *Primitive Rebels: Studies in Archaic Forms of Social Movement in the 19th and 20th Centuries* (Manchester: Manchester University Press, 1959).

656 Robert Spencer, "Drug money sustaining al-Qaeda: US officials," *Jihad Watch*, December 30, 2003, http://www.jihadwatch.org/archives/000519.php; "Al-Qaeda And Drugs Fuel Afghan Fighting Says NATO Commander," AFP, Sep 14, 2006; http://www.spacewar.com/reports/Al_Qaeda_And_Drugs_Fuel_Afghan_Fighting_Says_NATO_Commander_999.html; Matthew Levitt, "Hezbollah drug ring broken up in Ecuador," The Counterterrorism Blog, June 22, 2005, http://counterterror.typepad.com/the_counterterrorism_blog/2005/06/hezbollah_drug_.html.

657 Barry Rubin & Judith Colp Rubin, *op.cit.*, p. 30.

658 Alastair Horne, *A Savage War of Peace: Algeria 1954–1962*, (Hammersworth: Penguin Books, 1979), p. 95.

659 Roger Le Tourneau, Maurice Flory and René Duchac, "The Revolution in Algeria," pp. 89-119, in P.J. Vatikiotis, ed., *Revolution in the Middle East and Other Case Studies*, p. 114.

660 Alastair Horne, *A Savage War of Peace, op.cit.*, p. 74. Horne's impressive study has used the best literature available on the subject, and confirms what, for instance, Yves Courrière's highly valuable contribution had reported. I have therefore chosen to use his book as the source for most of the incidents mentioned in this section; they are present in most of the other published accounts of the Algerian War.

661 Alastair Horne, *A Savage War of Peace, op.cit.*, p. 407.

662 Alastair Horne, *A Savage War of Peace, op.cit.*, p. 78.

663 Alastair Horne, *A Savage War of Peace, op.cit.*, p. 405.

664 Alastair Horne, *A Savage War of Peace, op.cit.*, p. 406.

665 Roger Le Tourneau *et al.*, *op.cit.*, 91.

666 Alastair Horne, *A Savage War of Peace, op.cit.*, 131.

667 Alastair Horne, *A Savage War of Peace, op.cit.*, pp. 24–26.

668 Roger Le Tourneau *et al.*, *op.cit.*, p. 89.

669 Alastair Horne, *A Savage War of Peace, op.cit.*, p. 118.

670 Alastair Horne, *A Savage War of Peace, op.cit.*, p. 101.

671 Alastair Horne, *A Savage War of Peace, op.cit.*, p. 112.

672 Alastair Horne, *A Savage War of Peace, op.cit.*, p. 134.

673 Alastair Horne, *A Savage War of Peace, op.cit.*, p. 135.

674 Alastair Horne, *A Savage War of Peace, op.cit.*, p. 214.

675 Alastair Horne, *A Savage War of Peace, op.cit.*, pp. 221–222.

676 Albert Camus, *Actuelles III, Chronique algérienne*, 1939–1958, (Paris: Gallimard, 1958).

677 Frantz Fanon, *Les damnés de la terre*, introduction by Jean-Paul Sartre, (Paris: F. Maspéro, 1961).

678 Alastair Horne, *A Savage War of Peace*, *op.cit.*, pp. 235, 238, 244.

679 Alastair Horne, *A Savage War of Peace*, *op.cit.*, p. 408.

680 Alastair Horne, *A Savage War of Peace*, *op.cit.*, p. 538.

681 Alastair Horne, *A Savage War of Peace*, *op.cit.*, p. 119.

682 Alastair Horne, *A Savage War of Peace*, *op.cit.*, p. 120.

683 Alastair Horne, *A Savage War of Peace*, *op.cit.*, p. 121.

684 Alastair Horne, *A Savage War of Peace*, *op.cit.*, pp. 128–129.

685 Alastair Horne, *A Savage War of Peace*, *op.cit.*, p. 497.

686 Alastair Horne, *A Savage War of Peace*, *op.cit.*, p. 526.

687 Ahmed Ben Bella, "Che Guevara, Cuba, and the Algerian Revolution," *The Militant*, Volume 2, No. 4, 2 February 1998. http://www.hartford.hwp.com/archives/40/058.html.

688 http://www.tolueislam.com/Bazm/Shahid/SM_001.htm.

689 Brigadier S.K. Malik, *The Quranic Concept of War*, (Lahore: National Book Foundation – M/S Istiqlal Press, 1979), xi.

690 S.K. Malik, *The Quranic Concept of War*, xiii.

691 S.K. Malik, *The Quranic Concept of War*, xiv.

692 S.K. Malik, *The Quranic Concept of War*, xix.

693 S.K. Malik, *The Quranic Concept of War*, xxi-xxii.

694 S.K. Malik, *The Quranic Concept of War*, pp. 23–24.

695 S.K. Malik, *The Quranic Concept of War*, p. 41.

696 S.K. Malik, *The Quranic Concept of War*, p. 54.

697 S.K. Malik, *The Quranic Concept of War*, p. 58.

698 S.K. Malik, *The Quranic Concept of War*, p. 58.

699 S.K. Malik, *The Quranic Concept of War*, pp. 58–59.

700 S.K. Malik, *The Quranic Concept of War*, p. 60.